ABOUT THE EDITOR

BILL FAWCETT is the author and editor of more than a dozen books, including *You Did What?* and *How to Lose a Battle.* He is also the author and editor of three historical mystery series and two oral histories of the U.S. Navy SEALs. He lives in Illinois.

HOW TO LOSE A
WAR

HOW TO LOSE A
WAR

MORE FOOLISH PLANS
AND GREAT MILITARY BLUNDERS

Edited by
BILL FAWCETT

HARPER

NEW YORK • LONDON • TORONTO • SYDNEY

HARPER

HarperCollins books may be purchased for educational, business, or sales promotional use. For information please write: Special Markets Department, HarperCollins Publishers, 10 East 53rd Street, New York, NY 10022.

FIRST EDITION

Library of Congress Cataloging-in-Publication Data is available upon request.

ISBN 978-0-06-135844-9

12 13   OV/RRD   10 9 8 7 6 5 4 3

DEDICATED TO
"noted scholar" Brian Thomsen
(1959–2008)

CONTENTS

MODERN MISTAKES

In this book we look not at the brilliant strategies of history's greatest generals and leaders, but at the failures of those who lost wars they should have won, or at least made it a fight. While any book whose subject is war deals with death and ruin in the most literal way and the results are often desperately hard on the citizens who are the real losers, there is an inescapable feeling of superiority as you look on what are, in 20/20 hindsight, obvious mistakes. It asks and then attempts to answer the question of why leaders who felt confident enough to start a war ended up losing it or why a side that should have won easily ended up suffering defeat. There are many more examples than could be included, Darius losing to the king of relatively tiny and poor Macedonia and ninety thousand Poles being thrashed by thirty thousand Mongols come to mind. Most are here because they are such prime examples of losing. A few wars have been included simply because the unlikely loss had a major effect. Many books concentrate on what went right or the brilliant moves of the winning leaders. This one looks at what went wrong.

We begin with a look at wars lost in modern times, examining with a critical eye the reasons for major defeats in the last sixty years. Now you might think that this means, if the last century's leaders learned from history, we should see mistakes that are different from those made in the past. Really, they should be different, not the same old errors. . . .

*No one won in Korea. At great cost, the situation was
restored to the status quo of before the war. From the
perspective of over fifty years later, it is easy to forget just
how close South Korea came to losing in the first weeks of
the North Korean invasion. The Pusan perimeter, a small area
in a corner of Korea, was all that remained in Allied hands.
Had the North Korean army made a few different decisions,
or the USA been less determined to stand by an ally,
it would have been all over in weeks.*

A COLD WAR IGNITES

Or, How the Communists Lost the Korean War:
Korea, 1950

DOUGLAS NILES

Just like another Sunday morning, nine years earlier at Pearl
Harbor, the United States on June 25, 1950, was at peace in an
uneasy world. That peace was rudely shattered as, before dawn,
the heavily armed and armored forces of the North Korean Army
(NKA) stunned their counterparts of the Republic of Korea (ROK)
with a massive and devastating attack along the length of their
shared border. Artillery barrages pounded villages and lightly
manned trenches, while tanks—powerful, durable Russian T-34s—
rumbled forward in mighty columns. Their immediate objective
was the South Korean capital, Seoul. For the first time since WWII,
armed forces of the communist bloc and the Western world were
engaged in large-scale combat.

Surprise was complete, and there was very little standing in the North Koreans' way.

The nation of Korea had been divided, almost capriciously and certainly with no intention of permanence, at the end of WWII. During conferences at Cairo and Potsdam during the war, the Allied powers had agreed that Korea's independence should be restored after the fall of Japan. Immediately following the end of that war, the victorious Allies decided that the Soviet Red Army, which had swept out of Siberia to occupy all of Manchuria during the final month of the war, would accept the surrender of Japanese troops in Korea, north of the 38th parallel of latitude. The Americans would take charge of the Japanese troops located south of that line, which more or less bisected the long, mountainous peninsula.

As with so many of the borders set up for occupation zones at the end of the war, the demarcation lines between the Soviets and the other Allies became de facto borders, delineating the boundary paralleling in Asia that which Winston Churchill so memorably described regarding Eastern Europe as the Iron Curtain. In the case of Korea, the Republic of Korea was established in the South during August 1947, with a right-wing capitalist, Syngman Rhee, as president. The capital was Seoul, the peninsula's major city, only about thirty miles south of the 38th parallel. Though dissent was repressed by Rhee's rather harsh regime, South Korea was in fact a democracy.

The USSR promptly declared Rhee's government to be illegal, and established the Democratic People's Republic of Korea, with its capital at Pyongyang, in the north. Kim Il Sung was established as the leader of that country, presiding over a Stalinist-type communist regime. By the late 1940s, the Soviet and American occupation forces had withdrawn, though both sides left advisory forces in the country.

In the south, the Korean Military Advisory Group (KMAG) was a small cadre of U.S. military officers and men. The army of the Republic of South Korea was basically a national police force, with men organized into divisions, but armed only with rifles and small automatic weapons. They had no armor or mechanized units, nor were they equipped with even the most rudimentary mortars, artillery, or bazookas. Neither did South Korea possess an air force. This was in part a political design, since the U.S. did not want their Korean allies to be perceived as taking an aggressive stance; neither the U.S. nor the ROK expected large-scale aggression from the north.

The NKA, on the other hand, was very well-equipped by the Soviets, and thoroughly trained by Russian advisers. Many of the troops were veterans of the Red Chinese army, some having fought against the Japanese during WWII, while many of them battled the Nationalist Chinese during the Chinese Civil War. Upon the successful conclusion of the latter conflict, these men returned to North Korea as intact battalions and divisions. The Soviets provided them with some 150 T-34s, which were very capable tanks even in the 1950s: they were heavily armored, armed with powerful guns, and mechanically reliable. Furthermore, North Korea had an air force of about 180 airplanes, WWII-vintage Yaks provided, of course, by the USSR.

During the nearly two years between the establishment of the opposing governments and the start of the war, the 38th parallel was the scene of many small skirmishes, propaganda raids, ambushes, and acts of sabotage. Nervous garrisons on both sides of the boundary occupied the frontier, and kept fingers near their triggers. Still, the South Koreans were comfortable in their independence, and felt little fear of their northern neighbors. Neither did the American advisers of KMAG suspect anything amiss. Indeed, Saturday night, June 24, was a typically festive weekend night, including a raucous gathering in Seoul at which U.S. Ambassador John Muccio was, as usual, the life of the party. (Later, many veterans of WWII would compare that night's revelry to the lively social gatherings that marked Honolulu on the night of December 6, 1941.)

When the onslaught came, before dawn on June 25, the NKA achieved complete strategic surprise. Kim's forces, organized into seven divisions and a brigade of tanks, plunged forward all along the front. The nearest American officer of the KMAG was in the city of Kaesong, practically on the frontier, and he fled in a careening jeep at dawn, chased out of the city in a hail of machine gun fire. By the time word of the attack, and complete confirmation, reached Seoul, the NKA was bearing down on the city like an unstoppable tide.

Further confirmation of hostilities came from North Korea itself, which announced the invasion as a "national defense against South Korean aggression." As soon as word of the attack reached the U.S., President Truman (who was at home in Missouri) made his way back to Washington, while in New York, the United Nations Security Council met in emergency session. Fortunately for the cause of South Korea, the USSR—a permanent member of the Security Council—boycotted the session, and thus did not have a chance to veto the actions of the UN, which called for an immediate withdrawal of North Korean forces and a cessation of hostilities. More significantly, the UN called upon member nations to assist South Korea in resisting the attack.

By the second day of the war, the NKA was approaching Seoul, driving the shattered remnant of the South Korean border garrisons before it. The wide Han River flows just to the south of Seoul, and the bridges over that flowage became critical choke points. A nervous officer of engineers prematurely blew up the main bridge, stranding many soldiers and civilians on the north bank; he was summarily executed for cowardice. The North Koreans occupied the capital, taking many prisoners, arresting many citizens judged to be reactionary, and swept onward.

In the meantime, Truman ordered General Douglas MacArthur, who was then in Tokyo commanding the United States occupation of Japan, to offer air and naval assistance to South Korea. MacArthur, for all his faults, was never one to avoid danger and, by June 28, he was personally reconnoitering the front, where he witnessed the remnants of the ROK forces falling back from the capital. The retreat was complicated by the masses of South Korean civilians mingling with the retreating army, clogging the roads, crowds churning along with growing panic. While his accompanying officers ducked bullets and bombs, MacArthur stood on a hilltop and observed the chaos. He immediately cabled the President with his assessment: the South Koreans would not be able to halt this attack without American troops on the ground.

At the time, U.S. assets in the Far East were slim. MacArthur had use of the Seventh Fleet and some eight combat groups of the Far East Air Force; he wasted no time in employing the ships to blockade the coast of North Korea, and committing the air forces to the battle in support of the ROK. His ground forces, however, were far from combat-ready. These consisted of four understrength divisions that had been softened by garrison duty in Japan. They lacked armor, supporting artillery, and anti-tank weapons, not to mention veteran soldiers. Still, by June 30th, the first of these—the 24th division, under General William Dean—began to move into the peninsula, arriving in bits and pieces at the southern port of Pusan.

In the meantime, the North Koreans continued to surge south-ward. On the eastern coast of the peninsula, moving against light to nonexistent resistance, the NKA columns had advanced three-quarters of the way toward the terminus of the peninsula, at Pusan, within the first four days of the war! Only a lack of supplies—they had outrun their support—and the absence of good roads approach-ing Pusan prevented the communists from attaining that ultimate objective the first week of the war.

The more intense combat occurred on the western side of the peninsula. It was here, on July 4, that the initial American forces made contact with a communist foe for the first time. Task Force Smith was an understrength infantry battalion (consisting of two, instead of the normal three, companies) under the command of Lieutenant Colonel Charles Smith. Supported by a single battery of artillery, TF Smith occupied a line just north of the city of Osan. The American companies were posted to either side of the main road into Osan, while ROK troops took up positions on both flanks.

The North Koreans attacked in a long column of trucks, with tanks in the lead. While the U.S. mortar, artillery, and machine gun fire played havoc with the enemy's trucks, the Americans had no answer for the T-34s. Their best anti-tank weapons were small (2.36") rocket launchers, commonly known as bazookas, and their projectiles typically bounced harmlessly off the heavily armored Russian tanks. In the meantime, the communist forces routed the ROK troops to either side of Task Force Smith, leaving the American force completely surrounded. During a furious battle, the U.S. troops held out until their ammunition was virtually exhausted; finally, the two companies began a retreat that quickly became a rout. Leaving much of their equipment behind, they were even forced to abandon the wounded who were incapable of walking— one officer could only offer a grenade to a wounded man, telling him it was "the best I can do for you." (More than half of the UN troops captured by the North Koreans would not survive their captivity.)

General Dean continued to commit his troops as they reached the front, and the sacrifice of the 24th division—mostly men who had been working at desk jobs up until the last week or two of their lives—did have an effect slowing the enemy advance. In the meantime, the 1st Cavalry Division and the 25th Infantry Division were hastily deployed from Japan. General Walton Walker took overall command of the troops that would soon become the U.S. Eighth Army, and he tried to use the remnants of the 24th Division to hold on while the rest of his troops could move into position.

The next key battleground was the city of Taejon. Here Walker thought he might be able to hold up the advance, but once again the collapse of ROK forces on the flanks exposed the Americans to envelopment and potential annihilation. Many troops were captured, including General Dean himself; stranded behind enemy lines, the division CO survived several weeks as a fugitive in enemy-occupied countryside before being betrayed into captivity by a civilian who had offered to lead him to friendly lines. Meanwhile, after being viciously attacked from three directions, the remnants of the battered 24th Division fell back, yielding Taejon to the enemy.

But now, finally, the momentum of the attackers was beginning to slow. One key NKA division, the 6th—a veteran of the Chinese Civil War—was ordered to clear out the resistance in the southwestern corner of the Korean peninsula, where virtually no defending troops were located. These tough fighters followed their orders, which relieved some of the pressure on Walker's units. Furthermore, the 25th Division was able to move into the line, replacing the all-but-destroyed 24th, while the 1st Cavalry Division and reorganized, re-equipped ROK formations began to show some stubbornness in the defense.

Back in the United States, the nation rallied behind President Truman, applauding his decision to meet communist aggression with force. On July 7, he had appointed MacArthur as Commander in Chief, United Nations Command. Truman had not asked for a declaration of war, so the Korean conflict was referred to as a "police action." Still, firm United Nations support for the South added international legitimacy to the campaign.

It was widely believed in the U.S. and Western Europe that the NKA was commanded by Russian advisers, and that the showdown in Korea was in fact a clash of the superpowers. In reality, while Stalin's men had trained and equipped Kim's army, and the Korean dictator thought that his invasion had tacit approval from the Soviet leader, the USSR pretty much kept its hands off the conflict—though Stalin surely relished the fact that the U.S. was paying so much attention to a relatively unimportant corner of the world, while the Communist Party leaders of the USSR kept their covetous eyes on Western Europe. The Chinese, too, remained watchfully aloof from the conflict, leaving Kim to his own devices. Still, in America, the idea of a monolithic communist conspiracy gave urgency to the war and bolstered popular support.

Ships of the Seventh Fleet sailed off both coasts of the Korean peninsula, providing gunnery support and launching air strikes from carriers. The Far East Air Force, now reinforced by an Australian group, had gained air superiority over the battlefield, and its planes harassed the NKA lines of communication and supply. These attacks blew bridges, strafed and bombed supply columns, and created a deadly gauntlet for the long supply line connecting the front line troops to their depots in the north.

One branch of the service that was quickly swept into the conflict was the United States Marine Corps. Like the Army, the Marines had been seriously depleted by post-WWII reductions in strength.

Still, as soon as the NKA attacked, officers of the USMC began to muster a force. At first this was merely a brigade-strength unit, created by pulling together active-service Marines from across the U.S. Hastily formed into platoons and companies, these men shipped out from California. An intended stop in Japan was cancelled, and the Marine brigade debarked at Pusan beginning August 2.

By then, Walker had pulled his defending forces—including three U.S. and four ROK divisions—back to their final position, issuing orders that there would be no more retreat. And, in fact, there was no place to fall back to. This ultimate defensive line, called the Pusan Perimeter, was an arc some ninety miles north-south and sixty miles east-west, defending the sole remaining port still held by United Nations forces. Pusan was located at the very southeastern tip of the peninsula. If it fell, all of Korea would be lost. Walker's Eighth Army was now being attacked by eleven NKA divisions, troops that were still riding the wave of initial success, determined to achieve ultimate victory. Kim Il Sung had thrown his entire army into the offensive, with the great majority of his troops occupying the front line, far to the south of the original border.

The key north/south line of the Pusan perimeter was anchored by the long Naktong River and the city of Taegu, and it was here that Walker was determined to make his final stand. Even so, the NKA pushed troops across the river in several places, driving wedges into the UN positions, threatening to blow the position wide open. The Marines arrived in the knick of time, their single formation—which included a dedicated USMC airgroup—serving quite literally as Walker's Fire Brigade. Many of the enlisted troops were fresh recruits, but their NCOs and officers included many veterans of WWII. There was no shortage of courage and determination along the perimeter, but the Marines truly excelled in this battle, in short order driving back one enemy penetration, then moving to counter another punch, and quickly returning to reclaim the ground gained by the initial attack when an enemy advance pushed out the troops that had relieved the Marines.

Enemy pressure remained strong all along the line, but as August eased into September, the situation began to stabilize. The NKA continued to attack, but there was little coordination to these offensives and, with his interior lines, Walker was able to shift reserves from one section to another as it became threatened. The shattered 24th Division was reconstituted with new arrivals, and became the Eighth Army's primary reserve. Walker was appalled when MacArthur ordered him to give up the Marine Brigade—though it was replaced with a British brigade, the 27th Infantry—but finally it was clear that the North Koreans had exhausted their punch.

As for MacArthur, he was just getting warmed up. Very early in the campaign he had formed a strategy, based on his experiences with amphibious operations during WWII, that he was certain would turn the tide. As the rest of the 1st Marine Division arrived in Asia, he did not commit it to the front—indeed, he brought the USMC brigade out of the Pusan perimeter in order to bring the division to full strength. Augmenting this with the U.S. 7th Infantry Division, he created X Corps, and announced plans for his lethal strike:

He intended to place X Corps ashore at Inchon, the port nearest to Seoul, and far behind the lines of battle at the Pusan perimeter. This daring stroke, MacArthur was certain, would lead to the annihilation of the enemy army and total victory in the war. Many others, including the Joint Chiefs of Staff, as well as his naval and amphibious force commanders, did not share the commanding general's enthusiasm. Inchon was a terribly dangerous place for an amphibious landing, with tides ranging up to thirty feet during a single day, strong currents, a narrow shipping channel, and mudflats along the beaches that were only passable to landing boats one day each month.

As usual, MacArthur was not to be deterred. He swept away the objections with his confidence, his articulate arguments, and his commanding presence—augmented by his reputation, only partially deserved, as a strategic genius of WWII operations. In the end, the Inchon landings were authorized, the decision made in mid-August for an attack on September 15. (If that date had been missed, a full month would pass before the next day of acceptable tide levels.) MacArthur appointed an officer from his own staff, General Edward Almond, as commander of X Corps, though Almond had little experience with combat operations or direct command of large troop formations. Still, he had been a loyal staff officer, and MacArthur liked him very much. With only a month of time to prepare—this was much less preparation than any similar operation had ever employed—the general staked his reputation, and the fate of the United Nations war effort, on what was, in effect, a breathtaking gamble.

And in this gamble, MacArthur must have been wearing his lucky shirt. The result was to be one of the quickest and most stunning reversals of military fortune in the history of war. The great amphibious fleet made its way down the long channel approaching Inchon. Despite several days of preliminary sea and aerial bombardment, the Marines landed at Inchon with virtually no opposition. Within two days they had captured Kimpo airport, the largest airport in South Korea, lying midway between Inchon and Seoul. The 7th Infantry Division followed the Marines ashore, and the two units closed in on the capital. Generals Almond and MacArthur were determined to announce the city liberated by September 25—three months after the start of the war—though the Marines who were doing the hard fighting, including division commander General Smith and famed WWII hero Colonel "Chesty" Puller, CO of the 1st Marine Regiment, insisted that they would not subject their men to extra casualties simply to meet that arbitrary date.

In the event, Almond and MacArthur declared the city liberated on September 26, though the actual fighting lasted several more days. Marines battled street to street, and even house to house, to clear the desperate NKA forces from the city. Casualties were heavy, but by the end of the campaign, the communist invaders were utterly defeated.

At the same time, Walker's men, spearheaded by the 1st Cavalry Division, broke out of the Pusan perimeter and counterattacked northward, a tank column shooting up the main highway toward the capital in true blitzkrieg fashion. The NKA troops on that line, exhausted by their long offensive and badly demoralized by the knowledge of a strong UN presence in their rear, collapsed. Many of them abandoned their weapons and simply dispersed into the countryside. Others fled northward, though they were generally unable to outrun the pursuing mechanized forces of the Americans. The 1st Cavalry linked up with Almond's X Corp troops at about the same time as Seoul was liberated. More than 100,000 NKA troops were captured; all of South Korea was liberated from the invaders.

Kim's ambitious attack, his attempt to unite the two Koreas under one communist regime, had failed and failed spectacularly. Yet it had come very close to success. The North Korean dictator and his allies made several key miscalculations which, together, allowed MacArthur's aggressive response to have a chance. For one thing, Kim was surprised by the vigorous American response. It seems likely that both Kim and Stalin expected the U.S. to remain aloof from the battle, which would have doomed South Korea in the first months of the war.

Furthermore, the Soviets blundered at the United Nations in their boycott of the Security Council meeting. Had the USSR representative vetoed the resolution to come to South Korea's aid, the resulting response would surely have been slower, and less robust.

Finally, the NKA underestimated the importance of American control of the sea, and failed to prepare a defense of Inchon even when MacArthur's intentions were made clear by the preliminary air raids and the approach of a large fleet.

As for MacArthur, his was already a career of legend, founded on well-deserved accolades for his speedy campaign up the islands of New Guinea and the Philippines as he closed in on Japan during WWII. His initial blunder in that war, when his large contingent of U.S. forces in the Philippines had been surprised by Japanese attack the day after Pearl Harbor was bombed, was long forgotten, and the audacious landing at Inchon was probably his finest hour as a commanding general.

With the liberation of Seoul, and the routing and destruction of the NKA, the Korean War for all intents and purposes was won, and won decisively.

*It wasn't over yet. It seemed at one point like the
weight-challenged mama-san had sung, but then things
changed. One side in Korea again seemed to be close to a
total victory, but this time with the Allies as the winners.
Then decisions were made that changed everything
and moved Korea from the win column to, at best, a draw.*

TO THE YALU,
AND AN ATTACK IN
A DIFFERENT DIRECTION

Or, How the United Nations Lost the Korean War:
Korea, 1950

DOUGLAS NILES

By the end of September, 1950, barely three and a half months
after a North Korean attack against the South started the Korean
War, the NKA was shattered, its major formations destroyed, scattered, or in chaotic retreat. The United Nations forces under General Douglas MacArthur had been pushed to the brink of defeat
until, sparked by the daring amphibious attack at Inchon, they had
completely turned the tide of battle in the course of two short
weeks. In the euphoria of the sudden and complete victory, it was
easy for the military and political leaders of the U.S. and South
Korea to overlook a few cracks in the façade of their great triumph.
But as that victory was heralded, with a formal ceremony reinstat-

ing Syngman Rhee as president of South Korea, those fissures were beginning to show.

Perhaps it was symptomatic that, despite the crucial contributions of the United States Marines, the senior army commanders—most notably Douglas MacArthur himself, as well as his hand-picked corps commander, General Almond—declined to invite any Marine representatives to the liberation ceremony at the National Palace. (Colonel Chesty Puller attended anyway, after instructing his driver to "run over" the nattily uniformed MP who tried to stop him.) As MacArthur formally declared to President Rhee that his country was being returned to him, the president of South Korea already possessed the same ambition as his counterpart to the north: he wanted to reunite the two Koreas into one state. This meant continuing the advance north of the 38th parallel, occupying the territory of Kim Il Sung's Democratic Peoples' Republic of Korea.

MacArthur, too, was determined to continue his pursuit of the shattered North Korean Army (NKA) units until that fighting force was completely destroyed. In this objective he had the support of President Truman and the Joint Chiefs of Staff. As soon as his seat was restored, President Rhee urged that the victorious American and ROK forces attack north of the 38th parallel. All of the signs marking this arbitrary border had been removed by the North Koreans during the early days of the war. There were very few NKA soldiers in position to resist this northward advance.

Truman and MacArthur did differ in their concerns about the war expanding beyond the Korean peninsula. The general chafed at restrictions on his command, most notably the orders that his air units could not attack, or even fly reconnaissance missions, north of the Yalu River, which formed the border between North Korea and the Communist Chinese territory of Manchuria. There were rumors and reports of larger Chinese forces gathering north of the river, but MacArthur was confident that Mao was bluffing, and would not enter the war. Truman was not so sure, and he issued the restricting orders to try to ensure that the communists would not fear an invasion of their homeland.

In the meantime, in Peking (Beijing), Communist China's supreme leader and de facto dictator, Chairman Mao Zedong, had carefully followed the misadventures of his erstwhile ally, Kim Il Sung, as the latter launched his surprise attack against South Korea. He had been pleased by the early successes of the communists, and alarmed by the stunning defeat inflicted upon the NKA in the wake of the Inchon landing and the breakout from the Pusan Perimeter.

In reacting to these developments, and the restoration of the ROK's government, the Chinese foreign minister went so far as to inform the Indian ambassador that the Chinese would intervene in the war if the UN forces advanced north of the 38th parallel. The Indian ambassador made certain that this news was carried to the west. But this crucial intelligence was discounted, since the Americans considered the ambassador to be an "unreliable reporter." The former Japanese ambassador to the United States, retired Admiral Kichisaburo Nakamura, also warned the U.S. government that, having issued the warning, the Chinese would be forced to intervene simply as a matter of saving face, if MacArthur's troops continued northward.

Nevertheless, units of the South Korean Army crossed the parallel on Oct 1st, under the overall command of General Douglas MacArthur, driving north along the east coast of the peninsula. American forces, spearheaded by the 1st Cavalry Division, advanced a few days later, moving north from the Seoul area. Walker's Eighth Army would drive on Pyongyang and clear the western half of North Korea. At the same time, Almond's X Corps embarked upon ships, sailed around the peninsula, and made course for an intended landing at Wonsan, the major port on the east coast of North Korea, some 100 miles north of the 38th parallel.

MacArthur's force, by now, had a true United Nations character. Although American and ROK units made up the bulk of the army, Turkey and Britain had each contributed a brigade, and Canadian, Australian, Philippine, Dutch, and Thai battalions rounded out the force. A sense of euphoria gripped the troops, and the folks back home, as there was a real sense that the war would be over before Christmas.

Truman was still worried about the possibility of Chinese intervention, and several of MacArthur's public remarks led him to believe that his commanding general did not share his apprehensions. The two men met face to face (for the only time during the war) on October 15th at a conference on Wake Island, a remote American base in the middle of the Pacific Ocean. MacArthur begrudged the time away from the battle—even though Truman flew nearly halfway around the world for the meeting—but the General was able to convince the President that he would proceed according to the wishes of the commander in chief.

On the peninsula, Walker's progress on the ground was swift, with Pyongyang falling to the Americans and South Koreans on October 20th. By the end of October, some ROK units had advanced to within sight of the Yalu. On the eastern flank, the fleet carrying X Corps approached Wonsan on October 19th, but an additional seven days were required to sweep mines from the harbor's approaches. The port itself had already been liberated by the rapidly advancing ROK vanguard, and when the Marines finally landed on Oct 26th—in a full-wave amphibious beach assault—they were chagrined to charge ashore to find signs inviting them to a USO show featuring Bob Hope, who was already in the city.

Still, the northward advance continued. There were warning signs in many places, including increasingly frequent reports of Chinese infiltration into Korea. Contrary to established doctrine, Eighth Army and X Corps did not maintain contact as they advanced. The heavily mountainous middle of the peninsula remained unoccupied and un-scouted. The UN forces, which were heavily mechanized, tended to stick to the roads, and gave little attention to threats that might be lurking in the trackless mountains.

On November 1st, a U.S. regiment was badly battered by a Chinese attack at Unsan, leaving no doubt that the Chicoms were present in Korea. Walker was becoming increasingly alarmed, and ordered his spearheads to slow down. He even pulled some of them back, establishing a position along the Chongchon River, where the Eighth Army would halt and await developments.

To the east, General Almond displayed no such misgiving, allowing X Corps to spread out across a very wide front, with his forward units advancing well beyond supporting range of their fellow formations. The ROK Capital Division reached the Manchurian border along the coast, while the U.S. 7th Division came into sight of Yalu at Hyesanjin. Despite steadily increasing reports, including interrogations of captured Chinese soldiers, Almond (and, by extension, MacArthur) continued to ignore the possibility of large-scale intervention by the Red Chinese.

On November 24th, MacArthur's "final" offensive began, with both Eighth Army and X Corps ordered to move northward. Once the Yalu was reached along a broad front, X Corps was to turn westward, and sweep all the remnants of the NKA into a vast trap. The war would be tidily ended, Korea unified and the troops on their way home by Christmas.

By the next day, however, that plan had been revealed as a pipe dream.

On November 25th, Walker's army was struck by a massive blow, with some 180,000 Chinese soldiers attacking across his front, the most powerful assault directed against the ROK II Corps on his right flank. That unit was shattered almost immediately, and the Chinese attack fell upon the U.S. 2nd Division, which lost some 4,000 men killed or captured and all of its artillery before fighting its way free of the trap. The Turkish Brigade moved up to fill the gap, suffering heavy losses, before the army extricated itself from the trap. Still, Walker's earlier caution paid dividends, as he was able to start his entire army retreating, with his right flank turned to repel the attacking Chicoms. By December 5th, he had withdrawn from immediate danger, and was able to continue a relatively orderly retreat down the western part of the Korean peninsula.

To the east, in the X Corps sector, an additional 120,000 Chinese attacked the widely dispersed units of Almond's men. On the coast, the ROK units started to withdraw immediately, and were able to pull back without serious losses. The Americans of the 1st Marine Division, and the 3rd and 7th Infantry, were not so lucky. They had advanced up both sides of the huge Chosin Reservoir and, when the Chinese attacked, these units were almost completely surrounded. One task force of Army infantry was completely wiped

out, and the two badly mauled infantry divisions fell back to the
ports of Hungnam and Wonsan, being forced to leave most of their
equipment behind.

On the west side of the reservoir, the Marines found themselves
completely surrounded. With temperatures plunging to well below zero (Fahrenheit), the men suffered tremendously from the
cold, and from the constant attacks. Nevertheless, the division
commander, General Smith, when asked what he thought about his
division being in retreat, angrily responded, "Retreat, hell! We're
just attacking in a different direction!"

And attack they did. In one of the epic sagas of American troops
in battle, the Marines of the 1st Division, with their wounded
packed into every available space on their trucks and jeeps, clawed
and battled and fought their way south down the single highway
leading them to the coast, against the constant resistance of the
Chinese. The road crossed a series of passes, some of them narrow
defiles, and in each case the Marines would send a company or two
to attack, seizing and holding the high ground to either side until
the long column was able to inch its way farther to the south. Supplies were dropped from the air, including, in one place, massive
sections of bridging so that the Marines could rebuild a destroyed
span across a gorge that would have been otherwise impassable.
After a running battle that lasted some thirteen days, the Marines
finally linked up with the 3rd Division and moved into the temporary safety of the defensive perimeter around the port city of
Hungnam.

With both ports protected by entrenched positions, Almond
ordered his corps evacuated by sea. Despite relentless pressure
from the Chinese, the debarkation of the corps went smoothly.
Some 100,000 troops, as well as nearly that many civilians and
more than 17,000 vehicles, were pulled all the way down to Pusan.
There, finally, X Corps was placed under the command of the Eighth
Army, where it would return to battle as the strategic reserve.

MacArthur's invasion of North Korea was unquestionably a major defeat, though the skill and courage of his fighting men had prevented it from becoming an unmitigated disaster. Still, the Chinese

went on to recapture Pyongyang and drive the UN forces all the way back to the 38th parallel. (Kim presided over an abbreviated, indoor ceremony when his capital was restored, since he was still worried about UN air attacks.)

But MacArthur, Almond, and to some extent Walker, had all failed to heed the warning signs of Chinese intervention. Almond's force, in particular, was caught flatfooted and terribly exposed when that intervention became manifest. MacArthur never accepted the restrictions implicit in a limited war—even advocating the use of atomic weapons against China—and eventually, when his public protests grew to an intolerable extent, Truman would have to remove him from command. Seoul would fall again, and be liberated, as the two sides engaged in two and a half years more of a war that each side had seemingly won, and lost, in the first months of the conflict.

As a final coda to the campaign, General Walker was killed in an accident in late December of 1950, when his jeep was struck by a truck that was trying to pass forward in a long convoy of vehicles. Lieutenant General Matthew Ridgway, a decorated commander of airborne forces during WWII, was sent to Korea to take his place. He would retain command of the United Nations forces for the duration of the conflict—and in fact, even before his relief, MacArthur turned over the management of the war to Ridgway to an extent he never did with Walker.

The war would sputter on for many more months, and many more lives. When a ceasefire was finally arranged, the boundary between North and South Korea remained pretty much where it had been since 1945, in the general vicinity of the 38th parallel of latitude.

*Taking a historical look at what happened to the American
military in Vietnam remains an emotional action. Too many
of us remain who lost friends or family in the war. But
on another level, the lessons learned there have made a
dramatic difference not only in military planning,
but also in how the civilian commanders became
involved or not involved in the conflicts that have followed.*

VIETNAM

1968

WILLIAM TERDOSLAVICH

The Vietnam War is over.

The fighting continues.

The United States cannot escape the ghost of the Vietnam War.
It haunts foreign policy, scaring presidents, generals, and congress-
men every time the armed forces must be sent into harm's way.
Every deployment runs the risk of turning into a quagmire, an un-
ending, unwinnable conflict against an elusive foe. Policymakers
don't talk about winning or losing, but of withdrawal dates and
exit strategies.

Put in overly simple terms: Liberals blamed conservatives for
losing Vietnam by charging headfirst into an alien land without
taking into account language and cultural barriers, differences in
understanding, and an appreciation for the limits of military power. Conservatives dished it right back, blaming liberals for being
too quick to appease, to surrender, and not going in with enough

force to get the job done quickly. Both like to blame the media presentation of the war.

Both sides overlook that maybe the enemy had something to do with the U.S. defeat. Had we won the war, there would be no controversy. Losing the war has driven an argument lasting decades, as many try to fix blame without understanding how to fix the problems the Vietnam War embodied.

Add up those problems and you have a near-perfect story on how to lose a war.

Did we ever learn from the mistakes?

The Simple Chronology

The tragedy of the Vietnam War reads like a five-act tragedy. Following France's defeat at Dien Bien Phu and their withdrawal, the U.S. first became involved in what was called the Advisory Period (1955–65), providing military aid to South Vietnam to resist invasion from communist North Vietnam. Lyndon Johnson's War (1965–68) committed U.S. ground forces to directly defend South Vietnam from communist aggression. The Tet Offensive (1968) marked the war's surprising and bloody climax, as North Vietnam attacked all of South Vietnam's provincial capitals and major cities, losing every battle but unintentionally breaking the political will of the American people to continue the war. Richard Nixon's War (1969–73) saw the withdrawal of all U.S. troops from South Vietnam and a negotiated settlement with North Vietnam. The final act was the tragic fall of South Vietnam (1973–75), when North Vietnam staged its last offensive, sweeping aside mediocre resistance in less than two months. In the end, the U.S. failed to help its ally stem the onslaught.

This merely sketches out the chronology of the war. The truth—and the errors—lie underneath the contentious clichés and slogans. The side that made the fewest mistakes won the Vietnam War. The conflict was fraught with error, misunderstanding, and miscommunication. North Vietnam won the war, but it was a strategically pyrrhic victory that held the nation in the past, staying poor while the rest of Asia got rich.

So who goofed?
And when?

The Advisory Period: A Big Mistake?

The strategic outlines of the Vietnam War were laid down early, hardening into an unyielding reality until war's end.

For North Vietnam, Ho Chi Minh set an uncompromising goal: unification of all Vietnam under the communist banner. Winning the war of independence against the French (1946–54) was not enough. Ho grudgingly settled for a partition of Vietnam, which would then be joined after elections, which did not come to pass under the Geneva Accords. The communist government set up shop in Hanoi, while virtually all 500,000 Vietnamese Catholics fled south. The Americans replaced the colonial French and backed Catholic anti-French dissident Ngo Dinh Diem in forming a Vietnamese national government, with Saigon becoming the capital of the new South Vietnam. Eighty thousand South Vietnamese communists fled north.

Fighting communism was the main driver for U.S. aid to South Vietnam. It was all part of the Cold War, a political and sometimes military struggle between the democratic and capitalist United States and the communist Union of Soviet Socialist Republics (USSR). Any gain made by one side was a loss for the other, even if the conflict took place in marginal parts of the Third World. The USSR and the People's Republic of China supplied North Vietnam's needs in the name of "international communist solidarity," but in reality both sought to extend their influence for reasons more Machiavellian than Marxist. North Vietnam could be equally cynical, playing off both communist giants against each other to get the most aid in its effort to take South Vietnam.

In 1959, North Vietnam's defense minister Vo Nguyen Giap commissioned two studies to see if troops and supplies could be routed via Laos and Cambodia into South Vietnam. Once this primitive route through mountains and jungles proved feasible, North Vietnam began sending the first of 80,000 South Vietnamese communists back home to start a guerilla war against the Diem regime. (They would later be called the Viet Cong, or VC.) The supply route, later known as the Ho Chi Minh Trail, became the logistic foundation for North Vietnam's forces for the entire war. By obtaining the discrete permission of "neutral" Laos and Cambodia to move troops through their territories, North Vietnam shielded its supply line from harm. Any attack mounted by U.S. or South Vietnamese forces to cut the trail would be seen as a violation of Laos and Cambodia's neutrality. This ploy worked for most of the war.

The VC—and later the North Vietnamese Army—would implement Mao Zedong's classic three-step strategy for guerilla war. First, organize the villages to create secure base areas and stage hit-and-run raids against the Saigon government's outposts and patrols. Second, once the guerilla effort was strong enough, launch larger raids in company and battalion strength against the government's battalions. Third, concentrate in regimental and division strength to fight and win main force battles against the Saigon regime's army.

Popular support, whether obtained by threat or persuasion, was vital. The guerillas could only survive if they "were the fish" that would "swim among the people." This strategy allowed the Viet Cong to make significant gains against Diem's government, eventually controlling almost a third of South Vietnam's land area by the time the Americans came in force.

Skillful at raiding and ambush, the Viet Cong had no trouble arming itself at the expense of the Army of the Republic of Vietnam (ARVN). South Vietnam's army was trained by the United States to defend against a conventional North Vietnamese invasion. This is what the U.S. expected following its experience in the Korean War. The approach proved useless defending against guerilla infiltration, where controlling people was more important than controlling ground.

Following his election in 1960, President John F. Kennedy increased the number of advisors in South Vietnam from a few hundred to a peak of 16,000 in a few years. To fight the so-called "liberation movements," Kennedy wanted the U.S. Army to form the first Special Forces units, known to us as "The Green Berets." The institutional Army would not accept Special Forces as a branch of service at first, and willfully resisted Kennedy's call for development of a counterinsurgency capability.

The advisory effort was faltering by 1962. In the Battle of Ap Bac, the ARVN concentrated several infantry battalions and a company of armored personnel carriers to surround and destroy a two-company VC battalion. They failed. The VC got away. The Pentagon proclaimed victory because the ground was taken, but U.S. advisors knew that was not so. Skeptical reporting on the war began as the advisors leaked the reality to the *New York Times* and other press outlets, leading to the first of many heated exchanges between the media and the military over "negative reporting."

In 1963, Diem's regime began its fateful slide. The Catholic refugees were his political base, while the army was his prime tool to keep himself in power. That left no room for the Buddhist opposition groups. Excluded from government, they began massive street demonstrations. A few Buddhist monks set themselves on fire and burned to death in protest. Communists were making gains in the countryside. ARVN generals sensed defeat. Taking matters into their own hands that November, with less than certain approval from the United States, the generals ousted Diem in a coup, later executing him. (Coincidentally, President Kennedy would be assassinated a few weeks later.) South Vietnam then suffered a series of coups until 1965, as the generals struggled to run the government. "Do you all understand English?" an exasperated Ambassador Maxwell Taylor once yelled at the generals. "I told you all clearly . . . we Americans were tired of coups. . . . We cannot carry you forever if you do things like this." General Duong Van Minh gave way to the politically maladroit General Nguyen Khanh, who was then replaced briefly by Dr. Phan Huy Quat, who was then undercut by Air Vice Marshal Nguyen Cao Ky, who was then out-intrigued by General Nguyen Van Thieu.

Whew!

Thieu would become our man in Saigon until the bitter end in 1975, when he realized he only had one country to give for his life.

He wisely chose luxurious exile in Europe, financed by ill-gotten gains.

The United States had to intervene to save South Vietnam from itself—and the communists. An excuse was needed. President Lyndon Johnson exploited an August, 1964, skirmish between the U.S. Navy and North Vietnamese PT boats in the Gulf of Tonkin. In just twelve hours, based on muddled, incomplete information, Johnson ordered the first air strikes against North Vietnam. LBJ was going to be tough on Communism. So was Congress when it passed the Gulf of Tonkin Resolution by a wide margin, empowering the President to use the military as he saw fit, so long as Congress was kept informed.

As president, Johnson was the commander in chief of the world's most powerful military, but hobbled by divided counsel among the service chiefs and the foreign policy holdovers from the Kennedy Administration. Ultimately, the war would be run by Johnson, Defense Secretary Robert McNamara, Secretary of State Dean Rusk, a few select civilian appointees, and Joint Chiefs of Staff chairman General Earle Wheeler, the only military representative at the table. Critics point out that the lack of military input toward crafting strategy was a major mistake, and that the passive and divided service chiefs should have resigned rather than letting Vietnam strategy be guided by unknowing civilians. LBJ's foreign policy circle was heavily influenced by nuclear strategic theory, which "signaled intent" through fine gradations of escalating action. Critics rightly point out that this creeping incrementalism robbed the U.S. of its ability to apply overwhelming force to win the war.

This amplified Johnson's greatest error: his failure to deal with the war decisively. Getting Congress to declare war on North Vietnam would have forced LBJ to declare what the goal was, muster the resources needed to fight and win the war. At such a point, the division of labor is pretty clear. The President must use his political skills to mobilize and marshal public opinion to support the war. The generals use their martial expertise to fight and win, calling for more resources to do so if they are lacking.

A general wins a war by winning battles.

A president wins a war by taking credit for them.

And he has to, for a president must use battlefield success to show the war is being won, and in turn maintain popular support for a war, which will decline as time goes on. Rather than sell the war, Johnson preferred to focus his energies on passage of Civil Rights legislation and the Great Society programs that he hoped would eliminate poverty.

The threat of defeat became the whip that flogged Johnson to fight the war he did not want. Defeat would condemn the Democratic Party to evisceration by conservative Republican critics who were more hawkish on Vietnam. It would be a repeat of the McCarthy witch hunts of the 1950s after China's loss to the communists. LBJ could limit the war by citing the need to avoid provoking China and Russia into fighting a larger war, just as Truman reined in U.S. forces during the Korean War.

The generals were divided or simply unable to adjust to irregular warfare, Johnson deployed enough force to avoid losing, but never really knew from the start how to win. He relied on the tendency of the American people to support the president when U.S. troops were sent into harm's way. He kept his salesmanship of the war to a necessary minimum to curry the needed political support, but this policy of "minimum candor" did not build trust. The goodwill of the American people was not a blank check with an infinite balance that Johnson could draw on. Americans will support a war for about two to three years, abandoning support if results are lacking. By taking public support for granted, Johnson was taking a grave strategic risk. He had every resource to fight the war on his side, but he did not have all the time in the world.

LBJ laid the groundwork for defeat very early, before the first ground troops ever went over. He never delegated military strategy to his generals, keeping a tight grip on its formulation and implementation. His need to appear tough confronting communism in Southeast Asia kept his critics in check, but robbed him of the chance to cut losses early and shut the war down by negotiation in 1965.

McNamara would drive the war effort on Johnson's behalf with a mind geared toward statistical inputs and measurable results, as if the war was just a bigger version of Ford Motor Company, where he once ruled as chairman. As the war progressed, the jungle of statistics yielded no sign of a decisive victory, like a Gettysburg or a D-Day, that a president could point to and say "we're winning." It just pointed to more fighting, more body count, more weapons seized, more of the same footage on the TV news every night, reminding Americans that it was the same old war, but fought on a different day.

Johnson increased the war's tempo in late 1964 by ordering Operation Rolling Thunder, an air campaign against North Vietnam. He also contemplated the deployment of ground troops, especially needed for air base security after the VC attacked grounded U.S. aircraft at Pleiku. Deploying ground troops and bombing North Vietnam added up to a flawed strategy, though Johnson did not know it. The Sigma I wargame of April, 1964, followed by Sigma II the following September, concluded that airpower alone could not break North Vietnam's ability to fight. Hanoi only had to send 10 to 15 tons of supplies per day down the Ho Chi Minh Trail to support its war effort in the South. The Viet Cong obtained most of its supplies locally. Sigma II also concluded that deploying ground troops would not win the war, only hasten the erosion of political support at home—in effect making the war self-defeating.

These results never got the attention of the chief policymakers surrounding Johnson. The White House picked the targets and shackled the Air Force and Navy with restrictive rules of engagement. Johnson wanted to avoid any incident that could trigger greater Chinese or Russian intervention. The port of Haiphong was never mined, for fear of sinking a Soviet freighter. Air defenses were never suppressed, lest bombs and missiles kill Soviet or Chinese missile and gun crews. Worse, North Vietnam never had enough industry to bomb anyway. So as long as the U.S. never interdicted Soviet shipments or Chinese supply trains, North Vietnam's capacity to make war remained unhindered.

The combination of American military strengths and political weaknesses made no difference to North Vietnam. In late 1964, just as the U.S. was increasing its bombing campaign, the Hanoi regime began sending the first units of the North Vietnamese Army (NVA) to South Vietnam.

Things Get Ugly: Johnson's War

Rolling Thunder began with a few U.S. air units based in South Vietnam. Viet Cong and North Vietnamese troops attacked several of the airbases. This prompted General William Westmoreland to ask for ground units in early 1965, starting with two battalions of Marines to protect the airbase in Danang. Eventually the Marines would be running aggressive patrols outside of the airbase to keep the enemy off-balance. Committing ground troops ended the advisory period, opening up Lyndon Johnson's War.

North Vietnam was in a hurry to deliver the "knockout punch" against the Saigon regime before effective U.S. intervention. The NVA began deploying in South Vietnam while Hanoi denied its presence there, a lie repeated for much of the war. Westmoreland's response was deployment of forty-four infantry battalions to prevent South Vietnam's fall to the communists. It became a race to see who could build up their forces more quickly. The U.S. had to transport its units from half a world away, building seven ports and upgrading numerous airfields to handle the inflow. North Vietnam was closer, but it took weeks to get a division into South Vietnam via the Ho Chi Minh Trail.

The U.S. met its deployment goal.

But so did North Vietnam.

Unseen by the United States was the divided counsel shaping Hanoi's strategic decision making. Eager to get quick results, North Vietnamese premier Le Duan wanted the NVA to fight main force battles against American units. Defense minister Giap, victor of Dien Bien Phu, advised that a protracted guerilla war would be a better strategy. Guerillas would wear down the American troops, who would leave when their political support collapsed at home, just like the French before them.

Chinese leader Mao Zedong also backed the protracted war strategy—after all, it had worked for him. But the Hanoi leadership was suspicious of Chinese motives. Historically, the two nations never got along well. North Vietnam's Politburo saw Mao's suggestion as a plan to fight to the last Vietnamese, thus weakening North Vietnam relative to China. Johnson and his advisors feared Chinese intervention, but did not know that Mao was going to stay out of the Vietnam War, as he planned to use his army to implement his Cultural Revolution—a purge of real and imaginary enemies in China's bureaucracy.

China did spare about 100,000 troops to provide air defense for the two rail lines between its border and Hanoi, as well as keeping them in good repair. Its cooperation with North Vietnam was hampered throughout the 1960s by the Sino-Soviet split, with North Vietnam eventually preferring the USSR as its main ally and supplier.

Given the task of winning the war within the limits of Johnson's hopes and fears, Westmoreland proceeded to fight with an eye toward defeating the NVA/VC forces and retaking lost ground. Westmoreland's biggest fear was that the NVA would concentrate its forces in South Vietnam's Central Highlands, then make a 100-mile dash to the coastal provinces, where most of South Vietnam's population resided. His 44-battalion deployment was to defend this coastal area until 1966, when additional troops would allow the U.S. to go over to the offensive.

Rather than sit tight, Westmoreland tried to preempt the NVA buildup. He deployed the First Air Cavalry Division to the Central Highlands in October, 1965. The first clash with the NVA occurred in the Ia Drang Valley near the Cambodian border. (This became the subject of the book and movie *We Were Soldiers Once, and Young.*) A battalion of infantry was landed by helicopter amid an assembly area for two NVA regiments. Superior firepower and air support allowed the U.S. to prevail despite being outnumbered six to one on the ground. The U.S. suffered 79 killed and 121 wounded, while enemy losses were 634 killed and another 581 estimated killed.

Giap was shocked by the defeat. He expected the Americans to advance by road from the coast, where they could be whittled down by repeated ambushes (it worked on the French). The Cav simply used its helicopters to hop over the terrain—and the ambush sites. The NVA seriously examined the battle for its tactical lessons. They would later fight against U.S. troops at close range, thus negating American artillery and airpower. The arrival of heliborne troops was always announced by artillery prep fires, so NVA units moved away from the landing zones—or advanced toward the LZs to launch surprise attacks and inflict casualties. Once U.S. firebases were set up, NVA and VC units always transited local areas just outside of U.S. artillery range. The key was always to pick an advantageous time and place to fight the Americans.

The NVA would change the way it would fight.

The army under Westmoreland was going to re-fight WWII and Korea.

The Marines had a different idea.

Given the I Corps operating area in South Vietnam's northern three provinces, the Marines attacked the VC/NVA at the village level through its Combined Action Program (CAP). A squad of Marines would enter a village and coordinate its patrols and ambushes with the local militia platoon, training the Vietnamese unit by example until it became proficient at providing security for the villagers. The Marines would get to know the people they were protecting and funnel economic aid to the villages, thus providing a tangible good that would sway the sentiments of the villagers for Saigon and against the VC. That in turn robbed the VC/NVA of the local support they needed to operate.

The Marines expanded CAP to 57 villages in 1966, then up to 79 in 1967. Statistics were compiled showing fewer U.S. casualties with this strategy while obtaining above-average village security.

Westmoreland did not see it that way, instead focusing on the fifteen main force VC battalions that operated in the Danang area. Large enemy units were free to come and go without interference, free to recruit in their localities. The Marines were not taking the war to the enemy, Westmoreland contended, and the Army did not have the manpower to place CAP squads in every South Vietnamese village. Westmoreland feared such dispersal of forces would result in U.S. units being defeated in detail, as each squad was no match against a VC battalion if the enemy stayed concentrated.

By the end of 1965, the U.S. would have 175,000 troops looking to kill NVA and VC. Westmoreland went on the offensive in 1966, sending out entire brigades and divisions to sweep the jungle for weeks or months. These units tried to find and destroy the enemy with massive, annihilating firepower. The VC and NVA would simply move away from those operating areas, leaving some detachments to fight and inflict some casualties. Re-infiltrating an area just vacated by the Americans proved easy.

All it would take to win would be more reinforcements and more time. By the end of 1966, the United States would have over 400,000 men. As 1967 gave way to 1968, another 100,000 men would be fighting in South Vietnam. With each troop increase, victory was just a year or two away, as Westmoreland was confident that he was bleeding the enemy dry.

That did not matter to the enemy. As Giap explained it, "every minute, hundreds of thousands of people die on the earth. The life or death of a hundred, a thousand, tens of thousands of human beings, even our compatriots, means little." North Vietnam had already suffered 500,000 casualties by 1969, Giap admitted to Italian journalist Oriana Fallaci, and the regime was committed to fighting the United States for decades, if need be, to achieve victory.

Westmoreland could not destroy this attitude with all the firepower in the world. Nor did he see that the terrain he needed to protect in South Vietnam was human rather than physical. Likewise, he did not possess a monopoly on being blind to reality. The NVA leadership proved just as wedded to preconceived notions. NVA and VC units could obtain "popular support" at gunpoint just as easily as through political organization, and the communist leadership did not see that difference. To launch the Tet Offensive of 1968, North Vietnam's leadership thought they had the support of the South Vietnamese people.

They had much less, but didn't know it.

Tet: How to Lose the War by Winning, and Win the War by Losing

By 1968, the U.S. would have close to 500,000 men in South Vietnam. NVA and VC strength averaged around 100,000 and just had to exist to disprove American and ARVN control on the ground. Giap had to replace almost the entire sum of this force yearly because of casualties.

Anti-war sentiments heated up in both countries. In 1967, North Vietnam purged its anti-war dissidents from its Communist Party, when they questioned the lack of results after losing so many men. Sending anti-war dissidents to secret prisons was not an option for the United States, which suffered growing protests on the college campuses and eroding support in Congress. Still, public support was standing by LBJ.

North Vietnam had to win the war quickly. Ho Chi Minh was no longer exercising active leadership, but his goal of unity was still North Vietnam's strategic aim, whatever the price. Le Duan pushed for an offensive. Giap resisted, was overruled by the Politburo, and like a good soldier, followed orders.

Planning for the Tet Offensive was extensive. VC and NVA cadres cased targets throughout South Vietnam for the better part of a year. Weapons and ammo were stockpiled. New units were infiltrated into areas Westmoreland thought were already swept clean.

The opening act would not be the offensive itself, but an attack on the USMC outpost at Khe Sanh, located near the Laotian border in South Vietnam's Central Highlands. A single USMC battalion guarded a single runway, well-placed to observe and interdict any cross-border infiltration. Here Giap concentrated two infantry divisions to besiege the lone Marine battalion. Westmoreland reinforced with a Marine regiment. Westmoreland was determined to do whatever it took to keep this battle from becoming another defeat like Dien Bien Phu in 1954. Massive air strikes and artillery firepower were the keys to holding the besieged base. Westmoreland briefly considered the use of tactical nuclear weapons. Whenever the enemy concentrated his forces to attack, a rain of shells and bombs would inflict massive casualties.

The siege was heavily covered by the American news media. LBJ even had a 3-D model of the battlefield installed in the White House basement, just so he could track the battle's progress.

Which is what Giap wanted.

Khe Sanh would fix Westmoreland's strategic attention, while the NVA and VC concentrated without interference on preparing for the offensive, scheduled for Tet, the Lunar New Year, in February, 1968. The attack would shatter expectations on both sides.

Viet Cong and NVA units attacked every provincial capital and major city in South Vietnam. North Vietnam's leaders expected these attacks to spark a popular uprising of the South Vietnamese people against Thieu's regime. Hanoi did nothing to politically prepare the people to rise up, despite painstaking military planning. So the South Vietnamese people did nothing. Westmoreland still had to juggle brigades, sending units to put out one fire after another, but after a month, the communist offensive was truly defeated. With overwhelming firepower, U.S. forces destroyed VC and NVA units with ease, winning every battle. Enemy dead numbered 40,000—roughly half of all forces attacking. The Americans lost only 1,000 troops, the ARVN another 2,000. The Viet Cong was totally destroyed as a large-scale fighting force, never again to operate at battalion strength or greater.

The only communist success was Hue. The old imperial capital of Vietnam was one of the country's largest cities, sitting on the coast just north of the Hai Van pass, linking South Vietnam's two northern provinces with the rest of the nation. Westmoreland's nightmare came true this time, as nine VC and NVA battalions concentrated in the Central Highlands and made a mad 100-mile dash for Hue, taking and holding the city for a month. Marines and ARVN were sent in to clear out the enemy, coming upon the mass graves of government officials and anti-government dissidents, executed by the communists before their defeat.

The United States lost the Vietnam War because of Tet, even though it had won every battle. The U.S. media, especially TV news, showed the chaos of sudden fighting in areas once deemed under control. Even the U.S. Embassy in Saigon was attacked. TV viewers at home saw the pictures but did not see their substance. The U.S. military won every fight, but the media only saw the fighting. What they saw was what you got on the news.

The White House did not expect American public support for the war to collapse. Neither did the North Vietnamese Politburo—those guys were banking on a popular uprising of South Vietnamese. Political repercussions were felt immediately in the New Hampshire primary, where anti-war candidate Sen. Eugene McCarthy garnered forty percent of the vote against Lyndon Johnson. A successful sitting president would never suffer such a result at the hands of a challenger. Voters were deciding that the war in Vietnam was unwinnable and without end. CBS anchorman Walter Cronkite opined as much on his news show.

Defense Secretary Clark Clifford convened a meeting of the Democratic Party's former foreign policy leaders, known as "The Wise Men," among them Dean Acheson. On the table was Westmoreland's request for another 150,000 troops and 18 to 24 months to win the war. The call-up of reserves would be needed to make this happen—a politically costly move just as the public was losing heart. Backed by Clifford, an avowed hawk, the council of "wise men" counseled withdrawal. Sensing the end of his power, Johnson made a televised address, calling for a halt to the bombing of North Vietnam and the beginning of peace talks. He then surprised everyone by announcing he would not stand for re-election as president.

Exit Johnson. Enter Nixon.

Nixon's War began with almost 550,000 troops in South Vietnam.

Ironically, Nixon won election campaigning as a peace candidate possessing a secret plan to end the Vietnam War. That was nowhere near true. Peace would have to come, sooner or later, as the United States could no longer win the war. The best Nixon could hope for was ending the war on his terms, which could only be shaped by the interplay between events on the battlefield and the Paris peace talks. North Vietnam's objectives remained unchanged, despite the death of Ho Chi Minh in 1969. They were still fighting for national unification, regardless of the human cost.

Nixon first disarmed the growing anti-war movement by instituting troop withdrawals, supplementing the move with increased American aid to bring the ARVN up to parity with U.S. forces. He coupled this with a diplomatic strategy to engage China and the Soviet Union to see if their support for the Hanoi regime could be reduced or ended. This did not succeed entirely, but perturbed Hanoi.

He also kept the pressure on North Vietnam, fighting outside the war's boundaries. Secretly, he ordered B-52 bombers to lay waste to the Ho Chi Minh Trail in Cambodia. (Press leaks about the secret bombing also prompted Nixon to place illegal wiretaps on White House staffers—the beginnings of an abuse of power that would lead to the Watergate scandal that brought his downfall.) This prompted North Vietnam, through local proxies, to clamp down on Laos and increase operations against the Cambodian government, now headed by General Lon Nol, who, with American backing, had recently overthrown Prince Norodom Sihanouk.

Nixon also had a new general, as Creighton Abrams replaced Westmoreland, now promoted to Army Chief of Staff. Strategy changed immediately, as Abrams placed limits on U.S. air strikes and artillery fire in his theater of operations. Massive firepower always destroyed any enemy units. It also leveled villages and killed peasants, generating a lot of animosity against the U.S. Restricting massive firepower forced U.S. units to rely on small arms and crew-served weapons, making it harder to fight the NVA, but it cut down on needless civilian deaths, and the U.S. still won all the firefights, despite losses suffered.

Abrams then reversed tactics. Now U.S. units would forgo the hunt for VC and NVA units, concentrating instead on finding rice and weapons caches. NVA strategy required emplacement of supplies in friendly controlled areas before deploying its units. Take away these stockpiles and the NVA could not show up.

Supplementing this effort was the arming of South Vietnamese militias, known as Regional Forces/Popular Forces. RF/PF units operated at the village and province level, allowing volunteers to defend their localities from NVA encroachment. ARVN and U.S. units would supplement the effort, providing the overwhelming hammers that beat the enemy against the humble village-based anvils. Thieu had some misgivings about arming the people, for fear of suffering yet another resistance movement, but noticed that most of the South Vietnamese people would *not* side with the communists. Much of South Vietnam managed to "self-pacify" this way.

Abrams tightened cooperation and coordination with U.S. ambassador Ellsworth Bunker and CIA station chief William Colby. The Phoenix Program, run by Colby, targeted NVA political cadres for assassination. The program suffered some abuse by Thieu's corrupt crony generals, who used Phoenix assets to target non-communist opponents. But Phoenix did strike fear into the heart of the NVA. Cadre leaders could never be sure they were free of spies, spending more time in purges and second-guessing, thus hobbling their own efforts.

Still, Abrams did not have time on his side. He had to get results with the troops that he had before they went home. In 1970, U.S. and ARVN units invaded Cambodia, seizing supplies and pre-empting the build-up of NVA forces poised to attack South Vietnam. This triggered an explosion of anti-war protests in the U.S. Congress followed up by passing a law to deny funding to theater ground operations outside of South Vietnam. In 1971, the ARVN invaded Laos to cut the Ho Chi Minh Trail. The offensive bogged down as the ARVN proved to be incompetent, only being rescued from destruction by massive U.S. artillery and airpower. Congress followed that up by refusing to fund any air operations outside of South Vietnam by air units based there.

Nixon would withdraw 165,000 troops in 1970 and another

90,000 by the spring of 1971, shifting more of the fighting burden to the ARVN. They could hold their own when operating with American units, but the ARVN on their own still had problems, even after a decade's worth of U.S. training and arms.

Concurrent with those operations and troop withdrawals in 1971 and 1972 were the Paris Peace Talks held between National Security Advisor Henry Kissinger and North Vietnamese foreign secretary Le Duc Tho. Hanoi's position called for a coalition government in Saigon that met Viet Cong approval. This was a nonstarter for Kissinger, who pressed for total withdrawal of all "foreign troops" from South Vietnam. If the U.S. had to leave, so did the NVA. Of course, this was a nonstarter for Hanoi.

Negotiations dragged and lagged. North Vietnam's 1972 Easter Offensive sought to improve Hanoi's negotiating position by seizing more South Vietnamese real estate. The U.S. only had 6,000 combat troops remaining in South Vietnam out of 70,000 support troops still present. Hanoi launched the Easter Offensive, looking to destroy the remaining American presence, thus humiliating the U.S. and improving its negotiating position at the same time. The tactic had worked against the French.

It was to be a conventional attack, with NVA infantry divisions backed by armor and artillery. Despite Giap's upshift to conventional war at an opportune moment, the offensive was hobbled by the NVA's inability to operate infantry, armor, and artillery together under a combined arms doctrine. The primitive Ho Chi Minh Trail proved unable to supply a modern fight, as supplies that were painfully stockpiled for months got used up in days, much more quickly than expected. The attacks, on Quang Tri in the north, in the Central Highlands and at An Loc in the south, were all easily blunted and parried by ARVN units backstopped by U.S. advisors and airpower.

The offensive also prompted Nixon to renew the air war over North Vietnam that May. North Vietnam's Russian backers hardly protested. Linebacker was a nastier reincarnation of Rolling Thunder. Haiphong was mined and Hanoi bombed. There were no White House restrictions on targeting.

North Vietnam failed to destroy the ARVN and topple the Thieu regime.

The U.S. failed to compel North Vietnam to abandon its war effort.

Only winners can dictate peace terms.

By October, 1972, both sides had to compromise at the negotiating table. Kissinger dropped the demand for mutual withdrawal of forces, but coupled U.S. withdrawal with the release of American prisoners of war held by Hanoi. Le Duc Tho no longer insisted on Thieu's resignation, followed by a communist-influence coalition government.

Both sides could have agreed on these terms two years before, but the peace talks were not held in an atmosphere of mutual trust. To North Vietnam, it was just another front in the war, poorly reinforced by events on the battlefield. Le Duc Tho offered a standstill agreement—all NVA and VC forces stayed where they were in South Vietnam. All American concerns regarding U.S. troop withdrawal and PoW release would be resolved. Political considerations between Hanoi and Saigon would be postponed pending formation of a "council of reconciliation," a hazy fiction at best. There was no guarantee that communist forces, left intact in South Vietnam, would not renew the fight.

Thieu would have to be pressed by the United States to accept these terms. He balked. Nixon's decisive re-election in November forced the issue, as he promised aid to South Vietnam if the NVA revived the war. Kissinger still brought Thieu's objections, embodied in numerous amendments, back to the negotiating table. Le Duc Tho broke off talks to return to Hanoi for "consultations." The U.S. responded with Linebacker II, sending the B-52s back to North Vietnam to drop more bombs. Fifteen of these giant bombers would be lost to SAM missiles over Hanoi as bombing continued through the Christmas season.

By December 30, the U.S. had run out of targets.

North Vietnam ran out of SAMs.

The bombing was halted.

The peace talks resumed.

Final terms were hammered out.

The papers were signed in Paris in January, 1973, thus ending the war for the U.S.

But was the war truly over?

The Last Act

The U.S. officially exited the war, but it was not over yet. North Vietnam resumed planning for yet another offensive, set for 1975. The Ho Chi Minh Trail was paved all the way into South Vietnam's Central Highlands. The Arab oil embargo of late 1973, coupled with the doubling of oil prices, gutted South Vietnam's ability to keep its air force airborne and its mechanized army trained and operational.

North Vietnam renewed its attack in early 1975, first taking a provincial capital to see if the attack provoked renewed American involvement.

It did not.

The NVA went all out, just as it did in 1972, using artillery, armor, and infantry to fight a main force war against the ARVN, which collapsed in retreat. Thieu desperately gave up the Central Highlands, hoping to draw a more defensible line to protect South Vietnam's populous southern third.

The withdrawal turned into retreat, then into a rout, and finally became a panic as ARVN units fled, with hordes of refugees not far behind. In vain, Thieu reminded Nixon's successor, Gerald Ford, to make good on America's promise of aid in South Vietnam's dark hour of need.

American aircraft carriers returned to the waters off South Vietnam. No aircraft took off to save the ARVN one more time. No Marines were landed to fight alongside the ARVN to stabilize the front. No surge in supplies and arms came. The U.S. evacuated its embassy and aid personnel. Some South Vietnamese managed to fly out to the carriers. Flight deck crews quickly tipped the helicopters over the side to make room for the next arriving refugee flight.

Americans watched South Vietnam's death throes on television. Ford could not keep America's promise to an ally suffering defeat. Congress would not let him. The war was that unpopular.

It took less than two months for NVA tanks to reach Saigon. Complementary efforts placed communist regimes in power in Laos and Cambodia.

The war was over.

The bad guys won.

Was There a Better Way?

The United States and North Vietnam committed many errors in the Vietnam War, but victory eventually went to the side making the fewest mistakes.

For the United States, the biggest mistakes were institutional. No capability to wage counterinsurgency was built. The Army refused to learn from experience in the field (or from the U.S. Marines) until it was too late to win the war. American forces still won their battles, but political and military leadership figured out too late that it had to win the support of the South Vietnamese people to win the war and maintain public support at home. Taking ground and killing NVA was not enough.

One option not pursued by the U.S. was for a conventional invasion of Laos to cut the Ho Chi Minh trail. Westmoreland had one plan to push the First Cav and a Marine division through Tchepone, Laos, all the way to Savannakhet on the Mekong. The ARVN attempted to cut the Ho Chi Minh Trail in a more limited version of the plan in 1971. Success, however, was not guaranteed. The Sigma I and II studies concluded that little supply was needed by the VC to fight its war in South Vietnam, so such an offensive would have been eventually moot if nothing was done to eliminate the ability of the VC to operate in South Vietnam.

The alternative was for the U.S. to stick to a strictly defensive deployment of the coastal zones of South Vietnam, ceding the sparsely populated Central Highlands to the enemy. This plan would have required about 180,000 men, far less than the peak deployment of 550,000. Such a strategy would have been easier for the American public to support over time. It would have inflicted a stalemate on the firepower-disadvantaged NVA and VC infantry.

North Vietnam, on the other hand, also fought the war way above its means. Sacrificing 100,000 men a year for six years eventually paved the way toward victory, but the preparations for the 1975 offensive saw the nation literally strip itself of all available personnel just to man the army. Poor nations can ill afford to put its few college-educated people in the ranks, which is just what North Vietnam did for its final push. In retrospect, it would have been far easier to have fought a protracted guerilla war, making less resource and political demands on North Vietnam. It could have been a poor man's war fought well within its means. The United States still had the clock, but the North Vietnamese certainly had the time.

With so much effort and resources expended on the war, North Vietnam remained stuck in the past as much of Asia embraced capitalism and moved forward, increasing the standard of living for billions of people. Unified Vietnam could "take pride" in its "greatest generation," defeating two superpowers in thirty years.

Victory offers no lessons to the winner. Giap was dismissive of Westmoreland. "He came, he saw the problems, and requested 200,000 men . . . but if he thought 200,000 men would be enough, he was wrong." Giap was equally indifferent to Abrams. "He based his leadership on research. He studied his own and others' experiences to see what he could apply to the real situation here, but he believed he would win and was defeated." No matter who was in command of U.S. forces, they all shared the same error: "Their mistake was that of invading us, but that was the responsibility of the U.S. government."

A pithier anecdote came from Colonel Harry Summers, who recounts a dialogue between a U.S. officer and his NVA counterpart after war's end:

"You know, you never defeated us on the battlefield," said the American.

"That may be so, but that is also irrelevant," replied the NVA officer.

United Vietnam stood proudly in victory in the years after the war, but the nation nearly starved. The repressive government curtailed what few freedoms the South Vietnamese had. A half a million people fled the country by any means possible, even in flimsy boats, hoping to make landfall anywhere to get away from hunger and tyranny.

The war left the United States two legacies. First, the Army refocused its attention on conventional war and achieving excellence in set-piece battle. The results were seen in the decisive defeat of Iraq in the Gulf War of 1990–91.

The self-doubt of Vietnam was slain at last.

Or was it?

Which brings us to the second legacy, when the United States Army deliberately effaced Vietnam from its institutional memory. Gone were the hard-learned lessons of counterinsurgency. That neglect would haunt the United States as it tried to fight a counterinsurgency campaign in Iraq following its quick conventional victory of 2003.

Those who choose to ignore history are condemned to repeat it.

Or in this case, watch the rerun of the Vietnam War on TV, with a whole new cast in Washington, D.C. and Iraq, and Afghanistan.

Once more they should not have won. Outnumbered, outgunned, defending a small area, and on the defensive, there was no way for Israel to survive, much less defeat the united strength of the nations surrounding it. As is always the case when there is an unexpected and one-sided victory, this surprising Israeli victory was as much a case of what their attackers did wrong as their undeniably brilliant defense.

THE SIX-DAY WAR

ROBERT GREENBERGER

Egyptian President Gamal Abdel Nasser proclaimed in May, 1967, "The armies of Egypt, Jordan, Syria, and Lebanon are poised on the borders of Israel . . . to face the challenge, while standing behind us are the armies of Iraq, Algeria, Kuwait, Sudan, and the whole Arab nation. This act will astound the world. Today they will know that the Arabs are arranged for battle, the critical hour has arrived. We have reached the stage of serious action and not of more declarations."

If that was the case, how on Earth did Israel manage to defeat such formidable forces in a mere six days, redrawing the Middle Eastern map for years to come?

The nations Nasser mentioned were less than thrilled when the United Nations partitioned the land and formed Israel in 1948. The promise of a parallel Palestinian nation was never kept and the notion that a people they loathed now were given a piece of the Holy Land as their own irritated them. As a result, none officially recognized the new country and hostilities flared up almost immediately and lasted, well, through now.

Twice before, Israel and Egypt clashed and, in both cases, the new country prevailed, which fostered growing resentment.

The seeds for the latest conflict were sown as far back as 1964, but really heated up in the first half of 1967. After the Suez Crisis of 1956, Israel backed off the land it conquered after pressure from both the United States and the USSR. All sides agreed to the addition of the United Nations Emergency Force to occupy the Suez region as a buffer between the countries. Part of the agreement also led to Egypt reopening the Straits of Tiran to Israeli shipping.

Things remained relatively quiet until 1964, when Israel and its neighbors bickered over, of all things, water. When Israel began drawing water from the Jordan River, Jordan and Syria sought to master the life-giving water by controlling the Banias stream and depriving Israel of eleven percent of the water it currently enjoyed.

Israel's Defense Forces attacked Syria as part of the diversion plan in the spring and summer of 1965, escalating tensions in the region.

The following year, after three soldiers were killed by a mine, Israel struck back attacking the West Bank village of Es Samu, filled with Palestinian refugees. This was followed up with a series of armed engagements throughout the region that saw dozens killed. In America, it was considered an out of proportion retaliation that threatened to destabilize the region. To the countries involved, it hardened their resolve to eradicate the upstart nation. On the hook was King Hussein, who had been quietly negotiating peace with Israel's Golda Meir the previous three years, and suffered a bad loss in the West Bank.

Seeking to save face, Hussein signed a November, 1966, agreement with Nasser that pledged mutual military support in case of war, encouraged by the USSR, which sought to temper Syria's desire for revenge and keep the region stable.

The following year, Israel began talking to the press about their concerns that the Arab countries were conspiring for a new conflict. There was also growing desire to cultivate the DMZ, but the

Syrian army, based on the opposite side, would shoot at the first sign of movement. Each time Israeli tractors entered the land, they pushed further and further, forcing Syria's hand, and the Israelis fought back. Israel was definitely spoiling for a fight.

Syria and Israel finally engaged in something resembling a real battle, as aircraft from both sides engaged on April 7th. Syria lost half a dozen MiG-21s over the Golan Heights as politicians made speeches about the DMZ and who could best cultivate the land. They felt their hand was forced, as Israel continued to send tractors into the zone and, when the Syrian army fired, Israel merely sent in armor-plated tractors and tilled the land. Provoked, Syria began shelling the Kibbutz Gadot, dropping over three hundred shells in a mere forty minutes.

The stage having been set, Israel decided in early May that a strike against Syria was warranted and then threatened they would use force equal to the April 7th fight, although factions wanted something larger in scale to put Syria out of action, once and for all. It was also presumed, despite the pact, Nasser would keep his men out of a battle. Press reports at the time were somewhat erroneous but served to fan the flames for war, and had the region, and the world at large, concerned.

Similarly inflating matters was a false report from Soviet president Nikolai Podgorny to Egyptian vice president Anwar Sadat stating Israel armed forces were massing along the Syrian border. Syria responded by proclaiming they had the forces in position to repel the Zionists and crush them once and for all. One general called the moment a time for annihilation.

Ratcheting matters up, Egypt declared a state of emergency and issued the following:

Egyptian Battle Order No. 1, issued by Field Marshal Abd al-Hakim Amer, 14 May 1967:

In the past few days, reliable reports have disclosed that there are huge Israeli troop concentrations on the Syrian borders. Their intention is to intervene on Syrian territory in order to:

1. *Overthrow the Arab liberated regime and establish a hired reactionary regime in Syria;*
2. *Suppress the movement for the liberation of Palestine.*

This was supported by the aggressive declarations, characterized by their impudence, which were made by the Israeli prime minister and chief of staff of the Israeli army, and which represent an undisguised provocation of the Arab liberated forces, at the head of which is the United Arab Republic. . . .

But, after considering all the possibilities, we decided to take a firm stand against the Israeli military threats and intervene immediately in case of any aggressive action taken by Israel against Syria. . . .

The following orders have been issued:

1. *Mobilization of the armed forces;*
2. *Raising the level of preparedness to full alert for war, beginning 14.30, 14 May 1967;*
3. *The formations and units indicated by the operation plans will move from their present stations to their appointed grouping areas;*
4. *The armed forces will be at full alert to carry out their battle assignment on the Israeli front according to developments in the situation.*

On May 16th, the United Arab Republic (called Egypt these days) tossed the UN forces out of the DMZ, figuring if Israel and Syria were ratcheting up for a war, it was better to get the peacekeepers out of the way. UN secretary-general U Thant tried to find a diplomatic solution before the shooting began, but was rebuffed by all sides. In fact, the UN forces, two days later, were told to get out—now. When U Thant suggested moving his peacekeepers to the Israeli side, his plan was rejected by the Knesset. On May 19th, U Thant ordered the forces out of the region.

The UAR then mobilized their forces and sent one thousand tanks and one hundred times that many soldiers to the border. And here's where they made their first mistake. Egypt began moving men and materiel three times within the space of a month, exhausting the troops, creating confusion, and affecting morale.

They also closed the Straits of Tiran and Gulf of Aqaba to any vessel flying the Israeli flag as of May 22nd. Problem was, Israel had more or less stopped using the straits, so it was basically an empty gesture to incite their allies to rail against the usurper nation. In fact, no Israeli ship used the straits in the previous two years, instead using Mediterranean ports for its shipping traffic. However, in 1957, Israel had stated that closing the straits would be considered by them an act of war, something Egypt knew, so the act was certainly designed to provoke a reaction. Gamal Abdel Nasser said before the Egyptian parliament, "The problem before the Arab countries is not whether the port of Eilat should be blockaded or how to blockade it—but how to totally exterminate the State of Israel for all time." Clearly, they were spoiling for a war.

Mohammed Heikal, a journalist, wrote in the Egyptian newspaper *Al Ahram*, "Hence I say that Israel must resort to arms. Therefore I say that an armed clash between the UAR and the Israeli enemy is inevitable."

Abba Eban, Israel's Foreign Defense Minister, traveled to Europe and Washington in an attempt to quash the brewing crisis. Meantime, Egypt was busily mobilizing its forces and enlisting support from across the Arab League.

On May 23rd, the Israeli cabinet approved a resolution calling for an armed response should the straits not be reopened to Israel within 48 hours. After hearing from U.S. Undersecretary of State Eugene Rostow, this was amended to a longer period of remediation, no more than two weeks. At this time, it became increasingly clear that, given the Arab forces amassing against them, a preemptive strike was in the country's best interests for survival.

Abdel Hakim Amer, an Egyptian field marshal, had proposed a plan of attack calling for them to cut off Eilat early on May 27th. At much the same time, Abba Eban was in Washington, seeking assurances of how America would act in case war actually broke out. Upon arrival, he read a cable from home indicating their intelligence sources had learned of Amer's plan. An angry Eban had a series of meetings with Secretary of State Dean Rusk, Defense Secretary Robert McNamara, and President Lyndon Johnson. All assured Eban that their own intelligence indicated the Egyptian movements were all defensive ones. Eban was less than thrilled with his ally's response. He was convinced Egypt was ill-prepared to fight and was stalling.

Later, Johnson grew concerned that Israel's sources might be more accurate so he used the Hot Line to Russia to check with Alexey Kosygin and see what they could tell him. His note stressed that, should a fight break out, it might turn into a global conflict, something no one wanted.

Kosygin sent a note via Ambassador Dmitri Pojidaev to Nasser, essentially telling him not to launch an attack. If they did, the USSR would not support Egypt. Hours later, Amer canceled his planned attack.

Israel named Moshe Dayan its Defense Minister on June 1st and met with his commanders. They drew inspiration from their conflicts in 1948 and 1956, where they proved triumphant over Egypt. A quick victory was called for, and a decisive one, to quell anti-Israel feelings throughout the region. It was clear to them, striking soonest was in their best interest.

That night, Dayan met with Chief of Staff Yitzhak Rabin and Southern Command Brigadier General Yeshayahu Gavish. Each presented plans for attack with Dayan endorsing Gavish's more decisive notion that included destroying the Egyptian presence in the Sinai.

Israel and Egypt began fighting on June 5th, with the smaller country first saying they were the aggrieved party but later admitting they struck first. Their announcement stated it was a preemptive strike intended to forestall an invasion, but a later analysis showed that Israel had not expected an attack at that time.

Honoring the mutual defense treaty it signed a mere week earlier, Jordan came to Egypt's aid and attacked Jerusalem and Netanya at 11 a.m. Jordan felt it had little choice, sensing its people wanted conflict, while Israel beseeched King Hussein to stay out of the fight. Hussein, called an imperialist lackey by Nasser before the treaty was consummated, eagerly joined with Syria and Egypt, agreeing when Nasser said, "Our basic objective will be the destruction of Israel. The Arab people want to fight."

After the treaty was signed, Egypt's General Abdul Munim Riad was given command of the Jordanian forces. Two days before the war broke out, two battalions of Egyptian soldiers were flown to Amman; their mission was to provoke the Israeli army into attacking along the Jordanian border, distracting Israel and buying time for Egypt.

During this period of intensification, Israeli Foreign Minister Abba Eban remained convinced that Egypt was not ready to fully commit to a war. Even the *New York Times'* James Reston wrote that the larger country was not in a position to wage a war. Prophetically, he wrote, "But it has already accepted the possibility, even the likelihood, of war, as if it had lost control of the situation."

When the fighting finally broke out, Washington was unhappy, since it meant their ability to broker peace was disrupted. A planned visit by Egyptian Vice President, Zakkariya Muhieddin for June 7th was canceled and Rusk was disappointed with their Middle Eastern ally, Egypt.

Egypt wasn't ready to fight but they were certainly in the midst of preparations. At the time of the attack, they had four infantry, two armored and one mechanized division, totaling 100,000 men, in the Sinai. They were bolstered by four independent infantry and four independent armored brigades. All told, they had 950 tanks, 1,100 APCs, and more than 1,000 artillery pieces.

By this time, Nasser had been redirecting his forces for about a month, changing his orders four times over the previous few weeks. Each change required moving men and materiel, which taxed all concerned. Finally, around the time of the Israeli vote on the straits, Nasser ordered his commanders not to use their latest plan, called Qahir ("Victory"). Instead, he wanted a defense of the Sinai to be their main objective while bringing Syrian and Jordanian troops into the mix. At the time, Syria's troop force was a mere 75,000, while Jordan had even fewer men, 55,000. Ironically, Jordan was using mostly U.S. M48 Patton tanks, plus M113 APCs, and a paratrooper battalion that had been trained in a U.S.-built school. They also had 12 battalions of artillery and six batteries of 81mm and 120mm mortars.

Nasser had commanded that lines of defense be formed. The second line was farther back, some thirty to sixty miles from the border, composed of the Egyptian Third Division and a Special Task Force led by General Sa'ad al-Din Shazli.

A third line was near Bir Gifgafa and Bir Thamada, manned by the Fourth Armored Division and a motorized infantry brigade. As positioned, they were set to defend the Bir Gifgafa airbase, and to hold the Mitla and Gidi Mountain passes.

Compared to this, Israel had a maximum of 264,000 troops, including reservists.

At 7:45 a.m., Israel scrambled approximately 180 of its jet fighters to launch Operation Moked ("Focus"). En masse, they crossed the Egyptian border, unexpectedly coming from the Mediterranean, and concentrated their attack on the airfield, intending to obliterate the Egyptian air force. The timing was geared to take advantage of the Egyptian leaders most likely being caught in the usual weekday Cairo rush hour and unable to be contacted.

Egypt was ill equipped for such an attack, with none of their airfield properly prepared to protect their aircraft from bombs. Additionally, at that time, they unwisely chose to turn off their air defense system to avoid accidentally attacking a single plane, one carrying Amer and Lt.-Gen. Sidqi Mahmoud, en route from al-Maza to Bir Tamada in the Sinai.

The Israeli planes flew fast and low so that they were beneath radar detection and too low for the SA-2 surface-to-air missiles to be effective. The jets flew in three waves of four planes to each target so that as one wave finished, the second was approaching with the third right behind. By the time the third wave completed their run, the first wave had refueled and was back, allowing Israel to sustain a two-and-a-half-hour bombing sortie. The initial strafing runs and bombing destroyed more than 300 parked aircraft and rendered the runways unusable, crippling the Egyptian air defense in a single morning. Israel lost a mere nineteen planes, mostly due to their own mechanical or operational issues.

Another advantage Israel had was that their pilots and crews had trained hard to enable them to ready planes for the air in record time so each jet could accomplish four missions a day, compared with the Arab average of two. The increased number of sorties led the Egyptians to erroneously conclude Israel had foreign help.

In the years preceding the war, Israel had also obtained vital information about the MiGs flown by the Egyptians. A number of pilots from Egypt, Iraq, and Syria had defected with their aircraft to Israel since 1964, allowing Israeli pilots to test fly the MiGs and plan effective maneuvers.

Once Egypt's air might was crippled, Israel turned their attention to doing the same to the Jordanian, Syrian, and Iraqi air fleets. All were hit hard that first afternoon, catching the entire ill-prepared Middle East by surprise.

On the ground, Egypt was following Russian protocols and was positioned so the mobile armor was placed deep, providing cover for the ground troops, allowing Israel to attack first and get worn down before hitting the armored forces. This followed the pattern of a World War II conflict known as the Battle of the Kursk Salient. The Russians and Egyptians anticipated that Israel would attack in force-flank action from the southern and central routes to the Sinai and were positioned accordingly.

As a result, they were caught off guard when the ground attacks occurred at the same time as the air assault, and came from the northern and central routes using direct tank action. This allowed Israeli forces, under the command of Major General Israel Tal, to march into the Gaza Strip.

Major General Ariel Sharon managed to attack the heavily fortified Egyptian forces from the front, flanks, and rear simultaneously, using ground troops and paratroopers.

For three and a half days, the Israelis and Egyptians fought in what is now called Battle of Abu-Ageila, until Gaza fell to the Israelis. When word of the loss, among other attacks, reached Egyptian Minister of Defense Amer, he panicked. Over the next few hours, he issued order after order, many of them contradictory, until he finally sounded a retreat from the Sinai, essentially ceding it to Israel. Had he analyzed his forces, he would have realized there were enough men and equipment left to wage a defensive action.

Such ill-informed and uncoordinated actions were a hallmark of the Arab side of the conflict, granting Israeli superiority.

Amer's clear lack of control worried other commanders, who actually abandoned their troops and headed back to Cairo. Whereas Israel had a tight, focused command structure, the Egyptian army was nowhere near as disciplined, a large factor in their loss that week.

Rather than pursue the retreating Egyptians, the Israeli High Command sent their men headed west to reach the West Sinai's passes. Tal's men were positioned along the Suez Canal while Sharon's divisions blocked Mitla Pass and Gidi Pass. The Egyptian army, though, managed to get past these points and crossed the canal without major loss of life.

The capture of the Sinai was capped by the arrival of Israeli infantry on the west coast of the peninsula where the tip had already been secured by the Israeli navy.

King Hussein, despite having signed the accord, needed coaxing from Nasser to participate actively once the Israeli attack had begun. Nasser used subterfuge to convince his ally to commit forces.

In fact, Egypt concealed their losses from their allies and their own people. The state-controlled media reported victories within Israel's borders including the bombing of Tel Aviv. They claimed the Haifa oil refineries were aflame, among other "successes."

Once Hussein's Arab nationalism won out, he committed 45,000 troops, 270 tanks, and 200 artillery pieces to the West Bank. They were met by an Israeli force totaling 40,000 troops and 200 tanks.

Jordan surprised Israel on June 5th, when these troops overran Jerusalem, taking over Government House from UN observers, and then shelled the Israeli portion of the ancient city. Even Tel Aviv found itself under missile attack. That afternoon, though, the Israeli air force decimated the 24 UK Hawker Hunter fighters, the sum total of the Royal Jordanian Air Force.

That night, Jerusalem's infantry headed south, with paratroopers coming from the north. The following morning, the Battle of the Ammunition Hill began with the infantry attacking Latrun's fortress en route to Ramallah. By nightfall, the Israeli forces were victorious and Jordan's 60th Brigade had been destroyed.

Farther north, brigades managed to capture the western portion of the West Bank and Jenin.

June 7th saw additional Israel victories as they entered Jerusalem's Old City, capturing the Western Wall and the Temple Mount. Reinforced by troops from the Jerusalem brigade, they went on to take Judea, Gush Etzion, and Hebron.

Fighting in the West Bank was fairly evenly matched between the Israeli army and the Jordanian forces. The arrival of the still-intact Israeli air force turned the tide and routed the Jordanians. The United Nations helped arrange a ceasefire between Israel and Jordan that began as the sun set.

Early on, Egypt has erroneously reported major victories over the Israelis, going so far as to show radar images of returning Israeli jets and telling allies they were Egyptian planes en route to Tel Aviv. Such boasts enticed Syria, like Jordan, to enter the fray. Before committing troops, Syria began firing missiles into northern Israel. Soon after, the Israeli air force arrived and bombed their jets, reducing their fleet by two-thirds. By this point, the leadership knew Nasser had lied to them.

Upset at Egypt and fearing for their people, they refused to commit troops and resumed ineffectively shelling their enemy. As a result, Syria's lack of engagement encouraged Israel to take a bold step and go after the Golan Heights. Military leaders feared it would prove a costly and bloody goal and Moshe Dayan was against the idea. David Elazar, one of the fiercest military proponents for it, eventually gained Dayan's support.

The Syrians had nine brigades totaling 75,000 men in the area, able to move north and south on one side of the geographically tricky Golan. They had been bombarded for four days by the Israeli air force although their equipment remained largely intact. On June 9th, the air force stepped up its bombing and made it nearly impossible for the Syrians to redeploy their men and equipments effectively. As a result, by that night, Israel's brigades breached the plateau and threatened the Syrians. Aiding them was intelligence they gained through Mossad spy Eli Cohen, who had died two years earlier at the hands of Syria.

The morning of June 10th, the central and northern brigades used a pincer move, but found the field empty—the Syrians had retreated. The ground troops spread out, taking positions along the western volcanic hills.

While there were tremendous victories on the ground and in the air, the sea-based field of combat was relatively quiet. Six Israeli frogmen sunk an Egyptian minesweeper, then were captured in Alexandria while boat crews took possession of the empty Sharm el-Sheikh resort.

Syria had had enough of the fighting and at 6:30 p.m. on June 10th agreed to a ceasefire. Israel obtained possession of the Gaza Strip, the Sinai Peninsula, the West Bank of the Jordan River, and the Golan Heights. They suddenly became governor to one million Arabs living in those lands, few of them happy with the new status quo.

While the fighting did nothing to end the hostility toward the relatively new country, it did announce to their Middle Eastern neighbors that they were not to be underestimated. Their ground and air forces were considered formidable and less likely to be challenged in the future, and proved they would not need help from allied countries to protect their borders.

The toll was also in Israel's favor, as they lost only 1,020 men all told, compared with Egypt's 11,500 men, plus 700 soldiers from Jordan and 2,500 from Syria. All the countries lost millions of dollars worth of equipment from aircraft to tanks and munitions.

Things had grown so bleak that on June 9th, Nasser made a resignation speech. He was persuaded to remain in office after mass demonstrations across the Arab world. Still, it showed how demoralized the country was and how poorly Nasser had waged the war.

From the jets leaving Israel until the ceasefire, the war clocked in at 132 hours and 30 minutes. Of course, the Jordanian portion of the conflict was over within 72 hours and the Egyptians caved in after 96 hours. The Syrians turned out to drag the conflict out to the sixth day.

Why did the countries give in after a few days rather than try to regroup? At the time, the lost lands were considered too sparsely populated to be worth dragging out the battle. At the time of the ceasefire, Israel had forces less than seventy-five miles from Cairo and some thirty miles from Amman and Damascus and the notion of all three capital cities being occupied was frightening.

What did Egypt learn from this? Not a lot, to be honest. Six years later they launched a new offensive to regain its lost lands and weren't much smarter tactically.

LITTLE WARS, BIG MISTAKES

No war when it is being fought feels like a "little war." Little is a relative term. Since we have seen wars in the past century that involved millions of casualties, a mere fifty thousand dead seems less important. What a sad commentary. Many of the conflicts here are as large in scale as any other conflict in their time.

You can contrast how the mistakes that lead to defeat here differ from those of the world-changing wars of modern times. But even some of the errors made by leaders who operated on a much smaller scale will look very familiar; they just were made on a smaller scale.

One editorial decision was made here, to leave out a war that has encompassed the world since ancient times and that has been fought with amazing and often devious weapons. This is, of course, the War Between the Sexes. But since I am pretty sure my side lost a long time ago, and we just don't know it, what can be written?

It is not every day that your name lives on in history.
Unfortunately this can be a very dubious honor;
ask Charles Lynch, for whom "lynching"
was named. We have all heard costly battles described
as being a "pyrrhic victory," named for this man whose legacy
was to be famous for losing by winning.

GLORY OR BUST

WILLIAM TERDOSLAVICH

Achilles.

Alexander the Great.

Pyrrhus of Epirus?

They were all Greek warriors, but that is where the similarity ends.

Pyrrhus of Epirus certainly showed courage, had ambition, and sought glory. He just wasn't very good at finishing what he started. He knew how to fight—he just didn't know how to win. Pyrrhus did make a valuable, if obscure, contribution to our language. A "Pyrrhic" victory occurs when the battle's winner suffers greater loss than the loser. Pyrrhus managed to do this in spirit several times. One wonders if this guy could ever learn from his mistakes. If there ever was a version of *American Idol* for classical Greece, Pyrrhus would have been one talented but disappointing contestant.

Most military historians don't devote a lot of space to Pyrrhus. He gets his write-up by Plutarch of Boeotia, who included a chapter about Pyrrhus some two thousand years ago in his *Lives of Famous Men*, which even today is available in paperback. Plutarch's *Lives* paired comparable biographies of famous Romans and Greeks. He wanted to show examples worth emulating alongside those worth avoiding. Pyrrhus' was definitely among those lives to avoid emulating.

Glory is a bright star that casts a dark shadow, a shadow that can torment anyone with ambition who wants to shine in its light. Alexander the Great was that kind of star. Starting in impoverished Macedonia, Alexander took his army eastward, vanquishing Persia, all the way to the banks of the Indus, thousands of miles away. Alexander wanted to exceed all the glory heaped on Achilles, the great warrior immortalized by Homer in the *Iliad*. All Achilles did was raid the Aegean and participate in a decade-long siege of a minor city in northwestern Asia Minor. Even at his peak, Alexander lamented that he could not outdo Achilles. (Talk about having an inferiority complex.) But to everyone else, Alexander the Great was the ideal ruler and commander. Coming from Greece as well, living like all those who followed in Alexander's shadow, so Pyrrhus wanted to outshine him, and the way to do that was to prove his own military and strategic brilliance.

Alexander was dead from his excesses, or poison, in 323 B.C. He left no heir, bequeathing his massive empire to "the strongest." That gave his generals a green light to raise armies and fight each other for the best pieces. During the "War of the Successors," young Pyrrhus first appears, an ousted prince whose realm of Epirus encompassed what is now northwestern Greece and southern Albania, a very small disinheritance indeed. Fighting for the successor general Ptolemy, Pyrrhus distinguished himself in the Battle of Ipsus in 301 B.C. Antigonus, who had a chance at holding Alexander's empire together, was vanquished in this war by an alliance of the successors Seleucus Nicator, Cassander, Lysimachus, and Ptolemy.

With the war over, Pyrrhus was free to reclaim his throne. Epirus was then misruled by the usurper Neoptolemus. Pyrrhus returned to rule as "co-king" in 297 B.C., countering his rival's intrigues and killing him. For about the next fifteen years, Pyrrhus sought to extend his dominion at Macedonia's expense, mostly unsuccessfully.

Fate threw the king of Epirus a curve ball in 281 B.C., when Tarentum made a plea for Pyrrhus' assistance. At that time, much of southern Italy and much of Sicily was inhabited by Greeks. The Italian

Greeks were suffering from Roman encroachment and had no desire to pay tribute to Latin-speaking "barbarians." Epirus was about
sixty miles across open water from Italy's heel. Any major events
taking place in southern Italy would impact the security of Epirus.
The Tarentine plea was also politically clever, as they asked Pyrrhus
to aid all Italian Greeks, not just their city. At one stroke, the war
Pyrrhus had been asked to join had turned into a glorious crusade. A
crusade with him as the leader, whose success would mean he could
rule lands many times the size and wealth of Epirus.

The offer went to Pyrrhus' head.

Cineas, a key advisor, tried to make a reality check by asking his
king what he intended to gain from this military adventure.

"Italy," replied Pyrrhus.

"Then what is conquered after Italy?" Cineas asked.

"Sicily, a very rich province," answered Pyrrhus.

"And what after that?" Cineas inquired.

"Maybe Carthage, and Libya, too," Pyrrhus said.

"And what after that?" Cineas asked.

"Then we take our leisure, sit at the table, drink, talk, and enjoy
life," Pyrrhus explained.

Cineas took a hard look at his boss and told him they could
drink, talk, and enjoy life right now, without having to fight a series of wars first. "One does not attain glory through leisure," the
king may have corrected him. An Alexandrian-style conquest of
the Mediterranean world made no sense to Cineas, but meant everything to Pyrrhus.

Answering the Greek plea, Pyrrhus sent Cineas to garrison
Tarentum with 3,000 infantry, making an advance base to receive
the bulk of the Epirote army in 280 B.C. Pyrrhus gathered a fleet to
transport his army of 20,000 infantry, 3,000 cavalry, 2,500 light
infantry, and 20 war elephants. The summer season should have
allowed for safe crossings. It didn't. A freak north wind blew up
and scattered Pyrrhus' fleet south. While the heavier flagship carrying the king made landfall in Italy, much of the fleet did not.

Pyrrhus would start his campaign shorthanded.

Two Ways of Fighting

Pyrrhus' campaign pitted the late Greek phalanx against the early Roman legion. To the casual observer, the difference appears slight. One line of men with spears and shields clashed with another line of men armed with swords and shields. If Hollywood movies offer any guide, the battle should have looked like a scene out of *Lord of the Rings* or *300*.

The difference was more complex. The late Greek phalanx that was Pyrrhus' martial inheritance came from Macedonia. The traditional hoplite phalanx was refined by Philip of Macedon and used to great effect by his son, Alexander the Great. Philip had the shield reduced in size and the spear lengthened into an eighteen-foot-long pike called a *sarissa*. The infantry now lined up sixteen deep, instead of eight deep as they did in the old hoplite phalanx. The longer spear enabled the first five ranks to bring their blades to bear against the enemy. The remaining men in the rear ranks stood as reserves, ready to replace the rankers up front who fell dead or wounded.

Infantry used to be the decisive arm of combat, but Phillip and Alexander used it to pin the enemy line and hold it in bloody contact. The decisive arm had become the heavy cavalry, trained to charge at the right moment through any gap in the enemy line, and hopefully deliver the powerful blow on the enemy's flank or rear that won the battle. Alexander preferred to fight with his Companion Cavalry, personally judging the right moment to charge at the enemy's command group; his goal often was to kill the opposing general . . . or king. Which almost always resulted in the collapse of the opposing army.

Light infantry and light cavalry also had roles to play in Macedonian tactics. Light cavalry screened the army while on the march, performed reconnaissance, and pursued the broken enemy. Light infantry skirmished with the enemy at battle's start and protected the flanks. It was this system that Pyrrhus would bring to fight the early Roman legion.

The Romans were great admirers and imitators of Greek culture, but they always tweaked things a bit before putting them into practice. Like the Greeks, the Romans put their poorer men in the light infantry and the more prosperous volunteers in the heavy infantry. But beyond this the two armies were organized very differently. Heavy infantry was divided into three classes—*hastati*, *principes*, and *triarii*. The soldiers in each class were further organized into smaller centuries, or groups of about 60 to 120 men. (The Roman century rarely had exactly 100 men in it.) The centuries were then paired, the first century being *prior*, the second *posterior*. This gave the Romans smaller units to command and move on the battlefield than the powerful, but unwieldy phalanx.

The legion's infantry centuries were normally deployed in three lines with *hastati* first, then the *principes*, and in the rear the *triarii*. The first two classes were armed with large, oblong shields and short swords. In open order, they stood a few steps apart and twelve ranks deep. When battle was joined, the men would close up and condense to six ranks, shield to shield. The posterior century would step left or right and march forward a bit to fill the gaps normally left between the prior centuries in order to present a solid line.

When there was a pause in the battle, the *hastati* would pass back through the centuries of the *principes*. The fresh second line would then go to closed order and fight. If the enemy had not broken by the time the *principes* got tired, they exchanged ranks at the next lull with the *triarii*. The final class was comprised of veterans who fought with spears and shields lined up three ranks deep. They were the best armed, best armored, and most experienced. Things were considered to be really bad if a general had to send in the *triarii*.

Two centuries together were a maniple. One maniple each of *velites*, *hastati*, *principes*, and *triarii* made up a cohort. Bundle six to ten cohorts together and you had a legion. Four legions together made an army, led by a consul. Cavalry and any other light troops were provided by allies and posted on the flanks.

Three important advantages were gained by the Roman system. First, reserves were effectively built in and rotated throughout the battle. More important, the legions were able to practice changing ranks until it could be done smoothly and offer no openings to their foes. Some portion of the army was always fresh to fight.

Second, the Romans had greater articulation. The sub-units that made up a legion were smaller and more numerous, allowing more flexibility. This is reflected in the many parts of the legion, which could be deployed separately as the needs of the battle changed. In comparison, the phalanx was a thick, clunky block of spearmen that could not maneuver very well without breaking formation. Only by keeping ranks did the phalanx find its strength. It could not change facing to deal effectively with an attack on its flank, nor was it maneuverable, being able to march only straight ahead.

Third, a Roman consul never took up arms and fought in the line with the legionnaires. They stood back a bit, keeping a broader view of the action and only intervened at a trouble spot when an order had to be given or when morale had to be rallied. In the Greek way of war, the general fought in the ranks. This inspired his men, but limited his view of the battle to the fight around him. This reflected the Alexandrian system where most units were expected to continue to follow their initial orders throughout the battle. But that only works well when the battle goes as planned. Alexander could pull this off because he maintained his distance until the decisive moment, then led the army-breaking cavalry charge, relying on experienced officers elsewhere in the line to hold their units together. His imitators followed the technique, but lacked the genius to sense the right moment. The Romans expected the battle would not go as planned and the best of their generals were adept and reacting to those changes.

Roman Holiday

Meanwhile, back in sunny Southern Italy . . .

Cineas led out the Epirote garrison, met Pyrrhus, and brought him back to the city of Tarentum with any Greek forces that landed—about 2,000 infantry, very few cavalry, and two war elephants. The Tarentine Greeks thought they could fight to the last Epirote. They would watch as Pyrrhus' army did the hard work. Sadly, they were mistaken. Pyrrhus had the gymnasia and the public walks closed. He forbade dinner parties, drinking, and festivities. He drafted the local men into his army.

Any Tarentines who didn't like this could take a hike.

Many did.

Circumstances would goad Pyrrhus to act. Every day, more of the army scattered by the storm wandered into Tarentum. Knowing this, the Roman consul Laevinus was marching toward Tarentum at the head of a consular army. If he moved fast enough, he might be able to crush Pyrrhus before the scattered remnants of his forces found their way to the city. Pyrrhus could either wait for uncertain reinforcements as the men straggled in, or he could fight the Roman army with the forces he had on hand at a time and place of his own choosing. He chose the latter course.

On the River Siris, near Heraclea, Pyrrhus' force closed in on the Roman legions. He personally scouted their camp from a distance and marveled at how barbarian soldiers could operate with such discipline. The Romans also knew Pyrrhus was nearby. They left camp, formed ranks, and began crossing the Siris. Pyrrhus had his phalanxes formed up, but had them stand to as he led his cavalry forward. He hoped to defeat the Romans in detail as each unit arrived on his side of the river. Plutarch's account of the battle hints at ill-timing by Pyrrhus. The Romans had already crossed and lined up by the time they received the Greek cavalry charge. The Romans also had allies who provided cavalry, which were a match for the Thessalian horsemen fighting for Pyrrhus.

Repulsed, Pyrrhus and his mounted troopers fell back. He ordered his line of phalanxes forward. The infantry battle lasted the entire day, the battlefield said to have changed hands seven times. Prior to the battle, Pyrrhus lent his armor to another officer, who was later killed in the fighting. Seeing the man die in the king's armor, the Greeks mistakenly lost heart and gave ground. Pyrrhus had to ride the line, showing himself to rally the men. The Greeks renewed their advance against the Romans. The two Greek war elephants panicked the Roman cavalry into bolting. Once the Roman infantry became disordered by their own horsemen, Pyrrhus launched one last cavalry charge, broke the Roman ranks for good, and drove them from the field.

The Greeks took the Roman camp. Technically, this made them the winners. The Greek losses were another issue. Sources vary, but the Greeks suffered anywhere from 4,000 to 13,000 killed, while the Romans lost somewhere between 7,000 to 15,000. The Romans could replace their army easily. In fact, they already had several centuries of experience losing battles, replacing armies and winning wars. One of the Romans' greatest strengths was that they could replace armies lost. Pyrrhus had a much smaller population to draw troops from, so every soldier killed was a challenge to replace. The victory did bring Pyrrhus allies. The Samnites and Lucanians, native tribes of Italy, were then ready to join forces with the Epirotes and Tarentines.

Pyrrhus sent Cineas to Rome, bearing gifts and offering terms to end the war. The Romans refused the gifts. The terms were simple: friendship with Epirus, hands off Tarentum, and a possible alliance with Pyrrhus to subdue Italy for Rome. Many senators were inclined to accept the terms, but Appius Claudius rallied his fellow senators to continue the war. He stressed that Pyrrhus had failed to subdue puny Macedonia, so he wondered what Rome had to fear. Making peace with Pyrrhus would only make Rome look weak in the eyes of its enemies, and in turn invite further invasions.

The Senate rallied to Appius Claudius and voted to continue the war. So long as Pyrrhus stayed in Italy, Rome would fight him. Cineas saw the Romans rebuilding their army to twice its size, and realized there were many more Romans who had yet to take up arms. He wanted peace while Epirus was still considered a winner, but further talks came to naught.

Pyrrhus resumed the offensive in 279 B.C. At Asculum, he managed to bring another Roman army to battle. Plutarch's account of the clash is brief, but again hints at Pyrrhus' poor judgment as he fought the Romans on broken ground. The cavalry lacked the open spaces needed to maneuver and charge. The battle was fought near a steep-sided riverbank, which made it difficult for Pyrrhus to bring his elephants to bear against the Roman infantry.

Neither side broke by sundown.

The battle resumed the next day.

This time the fighting shifted to a good patch of level ground, though Plutarch offers no details how either side changed venue. Now Pyrrhus could use his cavalry and elephants to great effect. The Romans used their swords to hack off the Greek spearpoints and rush their line. The elephants charged. The Roman infantry broke and retreated to camp. Losses were greater on the Roman side, roughly 6,000 dead compared to half that many Greeks. But these losses were harder for the Greeks to replace. "One more victory like that over the Romans will destroy us," Pyrrhus complained. Having led from the front, many of his best officers were dead. Not surprisingly, since Epirus was not that large and the leaders would have known each other, many of the dead had been his friends. And the king knew the Romans would easily rebuild their army, while he would be lucky to scrounge up enough men just to refill his ranks.

The Romans could afford to lose many battles.

Pyrrhus could not afford to lose one.

The Romans knew this.

Sicily Beckons, Italy Reckons

Political events elsewhere offered Pyrrhus an opportunity to leave Italy. Northern Greece was overrun by a barbarian invasion. Sicilian Greeks needed protection from Carthage.

Seeing no future in fighting the ever-growing number of Romans, Pyrrhus chose to seek glory in Sicily. Sending Cineas to negotiate terms with the Sicilian Greeks, Pyrrhus moved his army to Tarentum. He left a garrison there, which doubled the displeasure of the Tarentines, already angry at their treatment by Epirus and at being left to face the Romans alone. He then crossed the Straits of Messina to Sicily. It was 277 B.C.

Most Greek cities went over to Pyrrhus' banner with ease. The few that did hold out did not suffer long, as Pyrrhus marched with 30,000 infantry, about 2,500 cavalry, backed by 200 warships in

Sicilian waters. He had no trouble taking western Sicily from the Carthaginians, storming their fortress at Eryx. He dispersed the Mamertines of Messina, who made their living raiding the Sicilian Greeks. Carthage asked for terms and offered money. Pyrrhus told them that peace would come once they left Sicily. This reply inspired Carthage to continue the war.

Now Pyrrhus was eyeing Libya. He needed more oarsmen for his fleet. Rather than hiring volunteers, he drafted the Sicilian Greeks, raising local resentment. The Sicilian Greeks put up with it at first, but the breaking point came quickly. Pyrrhus began to distrust two leading citizens of Syracuse who had earlier invited him to Sicily, putting one to death and driving the other into exile. Starting with Syracuse, the Greek cities in Sicily bolted, seeking alliances with Carthage, the Mamertines, anybody who could get this Greek tyrant off the island.

Now trouble stirred in Italy. The Romans were on the march again. The Samnites wrote to Pyrrhus for help. So did the Tarentines. Pyrrhus heeded their call and moved the army back to Italy in 275 B.C. But it was not an easy move. He had to vanquish a Carthaginian fleet that controlled the Straits of Messina. The Mamertines were on the other side, eager to get even. They would not face Pyrrhus in battle, but skirmished with his column and hammered his rearguard.

The Samnites who sent for Pyrrhus no longer wanted him around. They had suffered many defeats fighting the Romans while waiting for the Greeks to arrive, finally quitting the war. Pyrrhus would lack allies in the next round. Any losses he now took could probably not be made up and his army would become continually weaker.

Pyrrhus managed to get to Tarentum with 20,000 infantry and 3,000 cavalry. He skimmed off the best Tarentine troops for his army and marched on the Romans, somewhere to the north in Samnite territory. He detached a smaller force to hold the attention of a second consular army in Lucania. With the greater part of his forces, Pyrrhus found the consular army of Manius Curius at Beneventum. Curius went on the defensive, as he was expecting the Roman army in Lucania to join him soon.

Pyrrhus decided that the best way to tackle the Roman army was to stage a night attack.

What was he smoking?

Today, such a plan would not seem far-fetched. Troops can operate with night vision equipment and thermal sights that can turn the darkest night into brightest day. Radio keeps all sub-units in touch with the higher HQ. Reinforcements, fire support, and air strikes are on call. Coordinating these elements in a night fight is possible with well-practiced ease. Even with WWII-grade technology, night actions were still fought, sometimes by moonlight, sometimes by the light of star shells and flares. Pyrrhus was trying to stage a night attack over 2,000 years before any of this stuff was invented.

Before the twentieth century, night attacks were *always* risky. The possibility of surprising and defeating the enemy was heavily outweighed by the possibility of failure. At night, troops got lost, could not distinguish between friend and foe, or just showed up in the wrong place at the wrong time. Coordination was not possible. This rule made no exception for Pyrrhus. He chose a long, indirect route through a forest to cover his advance on the Roman camp.

Torches burned out.

Troops got lost in the dark.

Units became intermingled and had to be reorganized.

The sun came up.

The Greeks were just emerging from the woods in column after having marched all night long. All Curius did was line up his troops quickly and attack the partially deployed Greeks. Curius beat the Greeks in detail, first routing the advanced guard, then defeating a follow-on unit, then sweeping through the Greek main line in the open field. Plutarch does not write with a good feel for battle, so the details may seem a bit dodgy, but the outcome was clear. Curius won a victory over Pyrrhus, or perhaps the Greeks suffered a Pyrrhic defeat.

Beneventum capped six years of campaigning in Italy, Sicily, and Italy again. Pyrrhus accomplished nothing. He fought courageously in line with his men. He led by example. Most times, he knew how to handle his army on a battlefield. Pyrrhus knew tactics, but not strategy. Every victory won by his army was wasted, and every battle wasted his army.

Pyrrhus returned to Epirus with just 8,000 infantry and 500 cavalry—roughly one third of the troops he had in his Beneventum campaign. And he had to pay them. Quick, start another war! Macedonia under the rule of Antigonus Gonatas was looking weak, so Pyrrhus raided that country, taking some cities with his combined force of Epirotes and Gauls. Pyrrhus quickly alienated the "liberated" Macedonians by allowing the Gauls to pay themselves by plundering at the people's expense.

His last campaign took him to the Peloponnesus, where he lost his son Ptolemy in battle outside Sparta. By this time, Pyrrhus was suffering some sharp near-misses in combat: getting hit in the breastplate with a spear, getting slashed in the arm by an enemy blade, having a horse killed under him. Pyrrhus' number was bound to come up.

And so it came to pass that Pyrrhus was facing down a Macedonian army led by Antigonus Gonatas, outside Argos, in 272 B.C. The Argives wanted both armies to go away after recognizing the neutrality of Argos in the war between Epirus and Macedonia. Antigonus agreed and handed over one of his sons as hostage. Pyrrhus promised the same, but handed over no one, which made his promise suspect. In the night, Pyrrhus led his force into Argos after one of his confederates left a gate open. His force got as far as the marketplace when someone shouted the alarm. The Argives mustered their troops and seized the city's strongpoints, key intersections, and squares while sending word to Antigonus to send reinforcements.

The hazard of fighting a night action was compounded by the difficulty of fighting in a city. The troops got lost trying to pick their way back out of Argos. Confusion was great. There was lots of shouting and orders could not be heard. As dawn's light illuminated his situation, Pyrrhus could see enemy troops lining the square ahead of him. The tempo of street fighting increased. Misunderstood orders brought Pyrrhus' relief force into the city, compounding the chaos. A war elephant went berserk in the tight streets, trampling some of Pyrrhus' men. Other troops were packed in so tightly that they had no room to wield their weapons, wounding each other instead. In the melee, Pyrrhus fought all comers. Just as he was taking on an Argive soldier in single combat, he was felled—not by the warrior, but by an angry woman flinging a roof tile at his head. Another Argive did a sloppy job of cutting his head off as a bloody prize.

Pyrrhus started his military career seeking glory in battle.

He died losing it in a street brawl.

With a focus on heroism that bordered on myopia, Pyrrhus thought that winning a battle was all that needed to be done to conquer other lands. He was wrong, never seeing how to add those battles up to win a war. His thirst for glory made him strategically unsteady, as he dumped any unpromising campaign to seek the next best opportunity, never weighing the consequences of his actions. Pyrrhus had a tin ear for politics, managing to become an unpopular liberator with those he freed. He was in it for himself, never quite understanding that he was also fighting on behalf of those who asked for his help.

In the end, Pyrrhus didn't know how to lose a war.

He just didn't know how to win one.

Some losses are so lopsided that it is nearly impossible to explain what happened in just military terms. Sometimes it is the men, or man. Often, technology can make the difference. In this case, the very culture and attitudes that had worked wonderfully to maintain a large empire for centuries would also set the stage for its collapse and defeat. History repeats itself and an empire too successful, too comfortable, and too contented with itself to change can be as vulnerable today as this one was four hundred years ago.

THERE'S AUDACITY, AND THEN THERE'S HERNANDO CORTEZ

DOUGLAS R. NILES

Hernando Cortez was a professional soldier in the service of the king of Spain, but under the immediate authority of Diego de La Vasquez, the governor of Cuba. When Cortez landed on the coast of Mexico near Vera Cruz, he commanded some 400 conquistadors, and was accompanied by about fifteen horses and just a few small pieces of field artillery. It was February, 1519, and the small Spanish force had arrived on the shore of an unexplored continent, an area ruled by a vast and militaristic Aztec empire, a nation possessing an army that included *several hundred thousand* veteran, and nearly fearless, soldiers.

A little more than two and a half years later, that empire was in ruins, its fabulous capital city razed almost flat, the vast political network of allies and subject nations turned on end by the arrival of the conquistadors. The Spaniards had laid their stamp on the New World with sudden, brutal violence, ending the reign of an empire that had risen less than two hundred years earlier, but that had inherited the traditions and knowledge of civilizations originating well before the time of Christ.

How did it happen? What did the Aztec Empire do so wrong that one captain, however daring and fortunate he might be, could bring about such a radical, even historic, shift in power? The reasons are complex, but all of them revolve around one central truth: rarely in the course of military history have two such radically diverse cultures clashed in battle. Though neither the Spanish nor Aztecs were strangers to war and political power, the way they regarded those key elements were utterly different.

Although relative newcomers to power, the Aztecs had over the course of less than two centuries risen from a wandering, albeit warlike, tribe of nomads to the masters of most of central Mexico—with the notable exception of the city-state of Tlaxcala who were bitter enemies of the Aztecs and would have been the next Aztec conquest. They did it through cunning, treachery, diplomacy, and military might. They did it to honor their own bloodthirsty god, Huitzilopochtli ("Weet-zil-poach-li") and to slake what their priests perceived as the god's virtually insatiable hunger for human hearts and human blood. They waged nearly constant warfare with nearby tribes, almost exclusively for the purpose of capturing enemy warriors so that they could offer their hearts to their god.

The Aztecs ruled Mexico from their fabulous island city in the middle of Lake Texcoco, on what is now the site of Mexico City. They rose to power as one member of a triple alliance, but eventually came to conquer even their former allies, so that they ruled the country alone. In this rule they were hated, and feared, across the land. Tenochtitlan was a vibrant, colorful city, dominated by lofty pyramids that rivaled Egypt's, connected by long causeways to the shore of the vast, though shallow, lake. At the time of the conquest, it boasted a population of something like 100,000—more than twice the size of London, and half again the size of Paris. It was too large to support even its basic food needs, so the

Aztecs addressed this problem by claiming the bounty of their subjects.

The cities of the Aztecs' former allies, and now subjects, lined the shore of Lake Texcoco, and spilled across the countryside beyond. Tribute, in the form of gold, dye, feathers, food, slaves, and sacrificial victims, was delivered to the Aztecs from all across the land. A typical day sent a number of victims to their deaths in the temples atop the great pyramids, while celebrations and holidays called for a great extravaganza of bloodletting. It is reported that, when the great temple of Huitzilopochtli was dedicated, something between 10,000 and 100,000 captives were marched up the steep steps so that their hearts could be cut out and fed to the insatiable god.

For all their might, and their commerce, the Aztecs lacked certain things that had become commonplace across the ocean, in Europe. They utilized no beasts of burden, nor did they have any wheeled vehicles—though, oddly enough, they understood the concept of the wheel and axle insomuch as it was a common feature of children's toys. They worked soft, precious metals such as gold and silver with intricate skill, but they made no tools of iron or any hard metal. They knew nothing of gunpowder, or of sailing ships, thought they utilized canoes of various sizes on their lakes and rivers.

When the Spaniards came ashore, they brought a whole world of new equipment with them, including field artillery, handheld guns, metal armor, swords and crossbows, and, decisively, horses. They, too, were united in service to their faith—specifically, to the Pope and his Catholic Church. They, too, knew how to use diplomacy and treachery to further their own ends. And, whereas the Aztecs made war primarily with the goal of taking captives for sacrifice, the Spaniards came schooled in a kind of warfare that was disciplined, lethal, and focused upon the destruction of an enemy army and the conquest of his lands.

And, finally, Cortez was one of the luckiest soldiers who ever went to war. When he landed his force on the shore of Mexico, near the current city of Vera Cruz, he was already an outlaw. Though his mission had initially been authorized by the governor of Cuba,

Vasquez had been alarmed by the efficiency and speed of Cortez's preparations, and, regarding him as a rival, ordered him removed from command. Cortez sailed from Cuba before the order could be served, stopping to top off his supplies in Trinidad and other small Spanish ports in the Caribbean.

Upon landing, he was confronted by a force of the local state, the Totonacs. A battle broke out in which the Spanish cavalry proved decisive, the few horsemen routing the native army with a single charge. Still, the intensity of the resistance convinced Cortez that brute force would be insufficient for his purposes. Whereas the islands of the Indies had been subjugated by Spanish arms, here, on the mainland, he would need to add a dose of diplomacy.

Summoning the Totonac chiefs to a parley, he gave them a demonstration of his artillery—guns that he implied were living creatures which played to their superstitions—and, through interpreters, suggested that, if the local chiefs agreed to become vassals of the Spanish king, he would protect them. The chiefs agreed, and gave the Spanish many gifts, including women and gold. One of the women, a teenaged girl named Malinalli, would become Cortez's closest adviser, and would bear him a son.

For the moment, however, it was the gold that captured the Spaniards' attention. They were informed that it came from a place called Mexico, meaning the Aztec heartland. Cortez immediately opened up negotiations with the representatives of the Aztec leader, Montezuma. The Spaniard proposed journeying to the capital to visit Montezuma, but was informed that this was out of the question. Still, the Aztec leader sent a series of fabulous gifts, including a large, elaborate disk representing the sun, and a helmet full of pure gold dust, in an attempt to persuade the Spanish to stay away.

This, of course, was like trying to put out a fire by pouring gasoline on it. Cortez was determined to go to Tenochtitlan—he reasoned that he really had no choice, since he had disobeyed his governor by commencing the mission. Not all of his men shared his enthusiasm, however. So in order to end any debate, he ordered that all of his ships were to be sunk, thus ensuring that his men wouldn't lose heart and decide to return to Cuba. With no retreat possible, the party of conquistadors started their march into the interior of Mexico.

They next came to the lands of the Tlaxcalans—the one state that had resisted Aztec rule, even though it was surrounded by the lands of their enemies. Fierce warriors, they battled the Spanish over the course of many days, mustering an army that the conquistadors estimated at well over 100,000 men. Still, their metal armor protected the Spanish from suffering serious losses. They created and held a strong point on a hilltop, refusing to join in the mobile battle that their attackers preferred. Finally, the Tlaxcalans ended their attacks and submitted, suggesting they had only waged war since they assumed the conquistadors were allies of the Aztecs. Cortez sealed a pact with the Tlaxcalans, who would become his most loyal allies for the duration of his campaign.

In Tenochtitlan, Montezuma was becoming increasingly anxious as his agents brought him word of Spanish deeds and intentions. He may have worried that Cortez was a god—some legends predicted that an ancient deity would return out of the east to take his rightful place as ruler of Mexico. In any event, he remained paralyzed by inaction, merely waiting as the conquistadors marched closer.

Next, Cortez arrived at the holy city of Cholula which featured many temple pyramids, where a great feast was planned to welcome him. His consort, Malinalli (known to posterity as Doña Marina) warned him of treachery, saying that the Cholulans planned to attack the Spaniards, taking them by surprise. Cortez turned the tables, unleashing his Tlaxcalan allies and his own men in a massacre that devastated the town and sent shockwaves all the way to the capital.

Now the Aztecs were really worried. They sent more gifts, and provided guides to lead the Spanish to the capital. Malinalli and the Tlaxcalans were suspicious of these guides, however, and Cortez chose a different route, leading his expedition over a pass between the two great volcanoes that still dominate the sky east of Mexico City. As the invaders marched into the lowlands, they passed through more of the Aztec vassal states, meeting more local leaders who almost invariably complained about Aztec oppression.

By the time Cortez entered Tenochtitlan, he had established himself in the minds of many of the Aztecs' subjects as more of a liberator than an invader. The Spanish were welcomed as guests by Montezuma, and given a palace to serve as their quarters. As they explored the city, they also became aware of the grisly sacrificial practices of their hosts, witnessing a vast wall made from the skulls of the slain, and seeing the bloody altars in the temples. The conquistadors clashed with the Aztec priests when they insisted upon setting up a cross in one of the temples. This uneasy state lasted for about a month, the Spanish increasingly worried about the possibility of Aztec treachery.

Finally, Cortez seized Montezuma and held him as a prisoner in his own capital, though he presented the news to the Aztecs as if their leader was his guest. The Spanish continued to amass treasure, while the situation grew increasingly tense. Cortez had sensed that his diplomatic opportunities were expiring, and was preparing for armed conflict, when word arrived from the coast: another Spanish expedition, numbering some 1,500 men, had arrived. It was commanded by Panfilo de Narvaez, who was under orders to arrest Cortez and to return him to Cuba in chains.

Cortez left half of his men in the capital, under the command of his chief lieutenant Pedro de Alvarado, and marched to the coast with the rest of his small force. He surprised and defeated Narvaez and his officers, and convinced the bulk of the new arrivals to enlist with him. Tales, and proof, of fabulous treasure were enough to bring the reinforcements over to Cortez's side.

The conquistadors quickly marched back to the capital, only to find that Alvarado's temper and harsh policies had at last driven the Aztecs to revolt. Cortez fought his way in to the palace, and tried to use Montezuma to placate the uprising. In the confusion, the Aztec leader was killed, though whether by his own people or the Spanish is unknown. In any event, the Aztecs attacked relentlessly, and the Spanish fought their way out of the city in a desperate, running battle—now remembered as *La Noche Triste*—"the Sad Night."

Hundreds of Spaniards, their pockets laden with gold looted from the city, drowned when they were dragged into the lake. Many more were captured—they would be marched up to the sacrificial altars the following day. Here, again, Cortez's amazing luck held. Though he fought on the front line of many of the skirmishes, and was undoubtedly recognized by his enemies, the Aztec warriors invariably tried to capture him instead of striking him a lethal blow.

Though he lost more than half of his men, Cortez was nothing if not a survivor. He withdrew to Tlaxcala, which welcomed him as a loyal ally. For nearly a year, he rebuilt his forces, established diplomatic ties to other rebellious states, and prepared for a new attack.

In these preparations he was aided by yet another advantage the invaders possessed. An African slave accompanying the Narvaez expedition was infected with smallpox, a disease to which Europeans had long evolved a degree of resistance. Yet it infected the native Mexicans as a lethal plague, and within months had reached the capital city. While Cortez was mustering allies, planning a campaign, bringing in more horses and cannon from other Spanish colonies, the Aztecs were dying in droves. It is estimated that something like half the population of Tenochtitlan, including Montezuma's successor as ruler of the Aztecs, perished from the scourge.

Even so, when Cortez attacked again, in May of 1521, he faced a desperate assault. The battle for the capital city was fought block to block, the Spanish using their artillery to literally blow the place to pieces, while the Aztecs fought every step of the way. Tens of thousands of native troops were allied with the conquistadors by now, and with their help, together with the use of small sailing ships on the lakes themselves, the Spanish finally brought the Aztecs to their knees. When the last of the nation's leaders, Cuauhtémoc, was captured trying to flee in a canoe, the resistance ended.

Cortez established Mexico City on the ruins of Tenochtitlan. With the ruling empire shattered, the other tribes of native Mexicans were placed under the yoke of Spanish rule, while still more conquistadors spread out to place the Spanish footprint on the rest of Central and South America. Because their concept of what war was all about left them vulnerable, the greatest empire of the Americas fell.

Here is a war lost because the one side simply did not accept the modern world. It featured fanatic Wahhabists against a modernized army. Modern weapons and tactics won every battle, but the survivors fled and eventually formed the nation of Saudi Arabia. The supposed winner was the now defunct Ottoman Empire. So who really won? Or perhaps considering the modern, terrorist Wahabist movement, is the war still going on? What this does also is explain a lot about why modern Saudi Arabia acts as it does.

EGYPTIAN-WAHHABI WAR

1811–1818

ROBERT GREENBERGER

Religious fervor will take you only so far. It may grant you clarity of vision, but on the field of battle, it just isn't enough.

The Wahhabi sect learned that hard lesson over the course of a conflict with Egypt in the nineteenth century, their loss against that nation dealing their faith a serious blow and retarding its growth.

Founded in the eighteenth century, Wahhabi considered the Koran a fundamental text as interpreted by Muhammad ibn-al-Wahhab. Those Muslims who seemed to be honoring other interpretations were the subject of a jihad as declared by Ibn-al-Wahhab. Part of the practice included a proactive component, compelling all to abide by these strict teachings. These extremist views were opposed by the Muslim scholars housed in Mecca and Medina. In 1744, al-Wahhab merged forces with Muhammad Ibn Saud, bringing their movement, known then as Muwahidun ("those who advocate oneness") to the Arabian Peninsula.

Interestingly, the zealous Wahhabi was critical of those who paid blind obedience to the scholars rather than families learning the divine commands on their own.

Located in central Arabia, they began a series of attacks on pilgrims crossing the desert en route to Mecca. Reports of the attacks reached Istanbul, the capital of the Ottoman Empire, which was protector of the holy land at the end of the eighteenth century. This began a series of conflicts that escalated the tensions between the Ottomans and the Wahhabis for decades. The first inevitable clash came in 1801, when the sultan directed his people to invade the land known then as eastern Arabia, prompting the Wahhabis to seize Karbala in Iraq. They proceeded to take control of the holy city of Mecca a year later.

By holding these two cities, the Wahhabi proved inspirational to those living in the region who disliked living under Ottoman rule. Additionally, settling in the cities allowed them to spread their beliefs, which proved to have long-lasting influence on the Muslim faith.

None of it, though, meant they had stable military or strategic commanders and in war, faith takes you only so far.

Given other concerns, the sultan, Selim III, was unable to act against the Wahhabis, letting them set down roots and get accustomed to their holdings. His successor, Mustafa IV, did little, but when he was killed and replaced by Mahmud II, things changed once and for all. The new sultan summoned Muhammad Ali Pasha, Egypt's viceroy, and assigned him the task of ridding the Ottomans of the pesky Wahhabi, whom he deemed heretics.

Muhammad Ali sent his son Tusun, then only sixteen, to lead the 8,000 men, including 2,000 horses, to confront the enemy. While impressive in number, they were at first stopped at the Pass of Jedeida, forced to retreat to Yembo. It took a year, but more reinforcements arrived and they finally took Medina, Jidda, and Mecca.

Muhammad Ali joined his son in Arabia for the glorious fight in 1813, leaving another son, Ibrahim, in charge of Egypt. The more treacherous terrain slowed him and cooled his own ardor for war. The Wahhabi also tested his patience with their fighting style, closer to guerilla harassment than the style of fighting the Egyptian leader was accustomed to.

In 1815, he managed to depose the Sharif of Mecca and then Saud II, the Wahhabi leader, died. Abdullah, Saud's son and successor, agreed to a treaty soon after. By then, news of Napoleon's escape from Elba distracted Muhammad Ali, and he returned to Egypt—just in case. He returned to his capital the day Napoleon met his fate at Waterloo.

He remained further distracted by rumor that the Turks were planning on an invasion of Egypt, having made these plans while he was protecting their interests in Arabia.

By 1816, Muhammad Ali decided the treaty was not being properly abided by and sought to settle things with the Wahhabi once and for all. He dispatched his forces that fall, led by his eldest born, Ibrahim Pasha. The young man fought with a fervor that made his father proud and, although it took until 1818, he gained success by taking the Wahhabi capital of Deriya.

For four years, Egypt and the Wahhabi battled back and forth with neither gaining any clear victory. Given the overwhelming number of Egyptian soldiers at the pasha's command, this said something for the fervor with which the Wahhabi fought.

Yet, a year later, Ibrahim Pasha, son of the viceroy, was given command of the Egyptian army. He surveyed the neighboring region and spent time listening to the tribal leaders' complaints about Wahhabi. He also plied them with lavish gifts from home and, as a result, favor was stockpiled.

When he was done listening, he marshaled his forces and marched into central Arabia and took up positions in Unayzah, Buraydah, and Shaqra. Bolstered with support from the Harb, Unayzah, Mutayr, and Banu Khalid tribes, Ibrahim appeared in the Wahhabi capital of ad-Diriyah in April, 1818. Thus began fierce combat, lasting six straight months.

Compared with fighting the Ottomans a decade earlier, the Wahhabi missed out on the modernization efforts credited to the Sultan Selim III. He modeled his forces after the European armies and, as a result, they were better trained and better able to deal with the fierce but undisciplined fight given by the Wahhabi. In some ways it contrasted Middle Eastern and European worldviews and, for a change, Europe won in the desert.

Abdullah I finally surrendered on September 9th and the sultan had him, his treasurer, and secretary sent to Constantinople to be beheaded. Members of the Saudi family were also imprisoned, a few escaping to the far reaches of the Middle East.

The sultan then ordered ad-Diriyah be razed, with Egyptian forces stationed in formerly principal Wahhabi towns. By then there was little resistance.

The surviving Wahhabi followers coalesced around the surviving members of the Saud family and they remained somewhat nomadic until circumstances allowed them to take control of Arabia in 1922, where they remain to this day.

There was little justification for the United States going to war against Mexico in 1846. Still, considering the relatively small size of the U.S. forces involved and the fact that the U.S. Army was fighting in the heart of Mexico, the outcome should have been very different. The soldiers of the Mexican army had courage, as demonstrated by the heroic stand of one hundred cadets. But the "Napoleon of the Americas" and a nation of several million citizens was defeated just outside their own capital by a force smaller than the Union losses (12,000 men) two decades later at Cold Harbor.

SOUTH OF THE BRAND-NEW BORDER

The Mexican War, 1846–1848

JOHN HELFERS

The war with Mexico that gave America most of its southwestern states and California was the culmination of almost thirty years of politics, warfare, dirty tricks, and suffering. In the end, our neighbor to the south ended up losing about half of its territory, and the continental United States of America expanded to its present-day borders. But this would all be bought at a high cost, with a lot of blood shed along the way, and even our own nation wouldn't be above committing what some might call outright theft to get what it wanted.

In the first two decades of the nineteenth century, the North American continent suffered growing pains equal to the trials of the first waves of colonization and wars that had swept it in the previous century. Borders of territories and states moved with alacrity as nations and independent republics rose and fell. Chief among these were the revolt of all the mainland Spanish colonies in the New World in 1821, but instead of banding together into a nation, they stayed independent, a fractious collection of weak, upstart countries. Of course, America also had to fight the War for Continued Independence, otherwise known as the War of 1812, defeating the British for good this time.

The U.S. was also expanding its borders, having purchased Florida from Spain in the Transcontinental Treaty of 1819, which also threw in the Oregon territory, making America truly a nation, "from sea to shining sea." However, Mexico's claim on the Southwest and California territories made it, at the time, as large as the nascent U.S. itself—bigger if Oregon was excluded. And, having just achieved its own independence, Mexico was a spirited competitor to its neighbor on the continent.

However, America was also feeling its expansionist oats, and made several overtures to purchase Texas, once by President John Quincy Adams in 1824, and again by Andrew Jackson in 1828. Both were indignantly refused by the Mexican government. At this same time, a flood of Americans poured into Texas, unhindered by the Mexican government, in contrast to the New Mexico and California territories, where Americans weren't nearly as welcome and their ownership of land was highly restricted. Why Mexico encouraged this immigration has never been clearly understood; surely if they had wanted to keep these lands, they would have made more of an effort to send their own population there to colonize the area. But Mexico even made it easier for Americans to settle in the area by granting them large tracts of land to colonize, to the extent that one such community contained 20,000 Yankees, and 2,000 slaves, though slavery was illegal under Mexican law.

That was one of the first friction points between the two cultures, but more soon followed. Although the immigrating Americans had promised to abide by the rules of their new home, many did not. Most did not convert to Catholicism, although they had promised to do so, and the slavery issue was also a growing concern. For their part, the Americans found it difficult to abide by the laws of their new land, particularly when the rules kept changing, depending on who was in power from year to year. Also, there is no doubt that racial animosity played a key role in laying the seeds of conflict, with the Americans regarding the Mexicans as superstitious and indolent, and the Mexicans increasingly viewing the Americans as haughty and overly acquisitive.

By 1836, more than 30,000 Americans had entered Texas, not only settlers, but rough frontiersmen and speculators like Davy Crockett, Stephen Austin, and Jim and Rezin Bowie, who saw the wild lands of the Texas territory as a good way to get rich by speculating in land. Mexico had also undergone yet another change in government, with the temperamental General Antonio López de Santa Anna locking up the nation under his tight rule. He imposed a new constitution that removed the various states' rights, and tried to strictly control the Americans living north of the Rio Grande. Santa Anna should have studied the history of America a bit more before trying this; he then might have been ready for what happened after his attempt to control its citizens.

On March 2, 1836, the Texans answered his new policies by declaring themselves an independent republic, creating a provisional government and removing the Mexican garrison at San Antonio de Bexar. Santa Anna mustered a 4,500-man army and headed for the city. He met a small force of 176 men, jointly led by Jim Bowie and Colonel William Travis, at an old adobe mission called the Alamo. After thirteen days of fierce fighting, including two frontal assaults that were repelled by the defenders, the Mexicans overwhelmed the fort and killed everyone inside except for a few slaves, women, and children. Although rumor had it that the Texans had managed to kill 1,500 Mexican soldiers before being overrun, historians place the actual figure at closer to 200 killed and 400 wounded, still a high number considering the lopsided number of the opposing forces. Sam Houston would later defeat the Mexican army near the San Jacinto River, forcing Santa Anna to sign the Treaty of Velasco, which stated he was to evacuate the territory and also use his influence to get Texas recognized as a republic, with a border between the two nations at the Rio Grande. Santa Anna had no intention of living up to these promises, and neither did the Mexican government, which claimed he was not empowered to speak for the nation and refused to ratify the treaty.

The battle became a rallying cry for not only the republic's citizens, but for the American government, which still coveted the vast Texas prairie. The brand-new republic sent its elected president, Sam Houston, to Washington to ask for either recognition as a sovereign nation or annexation to the United States. President Andrew Jackson recognized the nation on the last day of his term in order to insure a smooth transition of power to his vice president, Martin Van Buren. Van Buren did nothing about the Texas question, and neither did his successor, William Henry Harrison, primarily because the 68-year-old president died one month after taking office, a victim of pneumonia. His vice president, John Tyler, also wanted Texas as part of the Union, but again waited until the last day of his term before notifying Houston that Texas had been admitted into the United States by a resolution of Congress on December 29, 1845.

The next president of the United States, James K. Polk, had plans for the West as well. Not just Texas, but California too. America's expansionist dreams had been stoked even higher by John O'Sullivan, editor of the New York *Morning News*, who coined the phrase in an editorial the same month that Texas became our twenty-eighth state, writing of the nation's "manifest destiny to overspread and to possess the whole of the continent which Providence has given us for the development of the great experiment of liberty and federated self-government." Well, if it was good enough for a New York newspaper, it ought to be good enough for Mexico to just kindly step aside and let the U.S. take possession of the Western territories that were, according to O'Sullivan, rightfully ours in the first place.

There was only one small problem: Mexico had no intention of giving up California. Already incensed by the annexation of Texas, the country was practically demanding a war with the U.S. and wouldn't even consider an offer for the California Territory. Under the guise of defending (translation: expanding) U.S. interests, President Polk sent General Zachary Taylor down "on or near" the Rio Grande, further exacerbating the situation.

Not surprisingly Texas and Mexico had never seen eye-to-eye on where the border between them actually was. Texas claimed that the border was the Rio Grande; Mexico said it was the Nueces River, which flowed from forty to over a hundred miles farther north, leaving about a quarter of the state under Mexican control. When Taylor and his men arrived at the Rio Grande, Mexico said they were on Mexican soil, but the Texans said the soldiers were on American land. Texas' claim was much shakier, but that wouldn't have been obvious from Taylor's men camped on the river, looking like they were going to settle in for a long time.

Polk made one last try at purchasing the northern territories with cash instead of blood, offering to assume Mexico's national debt of $4.5 million, incurred by even more civil wars, $5 million for New Mexico, and for California, "money would be no object." He sent his minister to Mexico, John Slidell, down to try and negotiate the purchase. The Mexican government was appealing to France and Great Britain for political or even direct military help, but gained nothing from their pleas. They wouldn't receive Slidell even for an exploratory meeting, as their citizens were screaming that the Americans were coming to buy both Texas and California, and to deal with them in any way would be committing treason against their nation.

Mexico's supposed salvation came in the form of General Mariano Paredes y Arrillaga, who had taken over Mexico as a dictator. He wouldn't even meet with Slidell, and roused his countrymen into a frenzy of anger at their northern neighbor. Upon hearing the mission had failed, Polk met with his cabinet and found that all but one favored his request to ask Congress to declare war against Mexico. Polk wanted a reason—just about any would do—to declare a state of hostility, and ordered Taylor to take his men down to the left bank of the Rio Grande. On March 24, 1846, Taylor reached a point on the river near Matamoros—which the Mexicans still considered their sovereign territory.

The stage for battle was set, with infuriated Mexican soldiers prepared to repel what they saw as the invading Yankees. In their own minds, the Americans were simply there to protect their newest state. All that was required was a single spark, which came on April 25th. Under orders from commanding officer Mariano Arista, a force of 2,300 Mexicans crossed the Rio Grande and ambushed 63 U.S. dragoons, killing 11, wounding several others, and capturing the rest of the unit. The next day, Taylor informed Polk that, "hostilities may now be considered to be commenced." By May 10th, Polk had persuaded Congress that there was no choice; it would take a war to settle the restless Mexicans' hash, and the United States would be happy to be the cook. The votes passed overwhelmingly in the Senate and the House of Representatives, despite resistance from such leaders as Congressman Abraham Lincoln and former president John Quincy Adams, and Polk signed the bill on May 13, 1846.

The time had come to fight, and the Americans were ready to do so. The Mexicans' first mistake was their overconfidence. With 30,000 men at his disposal in 1845, Paredes dismissed the American soldiers as undisciplined foreign rabble, conveniently forgetting that their ancestors defeated Great Britain, one of the greatest military nations in the world—not once, but twice.

In fact, the U.S. military units sent to Mexico were probably among the finest ever fielded. Many who fought in the war would go on to distinction in the Civil War, including Ulysses S. Grant, George B. McClellan, Ambrose Burnside, Thomas "Stonewall" Jackson, James Longstreet, George Meade, and Robert E. Lee, as well as the future Confederate president Jefferson Davis. Led by "Old Rough and Ready" Zachary Taylor, the initial force of 4,000 men reached the Rio Grande on March 28th, and spent the next month building defenses along the river, including a fort, and preparing for battle.

General Arista was also ready to give it to them, and sallied forth to meet the enemy. Upon receiving word that the Mexicans were crossing the river on May 1st to try and cut off communication with Port Isabel, Taylor took 3,000 men out to meet him. The two forces found each other on May 8th. Although Arista commanded 4,000 men, the Mexican Army was officer-heavy, and not very well disciplined. Its men still used Napoleonic-era muskets, and often overfilled them with powder, leaving them to fire from the hip, instead of aiming and firing off the shoulder, meaning many of their shots went high.

The Americans were both better-trained and equipped, and had mastered the use of horse artillery, light 6- and 8-pound guns to be used against infantry, and the dozen such units Taylor had with him would make all the difference. The Mexicans fired first, their cannonballs coming at the Americans so slowly that the intended targets could often step out of the way of the projectile. But as the U.S. soldiers advanced, the shots became heavier, until they stopped, and Taylor brought his own artillery into play. Two 18-pound guns wreaked havoc on the Mexican line, preventing almost any sort of advance. A 1,000-man cavalry charge was dispersed by the Americans' accurate musket fire, while a section of the artillery blasted the two enemy cannon before they could fire a shot. The Americans might have defeated Arista's army completely, but lost their chance to press forward as night fell. As it was, the battle was a clear victory for the U.S., with 9 dead and 44 wounded, versus at least 250 Mexican casualties, and a retreating enemy army.

The next morning, Taylor and his men pursued the Mexicans to Resaca de Guerrero. Arista and the Mexican forces set up for the day in a defensive position on the road, but didn't believe the Americans would attack. Taylor sent his cavalry and horse artillery to try and take out Arista's cannons. Meanwhile, his infantry advanced through thick chaparral to encounter small pockets of the enemy leading to scattered fighting all over the area. After the cavalry charge overshot their objective, a furious Taylor sent in his infantry to claw the guns away from the Mexicans, which they did, then turned the captured cannons on the fleeing soldiers, sending them into the withering fire of Fort Brown, and scattering in panic across the Rio Grande. Again, Taylor might have destroyed Arista's army completely had he pursued them, but the Mexicans had taken all the boats, and Taylor was content to rest on the laurels he had gained so far. He had lost 48 men and suffered 128 wounded, but killed and wounded at least 500 Mexican soldiers.

The news of the victories in Mexico brought volunteers into the army at a rapid pace, swelling it by thousands of men seeking adventure south of the border. Polk, still looking for a way to end the war quickly, tried to smuggle Santa Anna, who had exiled himself to Cuba, back into Mexico, after extracting a promise that he would broker a deal with the United States, and would receive $2 million to purchase California. But the appropriations bill died in the Senate that August, infuriating Polk and ensuring the continuation of the conflict. Also, when Santa Anna was allowed back into Mexico at Vera Cruz Harbor in August, the opportunistic general immediately offered his services to the Mexican government, which had already removed General Paredes from power.

However, there was good news from the West Coast. The drive to claim the sparsely settled lands of California and New Mexico progressed well. Commodore John Sloat raised the Stars and Stripes in California on August 7th, although he would need Colonel John Kearny, who had already proclaimed American dominion over New Mexico on his way across the country, and his 150 dragoons to help keep the territory. After several months of small-scale skirmishes, Kearny and Commodore Robert Stockton would finally put down the last of the California resistance at the Battle of the San Gabriel River on January 8, 1847.

During this time, Taylor, his units swollen by volunteers to 6,000 men, marched on Monterrey, a strongly fortified city held by General Pedro de Ampudia, commanding 7,000 men and 40 guns. Although outnumbered again, Taylor wasn't worried, and split his forces into two units to take the city. Under Brigadier General William Worth, 2,000 men and cavalry circled north to approach the two fortified hills on the west of Monterrey. However, the end of the day found them still in the hills, and having to make camp there. Ampudia's best chance to defeat the split force was right in front of him, yet he didn't take advantage of it, apparently feeling his best offense was a good defense.

On September 21st, the battle for the city began in earnest.

Worth's men repelled a charge of Mexican cavalry, and attacked their assigned goal, Federation Hill, capturing it by nightfall, losing less than 20 men in the process. The eastern front, however, was a different story.

Brigadier General David Twiggs was supposed to assault a fortification called the Tannery, one of several fortifications in the area, ostensibly to provide a diversion for the units to the west. However, they had little artillery support, and a frontal advance turned into a bloodbath, with Mexican sharpshooters picking off the men from rooftops and loopholes on all sides. After several bloody charges, the small fort was taken, then Taylor ordered all of the troops to retreat except for the soldiers holding the Tannery.

Fighting resumed the next day, with Ampudia retreating on the western front after Worth's men took the second hill near the city, concentrating his men near the main plaza and in a structure called the Black Fort. In dusty urban fighting, Taylor's artillery swept the streets clear of Mexican soldiers, while the men dug through the sides of houses with pickaxes. Worth continued to press forward, trapping Ampudia and his men between the two forces, and making the Mexican general offer his surrender the next day.

Although the fighting had cost 128 killed and 368 wounded (Mexican killed and wounded were estimated at 367), Taylor was generous to his vanquished foe, allowing the army to leave with its arms, and even agreeing to an eight-week armistice, which angered Polk back in Washington. Taylor had little choice, however; with only 5,000 men and low on supplies in a hostile land, to keep pressing forward invited potential disaster.

However, the tide was already turning back in the U.S. The hard-fought victory at Monterrey, along with the not-so-surprising defection of Santa Anna in Mexico, made it clear to the U.S. Congress and citizens that this war would be a longer campaign than first thought. Faced with this reality, and discarding a defensive stance proposed by Taylor, Polk assigned Major General Winfield Scott to mount a campaign to take Mexico City, sending him to the port of Vera Cruz to begin his assault.

On the other side of the border, Santa Anna was on the march to defeat the Americans once and for all. Having received news of the Americans' disenchantment with the conflict, he planned to crush the U.S. army in the north with one decisive battle, then hold the area and harass the remaining forces until the American citizens would force their government to seek peace terms. He didn't concern himself with the possibility of an attack through Vera Cruz, as he figured the oncoming yellow fever season would immobilize any troops sent there. However, he was having enough problems of his own in trying to raise enough men to get the job done. The population of northern Mexico still regarded him with suspicion after his last dictatorial rule, and refused to help him, even when the volunteer backwoodsmen of the U.S. plundered their lands. The government was of no help; the treasury was empty, and Santa Anna was forced to seize Catholic Church property to fund his campaign, which further distanced himself from the people. Nevertheless, he led an army of 20,000 men north out of San Luis Potosí on January 27, 1847.

Taylor was ready to take the Mexican army on, but retreated to a defensive position near the Buena Vista ranch called "the Narrows," a tight defile passing through a plateau pocked with ravines on the east, which was fortified, and a confusion of gullies in front of a mountain on the right, which was considered impassible. Outnumbered four to one, Taylor set up his men in an arrowhead formation pointing south on the eastern side of the blocked road. After refusing Santa Anna's request for their surrender, Taylor braced for the Mexican assault, which came on February 22, 1846.

Santa Anna ordered his artillery to soften up the American lines, while General Ampudia tried to reach higher ground on the Americans' left, which was lightly held. The two forces picked at each other for the day, then the Americans withdrew at nightfall. During the night, Taylor traveled to Saltillo, fearing the Mexicans might have outflanked him and taken the city. His mistake made him double-time it back to the front, just as the Mexican artillery found their range on the summit of the nearby mountain—the one the Americans thought was impassable—and opened fire.

With the left threatening to crumble, Taylor arrived just in time, steadying his men as a group of Mexican infantry and cavalry were massing to charge. When they advanced, U.S. sharpshooters had a field day, picking off riders and runners left and right until the charge was broken. Another group of lancers decided to take on the infantry forward of the Buena Vista ranch. Mostly volunteers, the frontiersmen's response was to form a V, with the open end facing the enemy. The lancers charged in, then slowed to a walk in their confusion before all hell opened up on them from the U.S. muskets, destroying the head of the column, and tearing the rear into a dozen bloody pieces.

With the cavalry halted, the Mexican infantry retreated. Although the momentum had passed to the Americans, for reasons that may never be known, a flag of truce was run up, and both sides stopped fighting. During this time, Santa Anna made one last try to break the American line, sending men against what had been the center, and was now the left flank, but again was unsuccessful. The artillerymen saved the day, when two bold lieutenants, John Paul Jones O'Brien, and George Thomas brought their horse artillery up and sprayed the Mexicans' rear, buying enough time for volunteer units to come forward and plug the gap, driving the enemy back for the last time.

The battle had been won, but not without significant casualties for the Americans, 267 killed and 468 wounded. However, the Mexicans had fared far worse, with estimates ranging from 1,500 to 2,500 killed and wounded. Santa Anna returned to San Luis with approximately half the force he started out with, proclaiming victory. The American side knew the right of it, however, and the triumph revived our country's flagging morale when it was sorely needed. Taylor's part in the war was over, and he would return to begin a completely different battle, this one for the presidency of the United States.

On February 21, 1847, Major General Scott reached his staging point at Lobos Island, only to find the men in a small preliminary party waiting were already suffering from smallpox. Soon after, however, the rest of his soldiers arrived, and he set out at the head of 10,000 men, aided by soldiers such as P.G.T. Beauregard, George

Meade, Joe Johnston, Thomas Jackson, and Robert E. Lee, and sailed his flotilla of 80 paddle-wheelers and sailing vessels for Vera Cruz.

The landing army wanted to make an impression—this was America's first amphibious operation, and everyone wanted it to go smoothly. With the assistance of Commodore David Connor, and his specially designed, flat-bottomed, double-ended troop transports, he offloaded 8,600 men without a single loss in five hours on March 9th. By nightfall, the American army was on the beach, ready to take the fortified city.

The reason there wasn't a stronger force to oppose them was that Mexico was suffering yet another of its periodic civil conflicts. A democratic faction squabbled with a conservative merchant group, with the riches of the Catholic Church at stake to prop up the current, failing government. Fresh from his "victory" at Buena Vista, Santa Anna didn't publicly take a side; however, he was working against the democratic party—which also happened to be in power—and toward making peace with the Church. No one really trusted him, but they all figured he had to be better than the inept politicians currently in office, and on March 23rd they removed the sitting president and installed Santa Anna. But by the time all of this had happened, the Americans were beating at the walls of Vera Cruz.

Against the advice (and hopes) of his army officers, Scott assigned the breaking of the port city to his engineers, who created an investment line around the rear of the city, cut off its water supply, and prepared to shell it. On March 22nd, Scott gave its inhabitants one last chance to surrender. They refused, and suffered through four days of near-constant artillery fire, sometimes as thick as 180 shells an hour. On March 26th, a white flag rose, and Scott negotiated agreeable terms by the 29th. He had only lost 67 killed and wounded, with about 80 Mexican soldiers killed and 100 civilian deaths during the siege. Now it would be on to Mexico City, 220 miles away.

As soon as he heard of Vera Cruz's fall, Santa Anna mustered 6,000 men and marched out to stop the American invasion, but had no better luck than the first time around. He first met his enemy fifty miles from the ocean at Cerro Gordo. The "Liberator" had chosen his defensive site well: a fortified ridge lay to the road's south. Cerro Gordo, the "big hill," was also fortified, and another fortified hill, Atalaya, was a half-mile to the northeast. Anyone on the road would suffer the onslaught of not one, but two fields of fire. The south ridge was protected by a canyon and the Plan del Rio, and the north ridge was protected by terrain so rough it was impassable—or so the general thought.

The American engineers had a different opinion. After a daring reconnaissance by Robert E. Lee, they figured the Mexicans' left flank, on that north ridge, could be turned—if they could get enough men and artillery over there. Working in the suffocating heat, traversing ravines so steep horses couldn't climb them, the men worked toward the enemy position until they were discovered. Scott divided his men into two forces and sent them to take both hills at the same time. On April 18th, the two units did just that, routing the Mexicans by noon. American losses totaled 63 dead and 337 wounded, but the Mexican force was destroyed, with 1,000 killed, and 3,000 taken prisoner. Santa Anna left the battlefield in such haste he left his spare wooden leg behind in his belongings.

Scott took three months to reorganize his army, and on August 7th, marched out with 10,500 men, against what he thought was a force of at least 30,000 Mexican soldiers guarding an enemy city of 200,000 inhabitants.

Santa Anna had not spent that time lounging around, but had fortified his city well, creating narrow causeways between lakes that would be a killing ground should the U.S. soldiers try to cross them. The heavily fortified town of San Antonio blocked their way, along with the thick-walled, armed convent at San Mateo. After much reconnaissance, they found a passable route to San Antonio, but had to get through a Mexican unit led by General Gabriel Valencia, a glory hound of the first order who had deliberately disobeyed orders to meet the Americans. Scott's men surrounded his emplacement and overwhelmed him with an attack on the early morning of August 20th, killing 700 soldiers, capturing 800, and leaving the road to San Antonio wide open. However, disease was taking its toll, and the men were dropping with every mile traveled.

When Santa Anna learned of his unit's defeat, he retreated to the Churubusco River, placing his men behind the defenses on the far side. Scott decided to try to divide and conquer, sending divisions and brigade at the Mexican line at several different points. Although the Americans were heavily outnumbered—6,000 to 18,000—they held their own in battle for three hours. When Santa Anna's men ran low on ammunition, the Americans charged once more on three fronts—and broke through. A squadron of dragoons chased the fleeing Mexicans to the San Antonio gate, where enemy cannon chopped them into hamburger. Scott had won, but had suffered 1,000 killed and wounded. Santa Anna had lost 4,000 killed and wounded, and even worse, 3,200 soldiers had been captured, including eight generals.

Scott might have pressed on to take the city, but agreed to a two-week truce so that diplomats from both sides could try to work out peace terms. Santa Anna, however, was just using the time for a breather, and made such impossible demands that the U.S. general knew the fighting wasn't over yet.

The next battle occurred near Chapultepec, a castle that guarded the western approaches to Mexico City. It was heavily fortified and held by 8,000 soldiers. Scott wanted the position after hearing a rumor that Santa Anna was casting cannons there. He sent General William Worth and half his remaining men to take it. Worth was an old school officer who scorned artillery—in other words, a damned fool. After only light bombardment, his soldiers fixed bayonets and charged the walls on September 8th, with predictable results. They died by the dozens under the sweeping fire of Mexican muskets and cannons. Even under this barrage, the Americans managed to reach a gate, batter it down, and storm the fortifications, taking them after pitched fighting and beating off two Mexican counterattacks. It was some of the bloodiest fighting of the entire campaign, with 800 men killed and wounded in the attack. Even though they had won, and inflicted sizable damage (2,000 casualties and 680 prisoners), morale was low, with many officers thinking the army couldn't take many more of those kinds of victories and survive.

Scott understood all too well his army's precarious position. He was 250 miles from the coast, and yellow fever season would last until November, making it difficult to leave by way of Vera Cruz. There was nothing else to do but attack before Santa Anna realized he could defeat the smaller U.S. army. The only question was how to start? A council of his officers resulted in a consensus to go in through the western gates, taking the rest of Chapultepec and, from there, into the city itself.

On the morning of September 12th, the battle for Mexico City began. After retaking the abandoned Molino del Rey and Casa Mata fortifications, the Americans set out to conquer the rest of the complex, battering the thick walls with artillery. A diversion to the south had deceived Santa Anna, who had left less than 1,000 men to hold the western line, including 100 cadets from the Military College. The U.S. forces attacked from the east and the north, gained the walls, and drove the Mexicans off in fierce hand-to-hand combat. The cadets acquitted themselves valiantly, many fighting to the death, even after the regular soldiers had fled, but soon the Stars and Stripes flew over the roof of the college.

The only thing left to do was to take the rest of the city. By now Santa Anna realized the U.S. force was knocking at his very gates, with soldiers led by General John Quitman breaking through the Belén Gate into the outskirts of the city itself by early afternoon. The Liberator mounted fierce resistance from the massive Citadel nearby, as well as the Belén Prison, pinning the Americans at the gate.

However, a second force, led by General William Worth, aimed to take the San Cosmé Gate, but had to travel farther north before he could swing to the east and charge. When he learned of the second attack, Santa Anna hastily moved to protect that entrance, but it was too late. The U.S. soldiers broke through the defenses and moved into the city, fighting well into the night. Realizing all was lost, Santa Anna retreated to the Citadel again, and evacuated his remaining 5,400 soldiers, leaving 2,000 released convicts to harry the invaders.

On the morning of September 14, 1847, General Quitman arose prepared to clear the city of Mexican soldiers block by block if he had to, but received the news of Santa Anna's retreat instead. When he learned that criminals were looting the city, he formed up his men, marched them into the Grand Plaza in the middle of the city, and assigned the Marine contingent the job of clearing the National Palace of thieves and other ruffians. Later that morning, General Scott, in full dress uniform, galloped into the plaza escorted by dragoons, with officers and even a military band in tow. The men, and even the citizens of Mexico, cheered his arrival. The war with Mexico was over, except for the parceling out of the spoils.

With his five-month campaign, Scott added 1,193,061 square miles to the United States of America, including all of present-day California, Nevada, and Utah, and parts of Arizona, Colorado, New Mexico, and Wyoming. The U.S. agreed to pay Mexico $15 million—less than half of what they had offered to buy the land outright two years earlier—and assume $3.2 million of Mexican debt. The Treaty of Guadalupe Hidalgo was signed by both sides on February 2, 1848.

The U.S.–Mexican War is a classic example of how training and tactics can carry the day, even against a much larger force. It certainly didn't help Santa Anna that he was supremely overconfident that his much larger army would rout the smaller American forces, but his men were not trained to the exacting discipline of the U.S. armed services, which showed in every battle, as the Americans defeated armies two and three times their size. American ingenuity, from the skilled use of horse artillery to the troop-loading barges, also played a significant part in winning the campaign. Santa Anna's tactics seemed to rely largely on using his men to hold off any invasion, with no innovative ideas or new plans used to stop the relentless enemy advance. Although he styled himself "the Napoleon of the West," things might have gone differently if he had used Czar Alexander's strategy when Napoleon invaded Russia, and let the land itself whittle down the American army by disease before attempting to defeat them.

It also didn't help that Mexico had anything but a stable central government, with revolutions rocking the capital and the nation seemingly every few months—the removal of Santa Anna and his eventual return to power is a chief indicator of that.

Overall, it seems that the main mismatch between the two forces was that of determination—with the unstoppable fortitude that is a hallmark of the American soldier, Winfield Scott and his forces were not going to stop until they had either achieved their objectives or had been destroyed. Even though they were fighting for their homeland, with an unstable government backing him, and the people of Mexico unsure of his true motives, Santa Anna (who was president of Mexico 11 different times in 22 years) must have had to use all of his persuasive powers to convince his men to follow him, especially after the stunning defeat at Buena Vista.

It is notable to see how the winners and losers of this war fared afterward, with Zachary Taylor being elected President of the United States, Winfield Scott becoming the military general of Mexico City and, later, a failed presidential candidate, and Santa Anna becoming president of Mexico one last time, although this reign was no better than any of his others. He lived in exile in Cuba and the United States before returning to Mexico, where he died penniless and despondent in 1876. His era had passed long before he did.

In the Hollywood of old, it was an assumption that the small, but valiant, Western forces always defeat the barbarous and disorganized natives. These can be American Indians, Zulu, or Mahdists. Often this is the case, but even the British Empire at its peak managed to lose one occasionally. Here is how that happened.

THE ANGLO-SUDAN WAR

The Sudan, 1881–1885

BRIAN M. THOMSEN

The British Empire of the nineteenth century loved to highlight its heroes and victories in its holdings abroad.

The sun never set on the British Empire, after all, and the forces of civilization and superior technology and strategy would always prevail.

Certain historians' record will recite victory after victory in an offhanded manner that less than reflects the carnage and casualty that was a direct result of such affairs. Indeed there is a certain degree of relish that is afforded when talking of the heroic martyrdom of Chinese Gordon at Khartoum, and the empire's triumphant campaign in the Anglo-Sudan War that lasted from 1881–1899.

A great deal of relish, however, is not an acceptable substitute for objective accuracy, for the Anglo-Sudan War was in reality two wars or at least a war in two parts. And it is entirely accurate to point out that the first part, the so-called "Mahdist Revolt" did indeed end with the death of the Mahdi (Muhammad Ahmad ibn as

Sayyid Abd'allah) in 1885 (a few months after the fall of Khartoum and the death of Gordon which signaled the end of British and Egyptian influence in the Sudan and its replacement by the dominion of the forces of the Mahdi).

Prior to his death, this religious zealot leader had successfully engineered a campaign that disposed of British dominance in the Sudan and the expulsion of the empire forces from the area for a period of not less than ten years, at which point the British Empire in strategic alliance with Egypt and Italy returned in full force to displace the regime of the Mahdi's successor. And to equate these two conflicts as one war in which the British Empire emerged victoriously would be the equivalent of saying the Green Bay Packers' victories in Super Bowls I and II and then again in Super Bowl XXXI constituted thirty years of Green Bay dominance in the NFL.

The fact of the matter is that, though the empire emerged victorious from what might be known as the Anglo-Sudan war, there is little reason to conclude anything other than the fact that they quite conspicuously lost their war against the forces of the Mahdi.

Moreover, why they lost is also equally apparent, and indeed can be traced back to the reasons that fostered the revolt itself.

By the last quarter of the nineteenth century, the Sudan was ripe for revolt due to many years of oppression under a British-backed Egyptian regime that unfairly taxed its subjects and imposed Western values and culture on its people, which indeed culminated in a legalistic attempt to abolish slavery which was for many not just a necessary facet of the economy but also a divine right as passed on from Allah. In the words of Winston Churchill: "The reasons which forced the peoples of the Sudan to revolt were as strong as the defense which their oppressors could offer was feeble. Looking at the question from a purely political standpoint, we may say that upon the whole there exists no record of a better case for rebellion than presented itself to the Sudanese. Their country was being ruined; their property was plundered; their women were ravished; their liberties were curtailed; even their lives were threatened. Aliens ruled the inhabitants; the few oppressed the many; brave men were harried by cowards; the weak compelled the strong.

Here were sufficient reasons. Since any armed movement against an established Government can be justified only by success, strength is an important revolutionary virtue. It was a virtue that the Arabs might boast. They were indeed far stronger than they, their perse-cutors, or the outside world had yet learned. All were soon to be 'enlightened.' "

On to this scene of discontent arrived Muhammad Ahmad, a Muslim cleric who preached religious Islamic revival that would lead to the salvation of the faithful and a removal/subjugation of the infidel. Continuing the words of Churchill: "fostered by the discontents and justified by the miseries of the people of the Sudan, the Mahdi began to collect adherents and to extend his influence in all parts of the country. He made a second journey through Kordo-fan, and received everywhere promises of support from all classes. The most distant tribes sent assurances of devotion and reverence, and, what was of more importance, of armed assistance. The secret could not be long confined to those who welcomed the move-ment. As the ramifications of the plot spread they were perceived by the renowned Sheikh Sharif, who still nursed his chagrin and thirsted for revenge. He warned the Egyptian Government. They, knowing his envy and hatred of his former disciple, discounted his evidence and for some time paid no attention to the gathering of the storm. But presently more trustworthy witnesses confirmed his statements, and Raouf Pasha, then Governor-General, finding himself confronted with a growing agitation, determined to act. He accordingly sent a messenger to the island of Abba, to sum-mon Mohammed Ahmed to Khartoum to justify his behavior and explain his intentions. The news of the dispatch of the messenger was swiftly carried to the Mahdi! He consulted with his trusty lieu-tenant. They decided to risk everything, and without further delay to defy the Government. When it is remembered how easily an organized army, even though it be in a bad condition, can stamp out the beginnings of revolt among a population, the courage of their resolve must be admired."

So England started off with two major mistakes:

- They underestimated the discontent of the people at large.
- They underestimated the potential charisma of their newly prominent charismatic leader.

Still, they were the representatives of the British Empire, after all, and quite accustomed to getting their way. Moreover they underestimated the religious fervor that was permeating the citizenry.

The British looked at this as a political situation—mismanagement by the Egyptian government might cause some discontent but not a war, at least so they thought.

They were wrong.

This wasn't just a simple rebellion.

This was the beginning of a holy war, and the seeds of discontent that had been already sowed in the fertile ground of the oppressed Sudanese had sprouted forth jihad.

At first, the Egyptian colonial forces tried to take matters into their own hands—a minor show of force with a machine gun or two should have been more than enough to put the religious insurgents back in their place.

The problem was that, with the exception of the normal activities associated with day-to-day political corruption, the Egyptian puppets were pretty lame at everything else. As Churchill recalled in his book *The River War*:

> In the miserable, harassing warfare that accompanied the collection of taxes the Viceregal commanders gained more from fraud than force. No subterfuge, no treachery, was too mean for them to adopt: no oath or treaty was too sacred for them to break. Their methods were cruel, and if honor did not impede the achievement, mercy did not restrict the effects of their inglorious successes; and the effete administrators delighted to order their timid soldiery to carry out the most savage executions. The political methods and social style of the Governors-General were imitated more or less exactly by the subordinate officials according to their degree in the provinces. Since they were completely hidden from the eye of civilization, they enjoyed a greater license in their administration. As their education was inferior, so their habits became more gross. Meanwhile the

volcano on which they disported themselves was ominously silent. The Arab tribes obeyed, and the black population cowered.

The authority of a tyrannical Government was supported by the presence of a worthless army. Nearly forty thousand men were distributed among eight main and numerous minor garrisons. Isolated in a roadless country by enormous distances and natural obstacles, and living in the midst of large savage populations of fanatical character and warlike habits, whose exasperation was yearly growing with their miseries, the Viceregal forces might depend for their safety only on the skill of their officers, the excellence of their discipline, and the superiority of their weapons. But the Egyptian officers were at that time distinguished for nothing but their public incapacity and private misbehavior. The evil reputation of the Sudan and its climate deterred the more educated or wealthier from serving in such distant regions, and none went south who could avoid it. The army which the Khedives maintained in the Delta was, judged by European standards, only a rabble. It was badly trained, rarely paid, and very cowardly; and the scum of the army of the Delta was the cream of the army of the Sudan. The officers remained for long periods, many all their lives, in the obscurity of the remote provinces. Some had been sent there in disgrace, others in disfavor. Some had been forced to serve out of Egypt by extreme poverty, others were drawn to the Sudan by the hopes of gratifying peculiar tastes. The majority had harems of the women of the country, which were limited only by the amount of money they could lay their hands on by any method. Many were hopeless and habitual drunkards. Nearly all were dishonest. All were indolent and incapable. Under such leadership the finest soldiery would have soon degenerated. The Egyptians in the Sudan were not fine soldiers.

As a result they met with the forces of the Mahdi to tell them who was boss and were promptly rebuked.

The Egyptians took action and all hell broke loose as the ill-trained forces got themselves caught in their own crossfire allowing the Mahdi forces to withdraw, regroup, and attack.

Another expedition was sent after the Mahdi rebels, but they never returned, having been slaughtered by the now-thriving masses that made up the Mahdi army.

What happened next was summarized by Winston Churchill in *The River War*, at the time as follows: "The Egyptian administration in the Sudan, now thoroughly concerned by the scale of the uprising, assembled a force of four thousand troops under Yusef Pasha. This force approached the Mahdist gathering, whose members were poorly clothed, half starving, and armed only with sticks and stones. However, supreme overconfidence led the Egyptian army into camping within sight of the Mahdist 'army' without posting sentries. The Mahdi led a dawn assault and slaughtered the army to a man. The rebellion gained vast stores of arms and ammunition, military clothing, and other supplies."

Needless to say even the government of the Egyptians realized that they were in over their heads and quickly beseeched England for help in quelling the uprising.

And the military powers-that-be back in England did what every good group of bureaucrats would do when any of the conquered peoples of the empire are placed in jeopardy—they did a cost-benefit analysis and valiantly tried to do nothing, hoping that the problem would just go away.

Further begging from the Egyptians resulted in the authorization of a military expedition under a retired staff officer by the name of William Hicks, who with his staff led a column of about eight thousand combined Egyptian and British forces to reinforce the city of Khartoum and confront the forces of the Mahdi.

Hicks' force met the Mahdi's men, now close to forty thousand strong at El Obeid on November 3, 1883, and the British force that was meant to stare down the Sudanese rabble were summarily slaughtered.

Needless to say the bean counters back in England as well as those north of the Sudan in Egypt were none too pleased with these results and commissioned an audit that determined that these instances of fighting the Mahdi were costing the already stretched (by corruption and featherbedding) Egyptian colonial government over one hundred thousand pounds a year just to maintain the garrisons that they already had in place, without even taking into account the additional expense of further reinforce-

ment and/or replacement of those forces that had been slaughtered.

Both the bean counters in Africa and back in the United Kingdom agreed on the cheapest solution possible—withdraw the British
colonial forces and citizenry (along with their Egyptian collabora-
tors) from the affected areas of the Sudan until the Mahdi's influence
waned, at which point everybody could then move back and reclaim
their positions as if nothing had happened. This same parsimonious
brain-trust also decided the way to achieve this strategic relocation
of forces (the word retreat was *definitely* not used) promptly was to
send in a direct military representative of the British crown, whom
the rabble would never deign to affront.

The Egyptians applauded this move and immediately emulated
their counterparts in England by sitting back and doing nothing, glad
that someone else was going to be responsible for this problem.

Much to the chagrin of the British consul in Egypt, Charles "Chinese" Gordon, hero of both the Crimean and Opium Wars who was
adored by the public back in England, was appointed temporary
royal governor of the Sudan and tasked with the relocation.

Whether Gordon was only half-listening to his orders or just
decided to do what he thought was best or most honorable for
England is unclear.

The facts of the matter (previously related in the volume *How
to Lose a Battle*) were that Gordon set out for the Sudan, arrived at
Khartoum, and began a game of brinksmanship against the Mahdi's
forces with the expectation that England would reconsider their
cut and run strategy and send reinforcements to deal militarily
with the insurgent masses of the Mahdi.

The timeline of these events were as follows:

Gordon arrived at Khartoum on February 18, 1884.

Khartoum fell on January 25, 1885.

Critics maintain that the city was still evacuative up until Christmas and supposedly Gordon continually urged others to leave and
head north prior to that point.

Be that as it may, and despite the public and press outcry back
in London, such forces that may have fortified Gordon's position

never arrived and Khartoum fell to the Mahdi unevacuated, with the whole world watching as England was walloped by the desert army of religious fanatics.

An inadequate relief column was dispatched to the city with tersely worded orders instructing Gordon to do what he had been sent to do (this time the word "retreat" indeed might have been used) but they only came within sight of the besieged city (and Gordon's pikestaff-mounted head) two days after it had already fallen and its obstinate leader been killed.

The column quickly followed the orders that were intended for Gordon and retreated, leaving the other garrisons to the mercy of the Mahdi. Those who weren't killed and earned the religious leader's mercy were bound into slavery with no hope of escape.

All subtleties of the situation were lost as the greatest empire of that time was forced to turn tail and run, rather than deal with the desert army that they had never taken seriously.

Moreover they never defeated Muhammad Ahmad.

In the words of Winston Churchill from his critical (and extremely unpopular among the decision-making circles of Cairo and London) history *The River War*:

> In the middle of the month of June, scarcely five months after the completion of his victorious campaigns, the Mahdi fell sick. For a few days he did not appear at the mosque. The people were filled with alarm. . . . Presently those who attended him could doubt no longer that he was attacked by typhus fever. . . . All those who had shared his fortunes—the Khalifas he had appointed, the chief priests of the religion he had reformed, the leaders of the armies who had followed him to victory, and his own family whom he had hallowed—crowded the small room. For some hours he lay unconscious or in delirium, but as the end approached he rallied a little and, collecting his faculties by a great effort, declared his faithful follower and friend the Khalifa Abdullah his successor, and adjured the rest to show him honor. "He is of me, and I am of him; as you have obeyed me, so you should deal with him. May God have mercy upon me!" Then he immediately expired.

The only word that Churchill left out in this account was "victoriously." The Mahdi had bested the crown and had removed the forces of the empire from his homeland.

He had won and was now entitled to rest.

True, the empire reclaimed dominion over the Sudan two years later after the Mahdi had died, but no manner of spin can obscure the fact that the Mahdi had beaten them in *his* war.

*This wasn't a defeat in the sense that England lost the
Boer War, but rather that it cost them so much to win.
The measures they won by would seem today barbaric,
and those measures were necessary because of the
many tactical and strategic failures of the
British professional soldiers.*

THE BOER WAR

This Is Going to Be a Cakewalk
and We'll All Be Home by Christmas!
South Africa, 1899–1902

BRIAN M. THOMSEN

According to the *Handbook of the Boer War*, first published in 1910, a
rather wordy early assessment of the unrest in South Africa in 1899
would have been as follows:

> *An Army of 100,000 men is the utmost that Great Britain will be able to
> place in the field in South Africa, for the Indian and Colonial drafts must
> be provided for, and the Militia and other Auxiliary Forces, which are not
> of much account, are tethered to the country; but it will be sufficient for
> the purpose. Although the military system of Great Britain is hopelessly
> behind the times, she has always done wonders with her boomerangs,
> bows and arrows, and flint instruments. That Army will be fairly well
> furnished with modern weapons and equipment, and the excellent person-
> ality of the soldier will compensate to a great extent for incapacity in the*

Staff and superior officers. With this Army she will have to meet a brave but undisciplined opponent whose numbers cannot be estimated. Even if the Free Staters are included it is improbable that more than 100,000 men can be put into the field. These have had no military training; their leaders will be unprofessional officers who will be unable to make good use of the munitions of war which the two Republics have been strangely allowed to import through British ports and to accumulate in large quantities. If the burghers of the Orange Free State throw in their lot with the Transvaalers, which is improbable as they have no quarrel with Great Britain, the numbers opposed to her will certainly be augmented, but the task before her will be greatly simplified. Instead of having to send one portion of her Army by way of Natal to effect a junction in the Transvaal, with the other portion working northwards through Kimberley and Mafeking, a campaign which would involve two long and vulnerable lines of communication, she will be able to strike at once through the heart of the Free State and will advance without much difficulty to Johannesburg and Pretoria. The hardest part of her task will be the passage of the Vaal, where a great battle will be fought, and the capture of Pretoria, which is reported to be well fortified. With Bloemfontein, Johannesburg, Pretoria and the railways in the possession of Great Britain, the opposition will collapse in a very few weeks, for no nation has ever been able to carry on a struggle when its chief towns and means of communication are in the enemy's possession.

This was the way most "impartial" military strategists in the Ministry of War back in England saw what was to become known as the Boer War.

Basically, a quick and easy shock and awe style response that could be done on the cheap, especially since the locals would probably throw in with the British forces (dare I say, greeting them as liberators?).

And of course, such great military minds would have been wrong.

Indeed, the Boer War was not solved in such a quick, cheap manner.

The war lasted over two and a half years (1899–1902) and eventually required a force of not less than 500,000 men to control/suppress the rebellious Boer forces that probably mustered no more than 80,000.

So what went wrong?

Well, initially the empire came to the conclusion that the problem had already been dealt with. A rebellion in South Africa against the British annexation of the Transvaal and Orange Free State Republics had been quickly quelled back in 1881 and written off as the expected aggravation of a few bad apples trying to prevent the inevitable. Unfortunately the number of these bad apples soon grew when gold and diamonds were discovered in the Transvaal, and the repressive policies of the representatives of the Crown became more intense, so much so that a Boer force was mustered to fight back. (The Boers, as they were called—Boer from *trekboer*, being the Dutch word for farmer—were primarily Dutch and Huguenot immigrants who had come to South Africa in search of religious freedom during the eighteenth and nineteenth centuries.)

This is not to say that the folks back in England were surprised by this action. Many members of the government were egging them on in hopes of settling the matter of rebellion once and for all, and though cooler minds and public opinion tried to slow down the march to war in South Africa, moneyed and militaristic interests had their own agendas and joined the conflict with little or no support or planning.

Worse yet, once they made their intentions clear, they then sat on their hands for three months as if the matter would resolve itself with the forces currently in place.

This set in motion a series of missteps that resulted in turning what might have been a simple police action into a money-draining fiasco for almost all concerned.

In the words of Winston Churchill: "It is possible that had war broken out three months ago that loyalty would have been demonstrated for all time. War after three months of hesitation—for such it was considered—has proved too severe a test, and it is no exaggeration to say that a considerable part of the Colony trembles on the verge of rebellion. On such a state of public opinion the effect of any important military reverse would be lamentable." Churchill then cites the advantage the Boers attained by drawing first blood, and more pointedly put his finger on the biggest blunder of all, saying, "A democratic Government cannot go to war unless the country is behind it, and until it has general support must not place itself in a position whence, without fighting, there is no retreat." . . . Which indeed the forces of the crown never seemed to get around to doing.

However, it was not just the politicians back in England who got it wrong.

Their military yes-men in the field were equally clueless.

According to Churchill: "Sir Penn Symons, who had been commanding in the Colony, and who was presumably best qualified to form an opinion on the military necessities, extravagantly underrated the Boer fighting power. Some of his calculations of the force necessary to hold various places seem incredible in the light of recent events. But everyone was wrong about the Boers, and the more they knew the worse they erred. Symons laughed at the Boer military strength, and labored to impress his opinions on (those below him). . . . The defect in this plan was that there were not enough troops to carry it out. As we had underestimated the offensive vigor which the enemy was able to develop before the army could reach South Africa, so now we altogether miscalculated his extraordinary strength on the defensive."

Indeed despite repeated requests from men in the field, supplies, reinforcements, and indeed adequate arms, artillery, and armament were either slow in coming or never actually authorized. Back in the safety of England, there seemed to be little interest in actually incurring any "cost" in the war that they decided to wage, almost as little interest as there was in trying to justify their actions to begin with.

Moreover, it was almost as if certain powerbrokers wished to have the matter resolve itself so that the real reasons for the conflict, the securing of the assets provided by the discovery of diamonds and gold, would never be brought to the forefront—almost as if these war merchants anticipated a war dividend without any actual investment at all.

However, the mistakes in the management of this conflict were not solely confined to decisions made back home. More than a few key blunders occurred in the field as well.

Many of the in-the-field military leaders seemed to have trouble approaching the South African battlefield as more than a competition or boardroom game at large. It would have been difficult to discern from the bearing and demeanor of the typical officer whether he was at the moment a prisoner of war in the Model School at Pretoria or had just taken part in the magnificent cavalry charge by which Kimberley was relieved. The former plight did not greatly depress him, nor did the latter phase of military life greatly elate him. It is probable that the War would have been brought to a successful close at a much earlier date if throughout the British Army and especially among the officers hearty disgust and indignation at the failures of the first few months had taken the place of a light-hearted accommodation to circumstances:

> The British officer played at war in South Africa much in the same way that he hunted or played cricket or polo at home. He enjoyed the sport and the game, did his best for his own side, and rejoiced if he was successful, but was not greatly disturbed when he lost. A dictum attributed to the Duke of Wellington says that the Battle of Waterloo was won upon the Playing Fields at Eton. It would not be so very far from the truth to say that the guns at Sannah's Post were captured on the polo-ground at Hurlingham; that Magersfontein was lost at Lord's; that Spionkop was evacuated at Sandown; and that the war lingered on for thirty-two months in the Quorn and Pytchley coverts.
>
> The sporting view of War was recognized and confirmed in Army Orders and official reports, in which the words "bag," "drive," "stop," and some other sporting terms not infrequently appeared. No one would reasonably object to the judicious and illuminating use of metaphor, but there are metaphors which impair the dignity of a cause and degrade it in the eyes of those whose duty is to maintain that cause. When the advance

of a British Division at a critical period in the operations is frivolously
termed a "drive," and when the men extended at ten paces' interval over
a wide front are called "beaters," it is natural that the leaders should look
upon their work as analogous to the duties of a gamekeeper; and when an
artillery officer is instructed to "pitch his shells well up," he is encouraged
to regard failure as no worse than the loss of a cricket-match.

And indeed, initially the war-game went according to plan.

By 1900, armed British forces had confronted the Boer armies on
numerous occasions and had fought them to a stalemate, at which
point the forces of the crown were inclined to declare victory except for one small problem: the armies of the enemy disappeared.

It was almost as if some colonial governor had waved his hand
and ordered the Boers disbanded.

The British hierarchy in place took this as confirmation of their
initial assessment that their adversaries were indeed disorganized
and would only be a minor irritant to the colonial government.

Well, at least until they started laying traps for her majesty's
fighting men, blowing up railroads, and launching their own terror war on those they considered to be interlopers and invaders,
namely the British. And because they had forsaken the niceties of
battledress uniforms and regulation formation, these shadow warriors just blended right back into the civilian population whenever
an "escape" was necessary.

Moreover, even the uninvolved "non-insurgent" citizenry were
not much help in the exposure of the identities of these guerilla
fighters; not just because of their lack of sympathy and/or respect
for her majesty's forces (for which there was none) but also because these so-called terrorists were usually members of their own
families and fighting for a cause for which they were all most sympathetic. Their nationalism had been born of hundreds of years of
fighting against imperialist powers like the crown, battling the harsh
African climate, a strong sense of nationhood, as well as a staunch
conservative Christian belief. Indeed they were archetypally more
akin to the forces of Oliver Cromwell, whose rebellion led to both
regicide and reform back in England two centuries earlier.

And contrary to what the armchair leaders in England and the lawnchair leaders in South Africa believed, they were not going to cease their hostilities any time soon.

Further hampering the British military was the "on the cheap" strategy that pervaded the early years of the conflict.

Rather than sending cavalry, the first reinforcements were primarily foot soldiers who were ill-suited to the wide-ranging task of tracking down roving bands of guerilla fighters used to living off the land. And even after the need for equine support was realized, the supplies were still inadequate for the task. In the words of Lt. Wittin of the Bushveldt Carbineers, "The saddlery issued to these men was practically useless. How any man or body of men could pass such worthless shoddy is beyond comprehension, and reflects sadly on the judgment of the Supplies Board. The saddles were without a vestige of stuffing, and the stirrup-irons were cumbersome pieces of ironwork, weighing over 7 lbs., and so narrow that an ordinary-sized boot would not fit into them—just the kind of equipment to cripple the rider and ruin the horse at the same time."

Moreover, the strict regimented approach to the use of cavalry by the British military hierarchy was ill-suited for the Veldt, particularly when their opponents weren't playing by some previously agreed upon rules as to how war needed to be fought by gentlemen. It was only after the importation of irregulars from Australia, whose outback experiences had trained them for living off the land, that some of the guerillas were kept at bay.

Up until the introduction of these live-off-the-land horsemen, the forces of the crown had almost universally adopted a strategy of confronting the enemy directly in an effort to engage them in battle in which the British superiority in numbers would keep the Boers to a standstill, and then pause in order to wait for the insurgents to surrender.

Though there was often a pause in the action and even an occasional white flag, there was never a real surrender, and the insurgents would move on, regroup and re-attack at another time and in another place, all of which was considered to be less than cricket of them.

The reinforcements from Australia took a slightly different approach.

One typical incident, as described in *Scapegoats of the Empire* by George Witton, was as follows:

> *Pietersburg is an important town 180 miles north of Pretoria and the terminus of the railway. After the occupation of Pretoria in June, 1900, the Boer Government was set up here, and it was not until May, 1901, that the town was occupied and garrisoned by British troops. A tragic incident, in which two Tasmanian officers were killed, is related to have occurred on the day the troops entered Pietersburg. These two officers were going out to a magazine on the outskirts of the town, and were sniped at and shot dead by a Dutch schoolmaster who lay hidden in the long grass. When the troops ran up to see what was the matter, this gentleman jumped up, and, holding up his hands, shouted, "I surrender! I surrender! I surrender!" The men walked up to him, and without hesitation ran a bayonet through his body, and in the heat and stress of the battlefield this action of the soldiers was applauded.*

The little war to put down an understaffed and underfunded rebellion that just wouldn't stay down required much more serious measures than proper British soldiers were used to, but since everyone was getting impatient (after all there were gold and diamonds to lay claim to and mining corporations to move in) desperate measures were required and the horsemen from the former prison colony of Australia were just the folks to do it.

Concentration camps were set up to prevent captured supporters of the insurgents from blending back into the rest of the citizenry and resuming their caring and feeding of the enemy.

Supply trains that were constantly being derailed to prevent the arrival of reinforcements as well as ammunition and other supplies were protected from the incendiary and explosive plans of the enemy by packing an open car with captured Boers in front of each train as a deterrent to such destructive actions. (The move was considered quite successful, since train attacks declined from that point, the Boers obviously choosing the lives of their comrades over the strategic gains that might have been obtained by the destruction of the trains.)

And, of course, insurgents captured in the field were denied normal military protocols and many times subjected to summary executions without benefit of council or the option of surrender and imprisonment.

And along the way, these bush-hardened warriors also destroyed crops, burned homesteads and farms, poisoned wells, and terrorized the citizenry in an effort to bring everyone, not just the armed guerilla insurgents but their bystander relatives, as well, to heel.

Such actions were extremely distasteful, but the war had gone on too long and had become too costly and results were being demanded. Even the genteel forces of Lord Kitchener himself began to join in and, at last, this Scorched Earth policy began to seriously affect the Boers' fighting strength and freedom of maneuver, and made it harder and harder for the Boers and their families to survive.

By mid 1902, the last stragglers of Boer opposition finally agreed to put down their weapons.

The last of the Boers surrendered in May, 1902, and the war ended with the Treaty of Vereeniging which was signed on May 31, 1902. Despite the victory, the military high command of the crown was quite distressed at the actions that had to be taken to assure victory once their early ineffectual actions had allowed the little Dutch settler rebellion, so they quickly court-martialed several of the Australians who had engineered the strategies that had proven effective.

After all, no one wanted to sanction such an uncivilized way of conducting a war, no matter how effective it turned out to be.

Still the cost in treasure and men was quite substantial and all because no one had planned any strategies to maintain order or bring about a peace once the war had been declared.

Moreover, all the armchair experts who had made the crucial decisions (and subsequent excuses) had grossly underestimated everything.

Winston Churchill summed it all up thusly: "It reminds me of

Jules Verne's story of the men who planned to shift the axis of the earth by the discharge of a great cannon. Everything was arranged. The calculations were exact to the minutest fraction. The world stood aghast at the impending explosion. But the men of science, whose figures were otherwise so accurate, had left out a naught, and their whole plan came to nothing. So it was with the British. Their original design of a containing division in Natal, and an invading army of three divisions in the Free State, would have been excellent if only they had written army corps instead of division."

Churchill should know; he wasn't in a London armchair, he was there.

Today, insurgents seem to have the upper hand in "non-conventional warfare." Such efforts have been successful, within limited objectives, since Fabius faced Hannibal. But these tactics only work if you do them correctly. Not every insurgency has. This one became the textbook example of what not to do.

THE MAU MAU REBELLION

MIKE RESNICK

Before Kenya was plunged into war the thoughts of the leaders must have run something like this:

To the tribal leaders it must have looked so easy. They surveyed the situation and probably said to each other: "There are six million of us, and only a few hundred of them. We know the territory and they don't. We are an army and they are farmers. How can we lose?"

They found out.

It began with the land, as it almost always does in agricultural societies. The finest farmland in Kenya is the area in the vicinity of Mount Kenya and the Aberdares Mountains. The Kikuyu, Kenya's dominant tribe, had been living there for as long as anyone could remember.

Then Kenya became a British colony. The farther we get from the era of colonization, the more difficult it is to understand why any European country felt it had the right to colonize (i.e., dominate and economically plunder) an African, American, or Asian country, appropriate the land, and impose their laws and religion on the populace, but no one gave it a second thought prior to the last few decades of the twentieth century. Indeed, Sir Winston Churchill, considered a pillar of fair play and democracy, did nothing to harm his reputation by giving a famous speech in which he declared, "I will not preside over the dissolution of His Majesty's empire." Which is to say, "I won't return control of their land, their government, and their economies to the people who live in the countries we have appropriated."

Clearly, this is not an attitude designed to win friends and influence people in the lands you have colonized, and sure enough, by the early 1930s most Kenyans, and especially the Kikuyu, were starting to get "uppity notions" of freedom. The British didn't help much. They appropriated most of the Kikuyu homeland, which became known as the "White Highlands," a term that told one and all who could own farmland there and who, by omission, could not. The colonizers imposed a hut tax, a tax on each dwelling, which could only be paid in British currency—and the only way to get British currency was to work on now-British land for British farmers. By 1948, the ever-expanding White Highlands constituted more than eighty percent of the Kikuyu homeland, and employed more than one hundred and twenty thousand Kikuyu, who had no other way to raise the money required for the hut tax than to work on land they had previously owned and for which they had never been compensated. A huge number of Kikuyu opted to move to Nairobi, doubling its population during the decade of the 1940s, and turning almost all of it, except the area of tourist hotels and restaurants, into an enormous slum.

A few Kikuyu decided that there must be some means of gaining redress, and led by Harry Thuku, they formed the Kenyan African Union. No one paid it much attention. There were hardly any members, they had no means of reaching the bulk of the people, they were not allowed to carry arms or even spears, and if this let them blow a little steam off, why not, it probably eased the tensions.

Except that more than a few people listened, and one of them was a brilliant and charismatic man named Jomo Kenyatta. He had gone to Europe to school, and he understood not only how colonialism worked but also how to organize a political party. He proceeded to do this all during the 1940s. The British would ignore him for a while, then ban whatever party or group he was forming.

But discontent kept spreading. Kenyatta may have been the impetus, but it soon reached far beyond his control. The Kikuyu formed secret societies, administered terrible oaths to each other, murdered those who would not take those oaths, and brought swift death to those who took but ignored their oaths (one of which had to do with killing any Kikuyu who *didn't* take the oath). They paralyzed Nairobi for nine days with a general strike that was broken only by a massive display of British force. The leaders, of course, were arrested and imprisoned.

Kenyatta and his less radical followers sought political change without threatening violence. It was an exercise in futility. Kenyatta wanted twelve black Kenyans added to the Legislative Council that ran Kenya. Instead, the British Colonial Secretary reorganized the government as follows: the handful of white settlers got fourteen representatives, the hundred thousand Asians got six, the twenty-five thousand Arabs got one. And the six million black Kenyans? They got five, all named not by themselves but by the white government.

Radicals tried to wrest control of the Kenyan African Union from Kenyatta, but he outmaneuvered them, still hoping for a political solution. He was the public face of Kenyan unrest—but a bunch of private faces got tired of waiting, and started killing Kikuyu who were loyal to the British.

By 1952, the movement had a name—Mau Mau—and a purpose: to drive the British back to Britain. They torched some houses, mutilated some farm animals, and killed some more black loyalists. The British were sure Kenyatta was the movement's leader, and they brought him to trial on what proved to be trumped-up charges:

"You are the leader of this subversive group that calls itself the Mau Mau," accused the British.

"I do not even know what 'Mau Mau' means," was his honest reply. This was true—even today there is no agreement about the origins of the name or what it meant.

The British gave him a seven-year prison sentence to think about what it meant. He was put into a small cell in Kapenguria in the arid Northern Frontier District, a place that had no rail or phone communication with the rest of Kenya, and that, thought the British, was that. A State of Emergency had been declared the day Kenyatta was arrested, eight thousand Kikuyu were arrested within the next month, and when Kenyatta (who would later become Kenya's first president) was found guilty, it was assumed the danger was over.

Memo from the Kikuyu to their colonizers: Welcome to the real world. The first European was killed three weeks after Kenyatta was incarcerated.

The problem, of course, was that only Kenyatta really understood what his people were up against.

For example: if you are fighting a war, you want to win the hearts of the people to gain support for your cause. If you find someone is undecided as to which side is right, you talk to him and convince him that you are fighting for the right.

But the Mau Mau never tried to convince anyone to join them. What they did was *terrorize* people into joining. If you spoke out against the Mau Mau, if you mentioned that you were content working for the British, you were as likely to be speared to death or hacked to death with *pangas* in broad daylight as to be ignored. If you converted, it was not because of the arguments of the Mau Mau, but rather the knowledge of the consequences if you *didn't* convert.

So while they had a country of six million, most of whom had no use for the British and wanted to be free, a huge majority was terrified of them. The populace may not have loved the British, but they weren't afraid of them either.

The next thing you want is a brilliant field commander, a Douglas MacArthur or a Tommy Franks, especially when you are outnumbered and outgunned.

What they got were a bunch of countries.

Let me explain that. Most of the Mau Mau generals were as uneducated as their followers. They wanted names that would impress the rank and file, and being uneducated they were unaware of names like Alexander and Caesar and Napoleon. So what you got was General China, and General Tanganyika, and a bunch of General some-other-countries. It's doubtful than any of them except General Tanganyika could find their namesake on a map. In fact, it is doubtful that many of them could even read a map, which does make it difficult to plan a campaign.

They felt safe in the mountains, so they set up headquarters there. The problem is that it meant climbing down the mountain every time they engaged in a military action—it also meant, once it was known where they were hiding, that all the British had to do was station men at the base of the mountains to cut the Mau Mau supply lines.

The one general who kept his own name was Dedan Kimathi, and he led the British a merry chase through the Aberdares mountain range for a couple of years. He used the mountainous terrain to stay hidden, but when you're hiding on a relatively unpopulated mountain, you're not presenting much of a military threat until you come down off it—and of course the British were waiting for him at the base of the mountain.

Speaking of unpopulated mountains, let's talk about the battle-field terrain for a moment.

Where was the enemy?

Most of them were in Nairobi, Mombasa, and other cities. Once the British realized that they were up against a military operation, no matter how poorly organized, they fortified the cities, and the Mau Mau never made any successful forays against them.

In the course of four years, the Mau Mau actually killed very few colonists. Farm fields tended to be flat and out in the open, and everyone was on the alert. Most farmers kept guns, dogs, and loyal Kikuyu on hand to hold off any attacks.

So who *did* the Mau Mau attack?

With the white settlers and the cities too well protected, they went after the loyalist Kikuyu. They mutilated them, they chopped them to ribbons, they killed them wherever they found them—and then they wondered why they had so much trouble recruiting soldiers to their cause.

When it became obvious that they didn't have the sheer force of arms to win, they decided to try something a little different.

They would attack with such savagery, such brutality, such barbarism, that the British, being a weak and civilized race, would be convinced that they had no recourse in the face of such horrible things but to go home.

Well, they convinced the British, all right—they convinced them that they couldn't leave the colonists to face such hideous attacks.

They convinced someone else, too: a tabloid columnist, who spent most of his adult life hanging out in fancy New York nightclubs, reporting on the comings and goings of local celebrities, a rival to Walter Winchell. His name was Robert Ruark, and all his life he'd wanted to take a safari. So he took one in the late 1940s, loved it, and started going back every year—and began to see what the Mau Mau were capable of. So he gave up being a gossip columnist and sat down and wrote one of the bestselling novels of the decade: *Something of Value*. It was the story of the Mau Mau, told from the twin viewpoints of a second-generation white colonist to whom Kenya is the only home he's ever known, and a Mau Mau terrorist. The hideous blood oaths, the animal and human mutilations, the utter callousness of the Mau Mau campaign were all presented in vivid detail in the novel.

It is said the Mau Mau assumed America, which had overthrown the yoke of British colonialism 175 years earlier, would rush to the Kikuyu side, or at least send them money and weapons. The only conclusion one can draw is that none of the Mau Mau leaders ever read Ruark's novel, or understood the effect it had on a few million Americans who had no other knowledge of Kenya.

It had an effect on one Englishman, too. When they rushed the film (starring Rock Hudson and Sidney Poitier) into production, there was a brief introduction by Sir Winston Churchill, explaining to each of the millions of moviegoers that the Mau Mau depicted in the film were real and, if anything, more dangerous than Ruark made them seem.

So much for foreign aid.

Okay, if you can't outmaneuver them and you can't out-recruit them, then the next best thing is to outgun them.

The colonists all had firearms. Most had powerful rifles. Once the British military showed up, with their rapid-fire weapons, all-terrain vehicles (which certainly didn't hurt when hunting the Mau Mau at 10,000 to 15,000 feet of altitude on Mount Kenya and in the Aberdares), they even had airplanes. (Bombs dropped from the planes into heavy cover on the mountains killed a lot of Mau Mau. They also killed a lot of elephant, rhino, and buffalo, and more than their fair share of smaller animals too.)

What did the Mau Mau have to combat this?

Well, they stockpiled weapons for a year before the uprising, and when it began they possessed 460 modern rifles, spread over a country somewhat larger than the state of Ohio. They mostly came armed with spears, *kibokos* (a whip that cuts to the bone, made from treating and stretching the private parts of a male rhino), *simis* (short swords), and *pangas*, which were actually farm tools but which functioned as machetes for the Mau Mau.

They realized that they were outgunned, so they established a couple of secret "factories" where they created more guns. Problem is, most of them exploded when fired, and accounted for ten times as many Mau Mau deaths and injuries as British fire.

Okay, so you're trying to infiltrate the enemy's society (in this case the enemy being anyone who hasn't taken the Mau Mau oath), not only to find out what the British are planning but also to hide from the British army. After all, if they find you walking around Mount Kenya with a spear and a *panga*, they pretty much know who and what they're dealing with.

The trick, of course, is not to let your men be caught or arrested, because once they're incarcerated, there's no telling who might collaborate with the enemy, and what they might say.

So how did the Mau Mau fare in this respect?

Let me give you some figures.

On October 30, 1952, the British arrested 500 suspected Mau Mau.

On November 25, 1952, they arrested another 2,000.

On April 17, 1953, the British rounded up and arrested another 1,000.

It gets worse.

On April 24, 1954, the British arrested 40,000 suspected Mau Mau and sympathizers.

By October, 1955, some 70,000 suspected Mau Mau and sympathizers had been incarcerated, and huge camps had to be built to hold them.

Were they all Mau Mau?

Of course not.

Were enough of them Mau Mau that the British were able to get the intelligence they needed about the leadership and the military movements?

Absolutely.

So much for keeping your men out of enemy hands.

Well, what else is left?

One of the things most Americans were surprised to learn during World War II was that despite George Patton's aggression, despite the number of battles he fought and won, his men suffered very few casualties compared to those under other leaders. The man was a brilliant general, and he took care of his troops.

You'd have to say if you're outmanned, outgunned, and outmaneuvered, the very best thing you can do is preserve what you have in the way of manpower and not waste the lives of your troops.

How did the Mau Mau fare under the leadership of General China, General Tanganyika, et al?

When the dust cleared at the end of hostilities in 1956, more than a thousand Mau Mau had been hanged by the British military. It's estimated that over 50,000 Kikuyu were killed. Probably 15,000 or so were Mau Mau, another 15,000 were loyalists killed *by* the Mau Mau, and the rest just got in the way.

And how much damage did this army which shocked Churchill, angered Ruark, and terrified the British and Americans, inflict on the enemy?

Of their victims, records show that less that one hundred white colonists were killed during the four years of the Emergency.

So let's consider it one more time: how do you lose a war?

- You go up against an enemy with superior firepower.
- You fail to protect your supply lines.
- You fail to rally the people to your side.
- You fail to protect your troops.
- You choose uneducated, inadequate military leaders.
- You lose the propaganda war.
- You are underfinanced.

If you ever wanted to write a textbook on all the myriad ways to lose a war, you could do a lot worse than study the Mau Mau rebellion.

An army is not better than its leaders.
Which in this case is all that needs to be said.

THE UGANDA-TANZANIA WAR

Blood and Circuses

MIKE RESNICK

He was a clown with a difference—when he wasn't busy amusing the press, he killed some 300,000 of his own people and invaded a neighboring country. Even the war had aspects of a circus.

He was Idi Amin, of course. As a young man, he had enlisted in the Kenyan army, and had actually become its heavyweight boxing champion, holding the light heavyweight championship in Uganda from 1951 to 1960. When he returned to his native Uganda, he rose rapidly in the military, and when he could rise no higher, he overthrew in a military coup Dr. Milton Obote, who was himself certainly no Lincoln-in-the-making, and became president in 1971.

Obote fled next door to Tanzania, where the president of that nation, Julius Nyerere, gave him sanctuary—and when Amin decided it was easier to kill off his political opposition than win them over to his side with compelling arguments, Nyerere also offered sanctuary to some 20,000 Ugandans who were fleeing for their lives.

All this took place during the first two years of Amin's reign.

Amin, for reasons a lot of us have yet to comprehend, was the darling of the Western press—at least for a while being credited with cleaning up corruption and reform. But in bits and pieces, Uganda's darker secrets began coming out. He turned government buildings into mass torture chambers. He began committing genocide on any Ugandans who were not from his own tribe. He erected a statue of Adolf Hitler in the middle of the capital city of Kampala, declaring the Fuehrer to be his hero. Though Uganda's economy was pretty much run by, and dependant upon, Indians who were the merchants, bankers, and managers. Amin kicked them all out of the country. Then, when the economy tanked and inflation skyrocketed, he invited them back—only to kick the Indians out (and appropriate their property and their businesses) a second time. He couldn't afford to feed his army, so he allowed them to poach their meals in the game parks. It's said he even practiced cannibalism on his own infant (or unborn; the accounts differ) son.

He was just a real sweetie.

It took him seven years to bankrupt the country, kill off a sizable portion of its population, get rid of every Indian, get rid of every technocrat, and go a few billion dollars into debt. Then, just to be on the safe side, he converted to Islam in case he ever had to leave in a hurry; according to the tenets of the religion, no other Moslem could turn him away or fail to offer him sanctuary.

As you may have guessed, not every Ugandan was thrilled with the situation. In 1978, the Malire Mechanized Regiment mutinied, and others followed suit. Then the crack Simba Battalion joined them. They actually mounted an attack on the presidential lodge in Kampala, but Amin escaped by helicopter.

Amin sent those troops that were still loyal to him after the mutineers. Many mutineers were killed; the survivors fled across the border into Tanzania, where Nyerere was still providing sanctuary for Obote and those 20,000 others.

Amin's subjects were getting restless as the decade drew to a close. It was okay to kill a few rivals, but Big Daddy (one *Monitor* reporter's nickname for him) had carried things too far. At the rate he was going, pretty soon he'd be the only Ugandan left alive. They also weren't thrilled with the fact that it now took twenty million Ugandan shillings to purchase what you could buy with fifteen shillings before Amin took over. Streets, buildings, everything was in disrepair, though Amin lived in obscene luxury.

It has become traditional that no African leader criticizes another. It makes sense: most of them are corrupt dictators who attained their offices through murder, revolution, or rigged elections, and if Dictator A criticizes Dictator B, why, he leaves himself open to similar criticism, and honest criticism is not what any African dictator wants.

There were only two leaders in all of Africa who constantly spoke out against Amin, and not surprisingly, they were the two who weren't dictators. One was Sir Seretse Khama of Botswana, who was secure in his British knighthood and the fact that he was almost two thousand miles from Uganda. The other was Nyerere, known to his people as Mwalimu, "the teacher," and he was Amin's next-door neighbor.

So when Amin concluded that the Simba Battalion and the others might start giving his troops and his citizenry too many bothersome ideas about freedom, or at least about replacing him with another dictator, he decided to divert attention by following the few escapees of the rebellion into Tanzania.

That began one of the most futile wars ever waged on the African continent.

Now, on Amin's behalf, there were extenuating circumstances: he was barely literate, and had apprenticed as a boxer, a cannibal, and a genocidal maniac. Along the way, he had totally overlooked his education as a field general.

The first thing he did was annex seven hundred square miles of an area known as the Kagera Salient. The second thing he did was blow up the only bridge across the Kagera River, which certainly slowed any advance Nyerere's army might make, but didn't do a lot for any Ugandan troops who were forced to retreat.

And forced to retreat they were. Nyerere was able to put together a 40,000-man army on the spot: soldiers, policemen, national service, whatever. Within a month the non-dictator had rallied enough of his countrymen to expand the army to 100,000.

Amin took one look at what was facing him across the border, realized his army had never been tested in combat—killing children, old women, and unarmed men didn't really count—and decided he needed some help. So he contacted fellow dictator Muammar Qaddafi of Libya, who sent a couple of thousand well-trained heavily armed troops.

Should have made a difference, right?

Well, the Libyan troops get on the front lines, ready to duke it out with the Tanzanians, and what does Amin's army do?

As the Libyans move south to face Nyerere's soldiers, Amin's army starts looting and raping its way north, spreading HIV, and stealing the Libyans' trucks to hold all their plunder.

Nyerere's army was supported by 20,000 Ugandan exiles, and picked up more every day as they defeated the 2,000 Libyans and marched toward Kampala. Suddenly there were other armies as well. There was one commanded by General Tito Okello, who would follow Amin and the restored Obote as Uganda's third consecutive incompetent dictator. And there was Yoweri Museveni, Uganda's president for the past couple of decades, who eventually threw Okello out of office by leading what was literally a children's army, the adults all having been slaughtered during the previous three administrations.

But that was in the future. Amin took a look at the situation, and saw the handwriting on the wall: his own retreating army was doing more damage to Uganda than the conquering army would do, Qaddafi had been burned once and wasn't about to send any more troops, and no other dictator would come to his aid. What was he to do? How was he to save his ass?

He came up with a solution that could have occurred to no one else.

He called a press conference. You probably wouldn't believe it if I didn't give you an exact quote:

"I am keeping fit so that I can challenge President Nyerere in the boxing ring and fight it out there, rather than having the soldiers lose their lives on the field of battle." He suggested that Mohammed Ali would be the perfect referee, and since he, Amin, was a former boxing champ and outweighed the 57-year-old Nyerere by at least one hundred pounds, he would fight with one arm tied behind his back and his legs shackled with weights.

(I feel compelled to emphasize that I am not making this up.)

The press loved it. No one took it seriously, least of all Nyerere. After all, he *was* a small, thin man with no athletic experience—and, it wasn't *his* soldiers who were dying.

His men marched on Kampala in April of 1979 and Idi Amin, His Excellency President for Life, Field Marshal Al Hadji Doctor Idi Amin, VC, DSO, MC, Lord of All the Beasts of the Earth and Fishes of the Sea, and Conqueror of the British Empire in Africa in General and Uganda in Particular, fled to Libya. Ever the opportunist, he began plotting to overthrow Qaddafi, who gently urged him to find another sanctuary or die, and he wound up his life in exile at a luxurious estate in Jeddah, Saudi Arabia.

He took one brief vacation from Arabia during his later years. Convinced that his people would welcome him back after the inept reigns of Obote and Okello, he got as far as the Ugandan border, dead certain that he would be made president again by acclamation. President Museveni refused to allow him to cross the border, no one came to his defense, and, totally disillusioned, he went back to live out his life in Arabia.

What can an historian learn about the Uganda-Tanzania War?

1. After invading your enemy over a river, don't burn your bridges behind you (to coin a phrase).
2. Don't pay your soldiers with worthless money.
3. Never give poorly trained and untested troops access to vehicles they can retreat in while a battle is going on.
4. Sometimes converting to a new religion isn't enough.
5. Don't challenge skinny little intellectual wimps to boxing matches—or if you do, make sure that the outcome of the war doesn't depend on their being dumb enough to agree.

Uganda is a wonderful, beautiful country. It still suffers greatly from poverty, corruption, and tribal competition, but has great natural wealth. It's said that if you spit a peach pit out of the window of your car and come back a month later, there will be a peach tree growing there. Most of the wildlife came back from the army's butchery when they used hippos, elephants, and gazelles for food, and so, finally, have the people—no thanks to Big Daddy. He may have been the worst general in African history. It hasn't yet been decided if he was Africa's bloodiest madman or the continent's most idiotic clown.

Me, I vote for both.

NAPOLEONE BUONAPARTE

Or "Napoleon Bonaparte," if you prefer the spelling he changed to in order to have his name look less Corsican and more French.

There is a strange irony in this section. Napoleon was unquestionably a world class military genius. Many of his tactics and strategies from the battles and wars he fought are still used to train modern officers. Modern warfare as we know it, including citizen armies, began in his era. Bonaparte's reign perfected the Corp structure, massed artillery, skirmishers, and a dozen other innovations. Canning foods was invented for the French emperor to assist in feeding his troops during the invasion of Russia. Thousands of books have been written in praise of Napoleon's generalship and leadership skills, but what follows are several articles describing his failures and eventual downfall. Perhaps this is because General and then Emperor Napoleon was so good a commander and strategist that we are still trying to understand how he ended his life as a British prisoner on a small, rainy island in the South Atlantic.

*For over two generations, the model for the perfect
military had been Prussia. In uniform and drill, the other
nations of Europe had mimicked the Prussians since
Frederick the Great's (1712–1786) victories. When the
French and Prussian armies met in battle, all Europe,
including Germany, expected that the renowned Prussian
army would put the new French emperor in his place.*

TO LOSE A WAR, FIGHT THE LAST ONE

Germany, 1806

WILLIAM TERDOSLAVICH

If an army won its last war, it will fight the next war the same way. That is because armies learn little from winning.

Prussia's army proved the rule in 1806, when it had to defend the nation against a French invasion. If Frederick the Great had still been alive, he might have given Napoleon a run for his money. Sadly, Frederick's ghost was no match for the French emperor.

At first, the war was no contest. Napoleon unleashed a modern army of its day against a Prussian military still practicing war the way Frederick fought it, minus his genius. Thoroughly outclassed and beaten at the double battle of Jena-Auerstadt, most of the Prussian army eventually surrendered, though the Prussian king relied on Russian intervention to carry on the struggle for another year. The Russians fought no better than the Prussians, checked Napo-

leon at Eylau, yet lost decisively at Friedland. That left Napoleon to
re-order Europe as he saw fit.

War is a stern teacher. Prussia learned its lessons the hard way,
by losing the fight to France and accepting a humiliating peace.
In the next war, the Prussian army would fight not as well as the
French army, but well enough.

Napoleon vs. Frederick the Not-So-Great

After Napoleon's masterpiece victory at Austerlitz in late 1805,
Austria was knocked out of the war. Russia was still in, but not active. Prussia was neutral.

In typical heavy-handed fashion, Napoleon was redrawing the
map of Europe. One scheme called for amalgamating many of the
small west German states into a "Confederation of the Rhine" that
would serve French interests. Prussia preferred to form a "North
German League," under its control. Saxony, a rich German state to
the south of Prussia, was wooed to join the Confederation of the
Rhine with the offer of Hanover, a British possession at this time.
Of course, this did not go down well with the "war party" in the
Prussian government, which revolved around Queen Louise, not
King Frederick William III, the "not so great." In 1806 Napoleon,
who had ceded Hanover to Prussia just to tick off England, changed
his mind and offered Hanover back to England as a possible entice-
ment toward a peace treaty.

England didn't care for the offer.

Frederick William III, unfortunately, took offense, now that he
was under the growing influence of the war party at court.

In August, Prussia went to war with France. An alliance was secured with Russia, which could not help Russia right away, as it
still needed to muster an army and march it westward. Prussia then
played a traditional opening move, invading Saxony and incorpo-
rating the unenthusiastic Saxon army into its own.

Taking stock, it would seem that Prussia had the advantage over
France. It had a 245,000-man army, outnumbering Napoleon's
160,000-man Grande Armée, which was deployed throughout

southern Germany between the Rhine, the Main, and the Danube rivers. Look more closely and the odds become more even. Prussia detached many units to garrison its network of fortresses. That left 171,000 men to be divided into several armies that were expected to maneuver between these strong points, drawing on their pre-positioned supplies.

The Prussian Army's outdated generals would be commanding the army, using its outdated doctrines. The army's main field commander, the Duke of Brunswick, was 71. Prince Hohenlohe clocked in at 60. Even the aggressive maniac Blücher was 64, and he would soldier on to victory at Waterloo in 1815! Many division and brigade leaders were ripe for retirement. Napoleon was only 37 years old when he led his army to conquer Prussia. Many of his corps commanders were roughly the same age. They could put in long hours in the saddle, commanding their forces with energy and purpose.

Technology had not changed much in the time between Frederick the Great and Napoleon. Both armies equipped their soldiers with flintlock muskets. Horses still pulled the wagons and cannons. They still fielded cavalry to screen, probe, and charge.

If both armies were the same, what was different?

Brunswick was in charge of the Prussian Army, but the real commander was the ghost of Frederick the Great. At a glance, Frederick could size up a battle and concentrate his entire tiny army against a portion of the enemy line, defeat it, and force back the enemy in ignominious retreat. It didn't matter how badly the Prussians were outnumbered, Frederick always attacked with this goal in mind. Prussia fought the Seven Years' War (1756–63) surrounded by France, Austria, and Russia. Frederick turned that drawback into an advantage, being able to march his army to any point on Prussia's periphery to defeat the enemy du jour before all could combine against him.

It was like juggling to survive.

Frederick codified his fighting methods in a top-secret book that his generals were required to read. Alas, Frederick's genius did not rub off on the generals, but they were still confident. The Prussians beat the French at Rossbach in 1757, so they should win again, right?

Napoleon had no secret weapon that guaranteed victory. He just used the existing tools of war in a different way, beyond the boundaries of his enemy's expectations. Napoleon inherited a reformed army that he refined further through his use of corps, all operationally tied together by a good staff at HQ. Each corps, commanded by a general or marshal, was a "mini-army" of about 20,000 to 25,000 men, formed up as three infantry divisions, a cavalry division, and one or two brigades of artillery. Several corps would operate within supporting distance of each other, their movements guided by a larger plan that was executed by Napoleon's staff. When competently handled, a corps should be able to hold off an enemy army of any size for twenty-four hours, thus buying enough time for several nearby corps to "march to the sound of the guns" as reinforcements.

Napoleon would maneuver seven corps in this campaign's opening moves, commanded by Lannes (V Corps), Augereau (VII Corps), Bernadotte (I Corps), Davout (III Corps), Soult (IV Corps), and Ney (VI Corps), plus the cavalry corps under Murat. He just had to pick an invasion route, knowing that Russia was marching to Prussia's aid.

The easiest, most direct invasion route was to march across the North German plain to Berlin. Time would be lost moving the French army from southern Germany to the jump-off position in the Netherlands. The direct route crossed two major rivers—the Weser and the Elbe. The Prussians could easily retreat toward the advancing Russians and the Grande Armée would be too far away from recently defeated Austria to keep it from jumping back into the war. Napoleon skipped this option, but did form a smaller secondary army in the Netherlands, under the command of his brother Louis, just to make the Prussians worry that it might invade along the easy route.

Of course, Napoleon could try the second route, invading from Frankfurt through the Fulda Gap into Saxony. Once past the gap, rough terrain would favor the Prussian defense. Plus, the Prussians could retreat toward the Russians and join armies, so forget about this option.

The third way, while least direct, offered the most promise. From existing bases in southern Germany, Napoleon could march the Grande Armée north through the Thuringerwald (Thuringian forest). The army would be close enough to the Austrian border to act as a threat, lest the defeated emperor there got any stupid ideas.

But the plan's risk was also clear. The various French corps would have to march separately on the three roads that cut through the normally impassable Thuringerwald, a string of wooded hills that formed a natural barrier between Saxony and Franconia. These roads were not linked by a lateral road, so if any corps got into trouble, neighboring corps would not be able to march to its aid. Worse, if the enemy got wind of the Grande Armée's march, it could concentrate on the other side of the Thuringerwald and defeat Napoleon's corps one by one as they emerged from their narrow passages, just as Frederick had massed his army against the French vanguard at Rossbach in 1757.

It was Napoleon's intent to get his army between the Prussians and Berlin to force battle and destroy the Prussian force before the Russians arrived. Brunswick, unable to read Napoleon's mind, never saw this coming until it was too late. He obliged the Emperor by orienting Prussia's three armies westward toward the Rhine, hoping to defeat the French Army in detail as its corps concentrated on the frontier, preparing for invasion.

In early October, Napoleon set his plan in motion.

He expected victory.

So did Brunswick.

October Surprise

The Grande Armée marched as a block measuring thirty miles by thirty miles. On the left, Lanne's V Corps, followed by Augereau's VII Corps, crossed the Thuringerwald on its westernmost road. On the center road, Bernadotte pushed forward with I Corps, followed by Davout's III Corps. The easternmost road saw Soult's IV Corps march up, trailed by Ney's VI Corps. Murat dispersed his cavalry corps to screen all three lines of march, as well as to probe forward, looking to make contact with the enemy.

Where were the Prussians?

It took two days to get the Grande Armée to the other side of the Thuringerwald. Murat's cavalry, lead elements of Bernadotte's Corps, then Lannes' Corps, all brushed against Tauenzein's division, batting it to the northwest toward Jena. Tauenzein's division was the southernmost of Hohenlohe's scattered army of 42,000.

Where were the French?

Tauenzein's division was never intended to act as the tripwire, but it gave Hohenlohe enough notice to prompt him into ordering all his units to march on Jena. Brunswick's Army of 70,000 was at Erfurt, about 30 miles to the west of Jena. Rüchel's smaller army of 19,000 was at Eisenach, roughly 30 miles to the west of Brunswick's force. They both marched east toward Jena.

Just as the Prussians began to concentrate, Napoleon decided to throw a right hook. With Lannes' Corps in contact with Hohenlohe's force at Jena, Napoleon ordered his center column—Davout's III Corps and Bernadotte's I Corps—to march past Jena and go north about 20 miles to Naumburg. Napoleon would rely on his easternmost column, consisting of Soult and Ney's corps, to reinforce his contact at Jena, as well as calling up Augereau's corps to the south to reinforce Lannes. Davout and Bernadotte would cross the Ilm River around Naumburg, march another eight miles or so to Auerstadt, then make a left turn and march south for about another eight miles toward Apolda. From this position, the two corps could outflank the Prussian main body concentrating just west of Jena. Such an attack would destroy the enemy, busy defending itself from Napoleon's main attack.

That was the plan.

Couriers with orders making it so were sent out after midnight. Various corps HQs would be getting their orders in the dead of night and readying their divisions to march at dawn. Napoleon thought he would be pinning the main body of the Prussian Army, judging from the numerous campfires seen in the distance during the night of October 13.

Battle would come with the sunrise.

Instead, Napoleon faced the fog of war.

A thick mist covered the terrain to the west of the Landgrafenberg, a commanding height from which Napoleon staged his attack with Lannes' Corps.

It was 6:30 a.m.

Screw the fog.

If the French did not attack first, the Prussians would.

Lannes' Corps stepped off its line of departure, marching through the fog across the open ground. He was supposed to attack the town of Closwitz on the right and its adjoining wood. Not quite able to see the way, Lannes' force drifted left toward the village of Lutzeroda, bashing into Tauenzein's hapless division one more time.

On Lannes' left, Augereau tried to march his corps through a ravine, had a hard time pushing it through the bottleneck, but found open ground around 9:30. He formed his corps up on Lannes' left and began attacking.

A half hour after that, Soult began deploying the lead division of his corps on Lannes' right. The division marched through Closwitz and on toward the village of Rodigen. Soult's lead division then collided with the Prussian division commanded by Holtzendorf. Soult was on the scene, directing the division to outflank Holtzendorf's left and push on.

It was now 11.

Napoleon now had two corps and a part of a third in line attacking the Prussians. The sun climbed toward noon, burning off the morning mist. The French were taking ground readily.

Davout and Bernadotte had better hurry.

Napoleon was expecting their outflanking attack by mid-afternoon.

Where were they now?

In deep trouble.

Davout got his corps on the march from Naumburg promptly at

6:30, just as Lannes was attacking into a morning fog. He crossed his corps over the Ilm at the village of Kosen, ascending the heights on the other side of the river, then down toward a pass between two hills.

The same morning fog that vexed the French at Jena also shrouded an advance guard of Prussians marching up the road toward the village of Hassenhausen on the valley floor, about four miles east of Auerstadt. They ran into a squadron of French cavalry from Davout's corps.

Davout wasted no time taking the village and pushing the Prussians back. Two Prussian divisions now marched on Hassenhausen as Davout deployed two divisions of his corps, anchoring both flanks on the high ground to either side of the valley. The Prussians had no space to turn a flank. They would have to attack straight ahead.

The units belonged to Brunswick's main force, on the march toward Leipzig, desperately trying to take a position between Berlin and Napoleon's army. The old general had figured out Napoleon's plan. But would he be too late to stop it? His force outnumbered Davout's corps by about three to one. He should win this battle.

By 9, Brunswick had finally lined up two divisions and led the attack. It fizzled quickly when Brunswick took a bullet to the head, followed by the death of one of his two division commanders. Still, the attack caused the French line to waver, giving up Hassenhausen. The timely arrival of Morand's division of III Corps bolstered Davout's thin blue line. The French attacked and retook the village.

Brunswick never set down on paper who would take command of his army in the event he was killed. The lacuna was not unusual for the time, but had a devastating effect. Command devolved upon King Frederick William III, the not-so-great. He threw everything he had against Davout's line—the Prussian Guard, Blücher's infantry, even part of Kuhnheim's division. Brave as he was, Frederick William had no idea what he was doing. Brunswick never briefed his king on "the plan." Brunswick's chief of staff, Scharnhorst, was busy commanding the left flank of the army, not knowing his commander was dead and that the king was in charge.

With Hassenhausen secure in French hands, Morand wheeled

his division and took the Prussians in the right flank. Wasting no time, Davout ordered his entire corps forward. The Prussians, hammered from two sides, broke and retreated.

It was 1 p.m.

Where was Bernadotte?

He was supposed to reinforce Davout's Corps.

Back at Jena, the French faced a Prussian counterattack, held, then resumed their advance. After getting pushed back four miles to Vierzehnheiligen, Hohenlohe fought back, hoping for Rüchel's small army to arrive from Weimar. Napoleon had three corps formed up and a fourth soon to arrive. He called for a general attack. For an hour, the Prussians maintained their line, but lost ground. By 2:30, the Prussian line broke. Hohenlohe's army was retreating.

Where was Davout?

Where was Bernadotte?

Where was the flanking attack from Apolda?

Napoleon saw his army winning, but nothing was going according to plan.

Rüchel's army now arrived, going over to the attack just as if Frederick the Great was ordering it. Only Rüchel did not concentrate against a portion of Napoleon's line. He was attacking all three corps. Within thirty minutes, skirmishers from two French corps had riddled the Prussian line with shot. Rüchel's small army was repulsed. The surviving Prussian soldiers broke ranks and ran for it.

Where was Davout?

Where was Bernadotte?

Napoleon's army pursued the battered Prussians until 6 p.m. By this time, he began to figure out that he had not engaged the main Prussian Army, but had brought overwhelming force against the smaller portion of it, smashing it to bits. General reports came to him that Davout and Bernadotte were engaged in battle.

Well, that was half true. Davout was engaged in battle earlier that day. Bernadotte did not "march to the sound of the guns" near Auerstadt, but had reversed course, marching south to Dornburg, crossing his corps over the Ilm, and reaching Apolda, where he brushed away a few stray units of Prussians. There was no Prussian flank to attack. Bernadotte had misread his orders. Then he had the gall to suggest his march had saved Davout's skin.

Yeah, right.

Frenchmen Gone Wild

What was left of the Prussian Army now retreated northward in broken pieces. Hohenlohe gathered and rallied the remnants, concentrating on the fortress of Magdeburg. This town was more important than Berlin, sitting astride a strategic road-and-river junction. The fortress controlled Prussia's richest and most fertile districts. The Prussian treasury lay behind its walls. The Queen's court was based there. The nearby Elbe River was the highway that allowed plentiful supplies to be shipped to the fortress.

Magdeburg had been everything to Frederick the Great, worth defending at all costs.

To Napoleon, Magdeburg was nothing.

The Grande Armée's corps bypassed it, chasing the remnants of Hohenlohe's force and other units to the four corners of the realm. Some were crushed. Others were forced to surrender. Destroying the Prussian Army made the fortresses moot. Napoleon was not going to waste his time with sieges if he could take the country. His army lived off the land. It had no need for magazines and supply depots.

Frederick William III could have pulled together another army of about 60,000 if he had been willing to strip his fortresses of their garrisons and unite them with the unengaged portions and shattered remnants of his army. Prussia lacked that kind of "management expertise," so the brief opportunity was never exploited. The Prussian king retired toward Küstrin on the Oder River, east of Berlin. From there he hoped to move eastward to meet the Russian army, now on the march. Prussia then owned a good deal of Poland. It linked Prussia with East Prussia. Königsberg was that province's capital, the last major city in Prussia still unconquered and not far from the Russian border, the place where Frederick William was going. Nearby was Lestocq's corps-sized unit, the last major intact remnant of the Prussian army.

By early November, Berlin was in Napoleon's hands. His Grande Armée crossed the Oder. Napoleon then took the Polish capital of Warsaw—and his new mistress, Countess Maria Walewska—with ease. Out there somewhere to the north and east of Warsaw was a Russian army, commanded by Bennigsen and tasked with staying between Napoleon's army and Königsberg.

Throughout January, 1807, Napoleon and Bennigsen marched their armies around Poland and East Prussia, trying to bring on a battle—or avoid one. The deadly game of blind man's bluff ended on February 8, 1807, when the two armies made contact.

Awful Eylau

The land around Eylau is one of rolling hills studded with many ponds, streams, and marshes. On the day of battle, all of it lay frozen under one to three feet of snow. Bennigsen took advantage of the chain of hills running northwest to southeast to deploy his army of 60,000 on higher ground. His was an army of divisions, with insufficient staff at HQ to direct those units as part of a larger plan, if he had one. Bennigsen commanded, but had to tell each unit what to do.

Napoleon only had two corps on hand, those of Soult and Augereau. His line was, also posted on a chain of hills, centered on the town of Preussich-Eylau. It paralleled the Russian deployment, separated by roughly one thousand yards of open ground. Napoleon already issued orders to Ney, to the southwest, and Davout, off in the southeast, to hustle their corps to Eylau.

If Bennigsen had a plan, he did not write it down. His right flank was screened by frozen marshes and rested on no clearly defensible terrain. His left flank rested on the hilltop village of Serpallen. In the line's center, Bennigsen kept a reserve of two divisions, with a third off to the left-center behind the main line of three infantry divisions.

Napoleon deployed Soult's IV Corps to the left of Eylau, resting his left flank on a hill, with a screen of cavalry deployed farther to the left. With Soult acting as the pinning force, Napoleon hoped to maneuver Augereau's VII Corps past Soult's line to attack Bennigsen's left. Upon timely arrival, Davout would add to Augereau's attack, outflank Bennigsen's left, and roll up the Russian line.

The morning dawned late and gray. At 8 a.m., Russian cavalry attacked Soult's left, trying to pick off the hill that anchored his position. Soult held firm. The Russian attack failed.

It was now 10 a.m.

Russian artillery was pounding Soult's line. Losses were mounting.

Napoleon sized up the battle. He could wait for the right moment to launch the perfect converging attack, with Augereau and Davout's corps hitting Bennigsen's left from different angles. But Davout's corps was slow in coming on, meeting heavy resistance, barely pushing the Russians out of Serpallen. One French division from Soult's corps on Davout's left had already been repulsed supporting III Corps' attack. The Russians were fighting and dying hard. Could Napoleon relieve the pressure on Soult's line by ordering Auguereau's corps to attack right now? Would the early, imperfect attack help speed Davout's slow advance?

Napoleon took the chance.

VII Corps was ordered forward.

Augereau could barely mount his horse, so sick was he that day. He lined up two divisions and advanced across the open ground toward the Russian line. While Augereau commanded his corps, he could not command the weather.

A freak blizzard blew up from the east, smothering the battlefield with blinding, wind-driven snow. Augereau and his officers lost sight of their objective. The corps veered to the left, unknowingly presenting its flank to a battery of seventy-two Russian cannons. The Russians had the wind to their backs, barely making out a mass of Frenchmen to their front.

The target looked easy.

The Russian guns opened fire.

Augereau never saw it coming.

Russian cannonballs knocked over the French infantry like bloody bowling pins. Ordered ranks turned into disordered mobs. VII Corps was quickly ripped to bloody shreds, losing half of its men in just thirty minutes. Quickly, Bennigsen committed his cavalry reserve and an infantry division to make a follow-up attack.

When the blizzard let up, Napoleon saw what had happened to VII Corps. The troops were falling back in great disorder, the Russians in hot pursuit. Davout's corps was not yet fully deployed to fill the gap. Napoleon quickly sent Murat's cavalry corps to attack the Russians and cover VII Corp's retreat, now leaderless, as Augereau and both divisional commanders had been wounded.

Murat's horsemen suffered heavy losses, but pushed the Russians back, saved what was left of VII Corps and rattled Bennigsen's composure. Had Napoleon an extra corps ready then and there, he could have supported Murat's charge and won the battle. But he had to settle for watching Bennigsen pull back his left, refusing the flank. Davout built up a deliberate attack that slowly gathered momentum, pushing the Russians farther back. By 4 p.m., the Russian left flank was about to collapse. Bennigsen had no reserves left to bolster it, but help arrived in the proverbial nick of time.

Lestocq's corps of Prussians had been posted west of Bennigsen's position to screen Ney's VI Corps. It had spent the day fighting a desperate series of skirmishes and small battles, sometimes sacrificing rear guards, always escaping destruction by a hair's breadth, but delaying Ney's arrival. Lestocq showed up with only 7,600 men and 30 cannon. He dropped off a battalion to act as a rearguard at Althof, roughly one mile west of Bennigsen's line. The depleted Prussian corps marched about one-and-a-half miles across Bennigsen's rear to take up position on his threatened left flank. They enveloped the extreme right end of Davout's line. Bennigsen advanced the units on his left, pushing Davout's corps out of the hilltop village of Kuttschitten, forcing it back to an east-west line resting on hills and woods one mile north of Serpallen, where Bennigsen's left flank rested at the start of battle.

It was already night when Ney finally forced his way past Lestocq's rearguard at Althof, marching one mile to take the village of Schlottiden at 8 p.m. Ney had no idea that he had just trapped the Russian army. The village was located smack on the main road back to Königsberg. Bennigsen was cut off. He now refused his right flank, scrounged up five battalions of infantry, and attacked Ney's position at 10 p.m. Ney commanded his meager line to hold fire until the Russians got really close, at which time they shredded the attackers with repeated musket volleys. Ney had not yet brought up his whole corps, and did not know what he was facing. He dashed off a message to Napoleon's HQ, promising to hold Schlottiden until 2 a.m., but would give it up if attacks persisted. With no reply from Napoleon, Ney ordered his units to fall back to Althof, unknowingly opening the back door that allowed Bennigsen to escape.

When the battle ended, Napoleon had possession of the field. Technically, that made him the winner. But of what? He lost 20,000 to 25,000 men—roughly half the force he had deployed. Bennigsen suffered 11,000 dead and another 2,500 captured, and he still had his army to fight another day.

Both sides claimed victory.

Napoleon pulled the Grande Armée south and dispersed it to winter quarters.

He'd deal with Bennigsen—after he reorganized and refitted the Grande Armée.

Fearsome Friedland

Serious campaigning resumed in June, as Bennigsen struck southwest across the Passarge River against the dispersed French corps, posted along the river line in the role of a long, broad tripwire. He had divided his Russian army into several columns, hoping to work them between the corps of Soult and Davout, then cut off Ney's corps from reinforcement and defeat it. These detachments lost a series of small battles as they tried to implement Bennigsen's plan, leaving Ney's corps unharmed. But these clashes did alert Napoleon to the threat, and he concentrated his army, while ordering Soult, Ney, and Davout to hold their line on the Passarge.

By June 7, Napoleon planned his advance on Königsberg, following the line of the Alle River due north from his position on the Passarge. The goal was to get his army between Königsberg and Bennigsen's force, which was falling back toward the city. For the next three days, Napoleon marched his corps forward, looking to hook one around Bennigsen's line of retreat, but to no avail. But Bennigsen could not retreat forever. He was running out of Prussian territory to defend.

Lannes, now in command of the Reserve Corps, was closing in on Friedland as the sun set on June 13. Bennigsen, trying to keep his options open while covering Königsberg, heard of the move and rushed his cavalry to take the town and secure a river crossing there. Perhaps this would be an opportunity for the Russian army to destroy Napoleon's force by crushing it one detachment at a time. By midnight, the Russians had built three pontoon bridges across the Alle into Friedland proper and began moving across to concentrate west of the town.

Bennigsen had picked a lousy place to fight a battle, but that wasn't clear until sunrise on June 14. By 8 a.m., Bennigsen had his army deployed in a north-south line paralleling the Alle, about 1 to 2 miles to the east, behind his forces. A small river called the Muhlen ran east-west, bisecting his battle line. Friedland lay on its south bank. To the north of the river, Gortschakoff arrayed three infantry divisions and two cavalry units along a chain of hills. To the south of the Muhlen, Bagration held another series of hilltops with two divisions, his cavalry posted to his left along the edge of the Sortlack woods. Bennigsen held the Guard back as a reserve north of the Muhlen, with another infantry division and a cavalry unit on the east bank of the Alle. Four light bridges were built across the Muhlen to allow Bennigsen to shift units to either side of his line as needed.

Bennigsen rushed 45,000 men across the Alle to destroy what he thought was an isolated French division stalking Friedland.

What he was facing instead was the Grande Armée's Reserve Corps.

Lannes arrayed the Reserve Corps' three divisions on a series of hilltops running in an arc from the village of Henrichsdorf to his north, centering his line on the village of Posthenen, then down to the forest of Sortlack to the south, paralleling Bennigsen's line.

Fighting began at 6 a.m.

Bennigsen was hoping to pin Lannes' corps while delivering an attack with his right across open ground. But Lannes shifted units up and down his line, holding any position that got pressed, feeding arriving units from Mortier's VIII Corps into the line to hold the trouble spots. Lannes kept this up for nine hours, his 26,000-man corps holding at bay Bennigsen's total strength of 60,000. This bought time for Napoleon to send corps marching to the sound of Lannes' guns.

Napoleon arrived at Posthenen at 1 p.m. and began sizing up the situation. He decided to concentrate his attack against Bagration's wing to the south of the Muhlen. He wanted to pin the Russians against the Alle. The Sortlack Forest masked Ney's VI Corps as it concentrated for the assault. To keep Bennigsen from shifting units south to help Bagration, Napoleon would order a pinning attack by Mortier's VIII Corps to fix Gortscahkoff's wing. Victor's I Corps and the Imperial Guard would be kept in reserve, to be used if a good opportunity appeared.

Ney's corps attacked at 5 p.m., rolling Bagration's flank guard out of Sortlack village into the Alle, then wheeling north to continue the assault. Bagration fell back towards Friedland, holding a thin line between the Muhlen and a bend in the Alle. Ney's attack began to stall as both of his divisions suffered flanking fire and/or cavalry attacks. To Ney's left was some empty space where more force could be brought to bear. This was the opportunity that Napoleon seized, sending Victor's I Corps to march through the gap to support Ney. Victor's corps toted thirty guns, setting them up in two batteries to either side of the advance column, opening fire on Bagration's line at three hundred yards. Instead of cannonballs, case shot was used, turning each cannon into a giant shotgun. Four thousand Russians were mowed down in twenty-five bloody minutes.

Ney renewed his attack, Russian gunfire be damned. Bennigsen then committed his Guard infantry and cavalry units to hit the French columns in the flank by crossing the Muhlen. The French infantry simply stopped, faced left and opened fire, stopping the attack cold. Once the Russians were routed, some French units crossed the footbridges across the Muhlen to press the attack eastward toward the Alle. The Russian retreat was cut off when the three pontoon bridges crossing the Alle from Friedland caught fire, either from French cannons or panicking Russians.

On the French left, the corps of Mortier and Lannes, plus the cavalry corps under Grouchy, spent the day in outnumbered defense against Gortschakoff's wing, which failed to outflank or break through the French line.

By 7 p.m., Friedland was cleared of Russians. Napoleon ordered his left wing to attack, shattering Gortschakoff's forces, triggering a rout smack into the river. Some units found their way across the Alle by a local ford, but crossed in great disorder. Many fleeing soldiers drowned.

By 10:30 p.m., there was no more battle to fight.

The French lost 1,300 killed, another 9,000 wounded. The Russians left 11,000 dead on the battlefield. Poor record keeping cannot provide the total count of all losses.

No organized Russian army existed anymore to keep the French away from Königsberg, thirty miles to the north.

Frederick William III had finally lost his war after fighting to the last Prussian, then to the last Russian.

Surrender, Negotiation, Revenge

While battle raged at Friedland, the corps of Davout and Soult, along with Murat's cavalry, converged on Königsberg, pushing Lestocq's remaining Prussians into the fortress. Davout and Murat's forces were then called off to Friedland as reinforcements. Soult's corps was not big enough to surround the city. Once Lestocq received word of Bennigsen's defeat, he pulled out his troops and marched toward the Russian border. Like Bennigsen, he was making for Tilsit on the Neman River. Napoleon's pursuit columns skirmished with the enemy rearguards, but failed to overtake either Lestocq's or Bennigsen's retreating columns. They evacuated Tilsit and crossed into Russia. When Napoleon's army reached the Neman, they encountered Russian plenipotentiaries ready to negotiate an armistice, rather than a last-ditch defense.

Over the next month, Napoleon, Czar Alexander, and their retinues negotiated a peace treaty. Russia had to join Napoleon's Continental System, which would close its ports to English trade alongside those of Prussia, Austria, and France. Russia also got Bialystok, and a free hand to make war against Sweden and Ottoman Turkey.

While Russia suffered a slap on the wrist, Prussia got hosed.

All of Prussia west of the Elbe was taken from Frederick William III and joined to the new Kingdom of Westphalia under Napoleon's brother, Jerome. Saxony joined the Confederation of the Rhine. Prussia's Polish provinces became the Duchy of Warsaw. In effect, Prussia got rolled back to its 1772 borders and its army was limited to just 42,000 men—roughly one sixth of its former size.

Frederick William III had to eat these humiliating peace terms.

But he did not get mad. He got even.

The ghost of Frederick the Great was banished from command. Prussia could not summon forth this Great Captain's genius from his old writings. But Prussia could institutionalize competence. Frederick William appointed a commission of reformers, led by Scharnhorst, to rebuild the army. Prussia would fire up the national fervor of its people against the French. Serfdom was abolished. The diminished army trained and discharged troops at a ferocious rate, building a deep pool of trained manpower that could become an instant army when the time came to strike back. Hidebound officers were discharged and smarter ones were advanced by merit. Excellence was cultivated through training and study.

Napoleon would create Prussia's opportunity for revenge by invading Russia in 1812—and losing big.

Come 1813, Prussia would break free from France's grip and play a key role in driving Napoleon from Prussia, from Germany, then from France itself.

All this came about because Frederick William III, the Not-So-Great, knew how to lose a war.

Then he became smart enough to let others win the next war for him.

It is hard for those living today to remember that the English navy did not always rule the seas. The real dominance of the royal navy did not come until after a string of one-sided victories against Napoleon. But this was hardly a given in 1793. The French navy was well-trained, had good morale, and better designed ships than the British. Without them to stand and defeat the British at Yorktown in 1781, there would have been no American victory and a different end to the Revolution. But a decade later something changed. . . .

NAPOLEON'S SEAPOWER LOST AT SEA

The High Seas, 1793–1814

ROLAND J. GREEN

The naval campaigns of the Napoleonic Wars (1793–1814) were the high point of naval warfare under sail. They also have an abiding fascination to this day, as the multitudinous readers of C. S. Forester, Dudley Pope, and Patrick O'Brien bear witness.

They also mark the end of two centuries of British struggle for supremacy at sea, with a decisive victory that set the stage for the *Pax Britannica* of the next century. What happened to Britain's rivals, particularly the French? In the War of the American Revolution, only a generation before, the French had come closer to beating the British at sea than anybody since the Dutch in the mid-seventeenth century. (Americans should be glad of that, too. If the French navy had not been able to blockade Cornwallis at Yorktown, the final decisive victory of the Revolution might have "gone a-glimmering," as they said then.)

So what happened? A good part of it was the British navy's being more innovative in a number of areas.

In tactics, they began abandoning the traditional rigid adherence to the formal line of battle, which tended to lead to indecisive cannonades. Instead, Rodney set the precedence for breaking through the enemy's line, delivering more raking fire and, with luck, cutting off a portion of the enemy's fleet and overwhelming it.

In gunnery, the British introduced the carronade or "smasher." This was a short-barreled, large-bore, short-range piece mounted on a slide. It was much lighter than a conventional gun mounted on wheeled trucks, but able to deliver an equally heavy shot. Carronades allowed the British to give small vessels heavy broadsides, and mount additional heavy guns on the top decks of larger ships.

They also introduced improved gun tackles—the ropes used to control the guns. They could now aim a gun forward or aft the beam, as well as straight out. This allowed guns to be aimed at targets not directly abeam, or bring concentrated fire on portions of a close-range target.

Both were more useful because of British gunnery tactics, which emphasized close-range, rapid fire into the opponent's hull, wrecking guns and killing the crew. The French preferred to aim at the rigging, to disable an opponent, who could then be evaded or polished off as appropriate. The Dutch followed British practice—which made fighting them a bloody business. The Spanish had no particular doctrine, as their gun crews were frequently artillerymen drafted to sea from the army.

Shipboard health was another British advantage. The Royal Navy was in the vanguard of overcoming scurvy with citrus juices and fresh vegetables, and other diseases by a higher standard of shipboard sanitation. The juice was normally lime juice which preserves well in casks, and yes that is where the term "Limey" comes from. Treatment of wounds was still gruesomely primitive (no antiseptics or anesthetics), but at least a British sailor had a better chance of surviving until the shooting started.

The area in which the British still lagged behind was in ship design. British ships of the line were said to be "built by the mile, and cut off as required" and they were generally smaller in proportion to the number of guns they carried. This meant that French and Spanish ships could carry their guns higher above the waterline and fire in worse weather than the British—if their gunners were up to it.

So the British navy arrived at the year 1793 with a number of advantages over its opponents, even the French. They did not know at first that they had acquired several more, which in the long run may have accounted for a good part of their success.

First, the French fleet had been allowed to run down during the last impecunious years of the French monarchy. Many ships badly needed refitting, and the dockyards were desperately short of naval stores (timber, masts, sailcloth, cordage, tar, paint, salt provisions, even simple items like navigating instruments and sailors' clothing). The Revolutionary Republic was practically bankrupt, and while they could confiscate freely at home, they could not buy abroad without ready cash and then had the problem of shipping their purchases home past the blockade the British were establishing.

Second, Revolutionary politics had deprived the French navy of many of its most experienced senior officers. These were usually noblemen and often devout Catholics, anathema to an egalitarian and anti-clerical regime. In large numbers, they went to the guillotine, fled abroad, or were forcibly retired. Some were later reinstated, and some of the commanders who had been lieutenants, sailing masters, or even in the merchant marine proved brave and capable. But the decapitation of the French navy's leadership cast a long shadow. And the revolutionaries considered the corps of *canoniers marins* (maritime gunners, specialists in scientific gunnery) a relic of privilege and abolished it—along with much of the French chance of matching British gunnery.

The war at sea began with skirmishing off the French coast through 1793, mostly single-ship duels, with the British usually getting the better of it. Meanwhile, French privateers were making their appearance wherever they could hope to get at British merchant shipping.

They did not make their disappearance until the war was over, and they were always a nuisance and sometimes a serious menace. In the Channel and the North Sea, they were usually small coastal sailing vessels, with large crews who relied on boarding their prizes. Elsewhere, the French (and their allies, in due course) were more ambitious, setting to sea in well-armed, fast vessels, sometimes carrying crews of 160 men and enough guns to fight a regular warship.

The privateers tied up dozens, even hundreds of Britain's frigates and smaller vessels, and produced any number of swashbuckling battles now lost in the pages of multi-volume histories. They never succeeded in setting up a counter-blockade, as the German U-boats so nearly did in 1917, with nearly disastrous results. British experience in previous wars against France and Spain earlier in the seventeenth and eighteenth centuries led to the institution of a convoy system for the high seas merchant shipping that carried so much of the essential trade. The French privateers nipped at the heels of the convoys (some numbering four hundred ships) but seldom really sank their teeth disastrously into British foreign trade.

On the other hand, the number of able commanders and prime seamen who served in the privateers may have amounted to a major drain on French maritime resources. Robert Surcouf, the most famous of the privateers, could just as well have commanded a frigate in the Atlantic as a privateer in the Indian Ocean. And even the Revolution could not make it possible for one sailor to be simultaneously boarding a British coaster off Dover and pointing a gun aboard a seventy-four beating out of Brest.

The naval war escalated in 1794. The British Channel Fleet established a blockade of Brest, the main French Channel base, and Toulon, the principal Mediterranean one. The blockade of Brest was a "distant" blockade, with the British fleet snug in Spithead (the anchorage of Portsmouth), reducing wear and tear on the ships and the captains' separation from their wives.

In spite of this limitation, the Channel Fleet had the honor of the first fleet action of the war. The Brest fleet sailed to cover the arrival of a large grain convoy from the United States, whose cargoes would have saved France from famine.

The two fleets met on June 1st, some four hundred miles offshore, in rough weather and poor visibility. Even the conservative and elderly Admiral Lord Howe was prepared to break the line, however, and did so successfully, taking six French ships of the line (battleships) and sinking one. On the other hand, the French admiral had drawn the British away from the convoy, and so saved both France from famine and himself from the guillotine.

The British christened the battle "The Glorious First of June," but neither side needed to be ashamed of the outcome.

The British also struck a blow at Toulon, which French Royalists actually seized and opened to the British fleet. The French promptly besieged Toulon, with a promising young officer named Napoleon Bonaparte commanding their siege artillery. Eventually they forced the British out, and while the British took some French ships with them and burned others, there were enough left to form a substantial French Mediterranean fleet.

That fleet skirmished with the British throughout 1795. An English captain who distinguished himself was Horatio Nelson. Meanwhile, farther north, the French had overrun the Netherlands and captured the efficient Dutch fleet almost intact.

The years 1796–97 were probably the most critical period of the war for the British. To start with, Spain joined France in an alliance against its traditional enemy. The Spanish fleet was the third largest in the world, with many fine ships and some able officers. But it was poorly maintained and supplied, as well as undermanned. The alliance still opened a great many more ports to the French, both in Europe and in the Americas, where the British were already having trouble fighting French privateers and yellow fever.

In 1796, the French launched what might have been a deadly stroke, taking the Brest fleet to the west coast of Ireland with 20,000 troops on board. They hoped to raise a rebellion in an Ireland seething with discontent—and incidentally supplying most of the British navy's food. Their fate was to run into such bad weather that they could not beat up a rock-studded bay to a safe landing.

Be it noted that Ireland would hardly have been more independent under Napoleon than it was under the British. But taking it back, village by village, defeating a French army in the process, and then keeping it pacified would have been a colossal drain on British resources. The strain might have been enough to delay or prevent any British offensives against the French—and Napoleon was not a man to waste a free gift of time.

As it was, the British struck back effectively. On Valentine's Day of 1797, they defeated a superior Spanish fleet off Cape St. Vincent, capturing four ships. The now one-eyed Nelson distinguished himself by breaking into the Spanish rear and capturing two of the prizes. He was knighted; Sir John Jervis, the British admiral, became an earl.

That fall, the British also smashed the Dutch fleet in the North Sea at the Battle of Camperdown. This was an out and out slugfest, with eleven Dutch prizes taken but only two of them fit for anything but scrapping. Not less notable was that most of the British ships had been in a state of open mutiny during the summer.

There were actually two mutinies in the British fleet that year. The causes were numerous, including brutal officers, but mostly short and poor rations, ridiculously low pay (not raised since the reign of Charles II and often late), slow distribution of prize money (if any), and lack of shore leave (intended to prevent desertion).

The mutiny at Spithead was more of a sit-down strike. The mutineers were orderly and pledged to return to duty if the French came out, the Admiralty conceded a large part of their demands, and the popular Lord Howe presided over a settlement.

The mutiny at the Nore (the anchorage at the mouth of the Thames) was more serious, and the sailors more militant and more violent. There was bloodshed, and for a short time, the British capital was blockaded by its own navy. Cutting off supplies to the fleet and a general return to reason ended the affair; although some of the leaders ended on the gallows. The rest eventually sailed out to thrash the Dutch, under Admiral Duncan, who had subdued the mutiny on his own flagship almost by sheer force of personality, then blockaded the Dutch fleet with that flagship alone.

Nelson was to become the greatest of British admirals—but he was not the only illustrious name on that list.

Nelson (now one-armed as well as one-eyed) took another step toward fame in 1798, when Napoleon took the French Toulon fleet and a large troop convoy to Egypt. Desiring both to emulate Alexander the Great and damage the British Empire, he had his sights set on an advance to India.

Nelson had his sights set just as firmly on catching the French fleet. Unfortunately his shortage of scouting vessels kept him from doing so at sea, and perhaps ending Napoleon's career somewhat early. As it was, the French army was already ashore when the British found the French in Aboukir Bay, near the mouth of the Nile.

The French were anchored in a single line just offshore. Nelson calculated that there was enough room inshore for him to send half his fleet that way and the other offshore, thereby engaging each French ship in succession with two of his own.

It worked. The French were virtually annihilated, in spite of a stubborn resistance. The French army was marooned in Egypt, where the British rounded them up a couple of years later with an amphibious landing. Napoleon fled back home, to stage a coup and become First Consul.

Nelson was made a peer.

He also made a fool of himself, falling in love with the wife of the British ambassador in Sicily. She became his mistress and bore him a daughter, while keeping him on leading strings for most of a year that could have been better spent operating against French or French-held coasts. But Lady Hamilton played to Nelson's ego, which was large, and in the end caused nothing worse than embarrassment for Nelson's by-now numerous friends.

Nelson was not such an embarrassment that he was kept ashore. In 1801, he went to sea again as second in command of a fleet headed for the Baltic. Four Baltic powers—Sweden, Prussia, Russia, and Denmark—had formed a League of Armed Neutrality over interference with their trade by rigorous British enforcement of the blockade. This threatened Britain's access to the Baltic, the source of most of its naval stores.

The first objective was Copenhagen, where the Danish fleet was drawn up in front of their capital. Nelson's squadron approached the city by a route that bypassed most of the shore batteries. Then it was another slugfest, with British gunnery prevailing over Danish courage.

It was at this battle that Nelson disobeyed an order to withdraw by putting his telescope to his blind eye and claiming that he did not see the signal. Chutzpah can be as useful as a broadside.

The League of Armed Neutrality dissolved, partly due to the battle, partly due to the assassination of the czar of Russia. Nelson returned to the Mediterranean.

The British still had their hands full at sea, with escorting convoys, chasing privateers, catching blockade runners, and rounding up the occasional hostile squadron that got out. They did this particularly well in 1801, not far from Gibraltar, destroying most of a Franco-Spanish squadron—whose two largest ships, however, destroyed themselves by colliding, catching fire, and blowing up.

The British could be pardoned for thinking that Napoleon and his allies were land animals. They could also be pardoned for signing the Peace of Amiens in 1802, because further fighting promised to be expensive without achieving any important goals.

The Peace (or Truce) of Amiens lasted thirteen months, before the shooting resumed, and it broke down basically over maritime issues. The French wanted Malta back; the British wanted to hold on to it, to keep the French away from Egypt and Turkey. The British wanted the French to evacuate the Netherlands; the French wanted to keep it (and its fine ports) as a springboard to England's shores.

The British nearly shot themselves in the foot during the peace, because Earl St. Vincent as First Sea Lord (equivalent of Chief of Naval Operations) now tried to slug it out with the Admiralty's timber contractors. They were undeniably corrupt. However, the eve of another war was the wrong time to provoke them to their own mutiny. St. Vincent went back to sea, the timber contractors resumed deliveries, and the British literally hammered together a fleet in time for the new war.

Napoleon thought he was putting the time to better use. He had started assembling a massive fleet of landing craft at Boulogne on the English Channel before the peace; he now doubled the rate of construction. Men, timber, and everything else were robbed from the French fleet to build the invasion flotilla, in dozens of shipyards from Brest to the Netherlands.

Be it said here, and firmly, that Napoleon was probably spitting into the wind. Most of the vessels were flat-bottomed and flimsy, and low in the water with a full load. When a squall struck one squadron of them close inshore, 2,000 men drowned. A good storm in mid-Channel might have ended both the Grande Armée and its master.

Even if the Boulogne Flotilla had crossed a clear and calm Channel, its ordeal would not have ended. The British had plenty of light brigs and revenue cutters able to nip in close to shore and massacre the landing barges, where French heavy ships could not protect them. The French survivors who sloshed ashore would have been short of food, ammunition, and artillery, and practically without cavalry. The British had a small core of regular troops and a large force of militia, besides a warning system to summon reinforcements from all over the realm.

A bloody fight? Yes. So expensive that British offensive would have been put off for years? Probably. Napoleon dining in Buckingham Palace? Not unless George III chose to entertain him after he was captured.

The British, of course, took no chance that this Sword of Damocles had a blunt edge. The Channel Fleet, under Admiral Cornwallis (brother of the Yorktown general) practiced a close blockade of Brest, with light craft inshore, a squadron of heavier ships in signaling distance, and the bulk of the battle line cruising well out to sea.

If a gale blew in from the Atlantic, the Channel Fleet could retire to safe anchorages in Cornwall. The French in Brest would be wind-bound. If the wind shifted back to the east, the French could sail—but the Channel Fleet could sail after them.

It was this phase of the naval war that gave Alfred Thayer Mahan inspiration for an almost poetic turn of phrase:

"Those far-distant, storm-beaten ships, upon which the Grand Army never looked, stood between it and the dominion of the world."

Another British fleet, the Mediterranean, under Lord Nelson, held the seas off Toulon. However, the French admiral Villeneuve (a survivor of the Nile) got out of Toulon and sailed to the West Indies according to the plan for drawing off British strength.

Nelson, however, pursued him hotly. Villeneuve doubled back and met a detachment of the Channel Fleet off the Spanish port of Cadiz. For once, a British admiral did less than his duty. Villeneuve lost only two ships, and was now supposed to join with the Spanish from Cadiz and sail north, to be joined by the Brest fleet in a force strong enough to control the Channel. (Likely outcome was Cornwallis getting credit for the Great British Victory, instead of Nelson.)

Instead, Villeneuve went into Cadiz and was promptly blockaded by the British under Nelson. Napoleon fired Villeneuve and canceled the invasion, unknown to the British. Before his replacement arrived, however, Villeneuve sailed—to his doom.

Twenty-seven British ships met thirty-three French and Spanish off Cape Trafalgar on October 21, 1805. Nelson's instructions contained two pregnant phrases—"It will bring on a pell-mell battle" and "No captain can do very wrong who lays his ship alongside that of any enemy."

This wrote the epitaph of the hostile fleet. By sunset, the British had taken eighteen of them as prizes and sunk one. But Nelson was dead, cut down by a sharpshooter from the top of a French ship locked with his flagship, the *Victory*. (The French ship, aptly named *Redoubtable*, lost five-sixths of her crew, so a British sailor was speaking the truth when he said, "They fought us pretty tightish for French and Spanish.")

Trafalgar was not only the supreme epic of the Napoleonic War at sea, it was the last major fleet action. Not that the French gave up trying to maintain a fleet, or even sending squadrons to sea, and their privateers swarmed out from every friendly port to "annoy and distress" the British to the limits of their ability.

Nor did the British always carry things off as splendidly (and let it be remembered, Trafalgar cost them over 2.000 casualties and a dozen nearly wrecked ships of their own). They failed to make Turkey an ally in 1807. They botched an attack on Buenos Aires in 1808. They failed to destroy a French squadron on the Biscay coast in 1809, and that same year met nothing short of disaster when they tried to take Antwerp.

In Antwerp, the French were building a new fleet, as they could bring men and material along the internal waterways of Europe. The British launched a major combined assault, but army-navy cooperation broke down completely. So did the health of the British forces, thousands of them dying of malaria.

What did the British more harm than both privateers and their own blunders together was the Continental System. In a nutshell, this was Napoleon's ban on the importation of British goods to any part of his empire or its allies. Britain was the world's leading industrial power; its exports generated the revenue with which it paid for new ships of the line and lavish subsidies to France's enemies. Cut these financial sinews, and Britain might see reason (whatever Napoleon meant by that).

The system had some success, overall—but not enough. The Continent was not going to give up sugar and coffee, British woolens, tin ware, and pottery, simply on a Corsican's whim.

The British navy, accustomed to keeping smugglers out of Britain, now found itself escorting them to the Continent (Hamburg enjoyed a boom). The French tried to extend the enforcement of the Continental System farther and farther, but doing so stretched their resources thinner and thinner—and even the French army couldn't do without British overcoats.

Eventually, the Continental System laid the grounds for disaster, in two stages. The first disaster came in 1808, when Napoleon decided that Spain could be closed to British goods only if the French made it a puppet kingdom, like the Netherlands. He put his brother Joseph on the Spanish throne.

The Spanish promptly rose en masse. The French faced blown bridges, sniped sentries, messengers with their throats (or other parts) cut, supply convoys looted, and their enemies informed each time a French general took a new mistress.

They also faced an increasingly strong British military presence in the Iberian Peninsula, with a British army that had come of age and the leadership of one Sir Arthur Wellesley, better known to history as the Duke of Wellington. Wellington occasionally complained that the Royal Navy could not deliver all the supplies he needed when he needed them, or keep station off the more impossible parts of the Spanish coast all year round. But the navy ignored his beefs and went right on guarding his back and supply lines to home.

The war reached its second climax in 1811–12. Crop failures and privateer successes meant bread riots and bankruptcies in Britain. Only Sweden would sell Britain naval stores, and running them home across a stormy North Sea once cost the British three ships of the line wrecked, with 2,000 men drowned.

But the alliance with Spain had closed the Spanish Empire to French privateers and opened it to British trade. The French also lost their privateer bases on the Indian Ocean and the Dutch East Indies, which left that rich trade unmolested.

And in 1812, Napoleon invaded Russia with 400,000 men. He retreated from Russia that winter, leaving most of them behind—including many gunners drafted from the French fleet to man the Grande Armée's artillery.

It did not make much difference that, during the same summer, the United States of America declared war on Britain. Its grievances were ostensibly restrictions on neutral trade with the French Empire and impressments of American seamen—with both sides guilty of abuses.

Their real purpose (or at least hope) was to annex Canada. The Americans fared dismally on land. On the water, however, they won decisive victories on inland lakes, Erie and Champlain. They sent to sea a small but efficient navy, which proved itself the superior of the British in single-ship combat. Finally, they sent another swarm of privateers to join the diminishing ranks of the French, most of them ocean-going vessels that could show a clean pair of heels to any British warship.

The War of 1812 quickly became expensive. It failed to become dangerous because Napoleon did not do something that the British Admiralty dreaded. He never sold half a dozen of his best ships of the line to the Americans, to be sent out with American crews, smashing British blockading squadrons and ravaging British convoys almost at will.

Of course, by that time he had other things on his mind. The Continent was rising against him, rolling up his empire like a rug. Every time a new stretch of floor showed, that was one more country open to British goods and closed to French privateers and squadrons, and often a new army added to the ranks of his enemies.

He abdicated in 1814, with his enemies in sight of Paris. He made a brief comeback in the Hundred Days, but the Waterloo Campaign had no naval aspect.

The aftermath had a certain justice, however. Napoleon fled to England and then sailed to exile on St. Helena aboard British warships. The Grande Armée was no more, but its fallen master remained at the mercy of the Royal Navy's far-distant, storm-beaten ships.

While those in power today remember Vietnam and everyone reads about the day-to-day losses in Iraq and Afghanistan, these pale to the absolute disaster for Napoleon the quagmire of Spain proved to be. But how could the most brilliant commander in nineteenth-century Europe have gotten into such a situation?

THE WEEPING SPANISH WOUND

Spain, 1807

ROBERT GREENBERGER

Most people think Napoleon Bonaparte's expansion was finally crushed in Russia, but first, he badly miscalculated handling neighboring Spain and as a result, suffered his first major defeat. It just took him six years to realize he was defeated.

As the French Revolution seized the country and allowed Napoleon to become emperor, Spain was racked with the ineffectual rule of King Charles IV. Nearly broke, corrupt, and demoralized, the people were unhappy but not ready to revolt. The real power behind the throne proved to be advisor Manuel Godoy, lover to Charles' wife Maria Louisa. Godoy saw to it Spain was allied with France in 1795. Even at this early stage, he was Napoleon's puppet, having been promised a piece of Portugal for his support. Godoy ceded the Louisiana territory back to France and agreed to pay a subsidy to France. Godoy also saw to it that 15,000 troops were placed under Napoleon's control and were dispersed throughout Europe.

Spain's meager navy aided France in battle against the British Royal Navy a year later. The problems between France and England persisted, so Napoleon ordered the Continental Blockade against the country in 1806.

Bonaparte, by 1807, had mastered much of Eastern Europe, so he felt the timing was right to deal with the Iberian Peninsula, taming the weakened Spain while dispatching Portugal's mad Queen Maria. The emperor had grown tired of Portugal defying the blockade—as it honored its treaties dating back to 1373 with England—so he requested permission to send troops through Spain to deal with Portugal via the Treaty of Fontainebleau. The document, signed on October 27, 1807, also called for the soon-to-be conquered Portugal to be split into three parts: the Kingdom of Northern Lusitania, the Algarve, and Kingdom of Portugal (although which portion was promised to Godoy was unstated). Napoleon then issued Portugal one final invitation to join the Continental System, which John, the Prince Regent, refused. The Emperor dispatched General Jean-Andoche Junot, a former Ambassador to Portugal, toward the peninsula.

Along the way, though, Bonaparte cannily left troops in key spots throughout Spain, with General Dupont stationed near Cádiz in southwest Spain and Marshal Nicholas Soult headed for Corunna in Spain's northwest. At first, the people seemed to welcome the French troops crossing their land, which served to embolden Bonaparte. Spain's royal court initially asked for Portugal's help in repelling the French, but entered into a secret agreement with France in exchange for territory, while coveting Portugal's naval fleet.

Soult's march to Portugal was a success with Lisbon the first to fall with no real opposition on December 1st. Just days earlier, Queen Maria fled her country, relocating to Rio de Janeiro. Prince Regent John VI also left, but asserted somewhat weakened control over Portugal's holdings and armed forces from Brazil.

Napoleon finally acted to take control of Spain, seen as a stepping stone to crushing Portugal, in February, 1808. He ordered his commanders to seize Spanish cities, with Pamplona quickly falling into French hands. On February 29th, Barcelona followed.

The Spanish army was told to stand down, let the French take control, since after all, they were poorly outfitted and numbered at best 100,000 men scattered through the land. Their best forces, the Division of the North, were in Denmark, having been previously loaned to Napoleon. Effectively, Napoleon invaded and took over Spain without breaking a sweat.

The quarreling within the Spanish royal family led to unrest among the people. Bonaparte took advantage of the impending chaos to work with the Spanish aristocracy, forcing Charles IV to abdicate the throne. His son Ferdinand was installed on the throne until he and his family were taken by the French to Bayonne, and on May 5th, Ferdinand also abdicated. To rule the country, Bonaparte installed his brother Joseph, who had previously disappointed the emperor by being a poor military leader. He was to be disappointed again and this miscalculation was the beginning of Napoleon's defeat in the Peninsular War.

An influential body was the Afrancesados, Spanish aristocrats who wanted their country to follow the French model. In order to win their favor, King Joseph dissolved the religious houses without any thought to how this would be received by the peasants. The people, though, were ready to defend the churches. The revolt began in Zaragoza and they resisted the French for over a year. From Valencia, they managed to force the French forces from Madrid beginning in early May. If Napoleon did anything, he managed to unify a people that had been fractured under their native leadership.

It took Marshal Murat hours and the loss of 150 men to quell the initial uprising. The following day, May 3rd, French soldiers rounded up the protestors and had many of them shot. The scene in Madrid was repeated throughout the country, but rather than bring the people to heel, resistance persisted, giving rise to the name *guerilla*, meaning "little war."

One of Napoleon's miscalculations was thinking that the Spanish people, like their rulers, were weak and easily cowed. Instead, the local priests told the peasants that the French intended to destroy that which meant the most to them: their way of life, which largely centered on religion. Fearing the loss of saints and festivals if occupied by the anti-church and anti-papal French, who had banned all religious practices during the revolutionary years, the people were fighting to preserve their status quo, which had more to do with their villages than their throne.

At month's end, the people in Asturias declared war on Napoleon, unaware of what was happening in the rest of Spain. Some 338 citizens of French ancestry were killed in Valencia while ships anchored at Cádiz were sacked.

Things grew so frenzied that the French leader sent more and more troops to control the country, draining resources he needed for the rest of Europe.

Bonaparte had to contend with the arrival of the British army, led at this time by Sir Arthur Wellesley, later Duke of Wellington. The relatively inexperienced man was actually England's eighth choice (of the seven: some passed, one had died in battle, others were discredited in an abortive Dutch expedition) to lead a force into Spain but was also the best prepared for a conflict, commanding some 14,000 men who were rerouted from a planned trip to the Americas. The British government didn't want to see the emperor take control of the peninsula since, if it fell, all of Europe that would be left free was the British Isles. Early on, Bonaparte made the disastrous boast that he needed a mere 12,000 men to handle all Spain. By June 1808, though, the French tally reached 165,120, with 80,000 alone based on a stretch from Pamplona to Madrid. In Madrid, they were commanded by Bon-Adrien Jeannot de Moncey with Junot stuck in Portugal, separated by 300 miles. The plan was for Joseph to rule with an iron hand, allowing columns of French troops to crush uprisings with speed and force. General Pierre Dupont de l'Étang took 24,430 troops to the south, while Marshal Jean-Baptiste Bessières took 25,000 men to Aragon, and General Guillaume Philibert Duhesme used 12,710 troops to lay siege to Girona.

The two armies initially clashed at Vimiero with the French cut off from supplies, costing them the first battle, which set the tone for the coming war. This led to the Convention of Cintra, forcing the French out of Portugal. Harry Barrard, who had replaced Wellington in commanding Britain's forces in Portugal, granted favorable terms in order to bring things to a swift conclusion. The deal called for the English to transport their enemies and their arms back to France, keeping the enemy virtually intact.

The Spanish did not accept the occupation quietly and fought back in ways large and small, often frustrating the occupiers. Duhesme's siege failed and he was run out of Catalonia. Under General José de Palafox y Melzi, the Spanish people fought back time and again for three solid months until Charles, comte Lefebvre-Desnouettes, lifted the siege in August. Similarly, Moncey was beaten at Valencia and retreated, pursued by guerilla attacks the entire time.

Over the course of the next several years, France would commit upward of 250,000 troops to taking over the peninsula, while England would expend no more than 50,000 men, supported by Spanish militia and guerillas. Large numbers of the French were required to protect the supply and communications lines, which were under constant attack by the local citizens. Given the overwhelming odds, on paper, things looked to favor Bonaparte, but time and again he miscalculated, allowing victory to remain elusive.

As the French retreated in the south, there was a victory in the north when General Antoine Charles Louis Lasalle won over the Spanish General Cuesta in Cabezón. Later, Cuesta made a crucial error after leaving a gap between his forces and that of the British leader Blake. The French exploited this and regained Old Castile. Napoleon gloated over the victory, ignoring the defeats in Girona, Valencia, and Zaragoza. He was disappointed when Dupont was badly beaten in Bailén, surrendering his army totaling 24,000 men, to General Castaños.

Joseph fled Madrid, and word rapidly spread across Europe that Napoleon was not invincible after all.

At first, the French retreated from much of the country, surprised as they were. Instead, Napoleon himself took control of the forces now stacked up in Navarre and Catalonia, defeating the ill-equipped Spanish army, and reasserting control in Madrid. The Spanish resistance seemed to crumble without the royal family present to unite the people. Local juntas appeared in control and there was panic among the citizens from border to border. Napoleon, commanding the Grande Armée of 100,000 battle-tested men, arrived that fall and forced the British army to the coast. He said at the time, "I am here with the soldiers who conquered at Austerlitz, at Jena, at Eylau. Who can withstand them? Certainly not your wretched Spanish troops who do not know how to fight. I shall conquer Spain in two months and acquire the rights of a conqueror."

Instead, the emperor could not press his advantage because Austria, emboldened by the Spanish resistance, threatened war and he rushed back to France.

As fall gave way to winter, the British seemed defeated or at best, stalled, allowing Bonaparte to solidify his control. General Blake and his men set up camp in Espinosa beginning in mid-November. They were attacked by Soult and held out until they could organize and quickly retreat to Santander, avoiding capture. Napoleon ordered 45,000 men into the Sierra de Guadarrama to protect Madrid and fight the remnants of the Spanish army. At month's end, the French enjoyed yet another victory, this time at Somosierra pass, when Polish and French cavalry defeated General San Juan. Napoleon's men arrived in Madrid on December 1st and took the city within four days. Joseph regained the throne while San Juan ran west to Talavera. His men mutinied and shot him before scattering.

The British rallied and attacked, trying to free Madrid under General John Moore but his force was too small and he was forced into a hasty retreat.

In mid-December, the Spanish army was badly beaten at Cardedeu by Marshal Laurent Gouvion Saint-Cyr, who proved adept at marching his men to surprise the enemy. St. Cyr pursued the fleeing Spanish forces and captured some 1,200 men near Molins de Rey.

Palafox's army was nearly destroyed to the man but they did manage to keep the Grande Armée stalled at the Ebro river.

Within weeks, as 1809 dawned, Soult and the French fighting forces appeared to have routed the English and Spanish armies. Moore died during the conflict and 7,000 Britons were killed before 26,000 others returned home.

General Theodor von Reding rebuilt his army and in February attacked the French army's right wing but were defeated by a better prepared cavalry. When the French left the area on the 20th, some 64,000 corpses were left littering the battlefield. It took Napoleon a little over two months to essentially reconquer Spain so he left for home, presuming his work was finished.

Soult resumed command and in March, once more attempted to stomp all over Portugal, this time coming from the north. Within four weeks, he was exceptionally successful despite continued resistance throughout the land.

Wellington took his refreshed forces to Talavera in April 1809, where Joseph and the French army were soundly defeated.

The English forces fell back to Torres Vedras, where Wellington oversaw the construction of 108 forts in three lines, linked by a semaphore system. This allowed Wellington to defend Lisbon and would prove the difference in 1810, when Masséna led the French army in a fresh offensive. Outnumbered and outgunned, the British had little choice but to retreat, following a scorched earth policy that left the Spanish citizens in desperate shape. The French took over the forts and wintered there en route to their ultimate goal, which remained Portugal, a country that had yet to capitulate.

Masséna, commanding 60,000 men, tried again in July 1810, but made several tactical blunders and was forced to retreat. By October 14th, it was considered a stalemate, and from that point on, the French attempt to conquer the peninsula never regained strength. Rather than give in, the Portuguese burned their homes and lands, resisting with their last breath, much as the Spanish were doing next door.

Unable to progress, low on supplies, Masséna gave up his goal and abandoned Torres Vedras in March 1811. He ultimately left Portugal in May after losing 25,000 men.

At much the same time, fresh British forces arrived and began a new offensive in Spain. They scored their first victory against the French at Barrosa on March 5. Men commanded by Marshal William Beresford managed a decisive victory over Soult on May 16th.

Soult was ordered to provide Masséna support, which allowed

General Graham to enter Cadiz and begin a siege against the French in the Battle of Barrosa. However, no one told Masséna that help was coming that spring, which resulted in decisions that proved fateful. First, Wellington outmaneuvered Masséna at Fuentes de Onoro, keeping the French from reaching Almeida. A rare French victory occurred when the garrison broke through the British lines, handing Wellington what he called "the most disgraceful military event that has yet occurred to us."

Things seesawed back and forth throughout the year, and it wasn't until 1812 that things finally turned England's way once and for all, spelling doom for the emperor. By then, Napoleon was suffering at the Russians' hands, forcing him to withdraw some 60,000 troops from the peninsula. The remaining troops were divided into three armies stationed around Spain, which provided clear targets for Wellington. On January 19, 1812, he attacked Ciudad Rodrigo, taking the town. The exhausted, elated soldiers celebrated by raping and pillaging the people they had liberated.

Napoleon, meantime, agreed that annexing Catalonia, dividing it into four sections, was an appropriate move. To appease the people, the emperor declared Catalan to be an official language alongside French. He once again miscalculated, ignoring the generations-old dislike between the Catalans and French. Guerilla activity resumed and the French were harried at every turn.

In early April, Wellington struck again, this time in Badajoz and repeated his January victory, although he lost 60 officers and 700 men with an estimated 3,500 killed and wounded. The city endured a three-day rampage at the hands of the victors. Salamanca was liberated on June 17th and he rested his troops there, knowing that Marshal Marmont was nearby. The two armies finally fought one another on July 22nd in the Battle of Salamanca, which proved costly to the French, allowing the allied forces to gain access to Madrid on August 6th.

Led by the Spanish General Burgos in October, they suffered losses from the French, so Wellington retreated from the center. He wintered and rested his men, plotting for a final campaign.

The change of fortunes accelerated in 1812, when Joseph was

forced to relinquish a throne for which he was ill-suited. Instead, Bonaparte named his brother head of the armed forces in Spain, yet another error in the making.

While Joseph proved his usual ineptness, the guerillas grew in strength and organization. The British navy secretly supplied them with tools and, most important, guns. While fragmented at first, by early 1813, they had coalesced into a fierce force numbering 7,000 under the leadership of Francisco Espoz y Mina. It was Espoz's men, not the Spanish army, who managed to blockade Pamplona, the capital of Navarre, breaking their supply line.

When four times their number of French troops arrived, Espoz dispersed his guerillas so the French had no one to fight.

It took Wellington until June of 1813 before he unleashed his well-rested, hardened forces. In a mere two days, they retook Burgos from the French and on the 21st arrived in Vitoria, bringing the war to the Pyrenees and France. While he hungered to enter France and bring the war to Bonaparte's homeland, Wellington knew he needed to gain control of the communications links, which meant conquering the fortress of San Sebastian on the Atlantic coast. He won the battle, but lost a significant number of men that August. These successes led Napoleon to once more dismiss Joseph, the titular commander of the armed forces at this point. Bonaparte turned command over to Soult in early July.

Soult reorganized his men and in August, set out to crush the Spanish in Maya, Roncesvalles, and Sorauren, collectively known as the Battle of the Pyrenees. He proved successful in Maya and Roncesvalles, but was routed in the Battle of Sorauren at month's end. On August 31st, Soult led his men in the Battle of San Marcial, at the same time Wellington was conducting his successful campaign to regain San Sebastian.

Lieutenant General Reille commanded the western corps, with Lieutenant General Clausel leading the central corps and Lieutenant General D'Erlon taking the eastern corps. Both Soult and Wellington intended their eastern flanks to feint, but both sides grew overzealous and a messy fight broke out. Early in the morning, Reille took his men across Bidassoa to gain control of San Marcial's main road. The Spanish forces proved tougher than expected and each advance was rebuffed. Late in the afternoon, Soult called the men off.

Also that morning, the center corps crossed the Bidassoa and headed east to meet with Reille's men. Combined, they seemed to scare off Wellington's army. As time progressed, though, the allied men remained steadfast and a change in weather pattern caused the river to swell and become impassable by nightfall. Clausel did not realize this, and when he sounded a mid-afternoon retreat, two of his divisions and much of the third, were caught on the wrong side of the Bidassoa. They found themselves surrounded and had little choice but to surrender.

The commander of the remaining men, Vandermaesen, chose to try for the little bridge five miles away which was being lightly guarded by the British. Marching in the dark, the men arrived at the bridge at about three in the morning of September 1st. Although it took them two hours to fight the meager British sentries, the French managed to gain access to the bridge and cross. Too eager for battle, Vandermaesen was among the first killed when they charged the bridge, one of 231 French soldiers to die that early morning.

Wellington was at first off guard, but rallied and took advantage of Soult's overstretched forces. The French retreated and built defenses along the Bidassoa, marking their final major assault on Spanish soil.

On October 7th, local French shrimpers guided the British army across the Bidassoa estuary, allowing them to outflank Soult and his forces who were busily crossing the Pyrenees. Other British troops were still laying siege to Pamplona, providing a distraction to the French.

The Treaty of Valençay was signed on December 11th, with Napoleon seeking peace so he could concentrate on the rest of Europe, which began to crumble in his grasp, beginning that fall with new hostilities in Germany. The treaty called for Ferdinand VII to assume the throne and be recognized by France. Still, the Spanish did not trust the little general and fighting continued into the New Year.

April 17, 1814, welcomed the Battle of Toulouse, the final engagement in the Peninsula War, conducted six days after Bonaparte abdicated. By then, he had logged a mere seventy-seven days in Spain, allowing his generals to conduct the six-year war, and his lack of personal attention may well be the biggest blunder of them all.

"This was what defeated me," Napoleon wrote about the peninsula. His arrogance, after easy victories elsewhere in Europe, seemingly blinded him to what it would take to conquer Portugal and Spain. He thought the people would acquiesce to his magnificence and the might of his well-trained, well-supplied soldiers. He never anticipated resistance, let alone continued resistance after he himself arrived to show his might.

He committed too few troops, misunderstood the people, and continued to rely on his ineffectual brother to rule or command. What was to have been a two-month campaign took six years and resulted in defeat. The losses in the peninsula allowed other countries to reconsider life under Bonaparte's heel and he began losing country after country, until his ultimate defeat at Waterloo.

In recent times, historians and critics have compared America's invasion of Iraq with Napoleon's ill-conceived move into Spain, and many parallels work, though the long-term outcome remains unknown at this writing. The losses are not likely to total the staggering half a million men Spain cost Napoleon.

The disaster for Napoleon that was Spain may have cost the emperor half a million men in a decade. But always efficient, in Russia he managed to lose almost that many in less than a year. And he did this while winning all the major battles.

A MARCH INTO AND OUT OF HELL

Napoleon's Russian Campaign, 1812

JOHN HELFERS

It should have been a relatively straightforward task: lead the largest army ever assembled on the European continent on a swift incursion into Russia to capture Moscow, forcing Czar Alexander's surrender, and creating a huge vassal nation that would leave Napoleon Bonaparte free to finish his conquest of Spain, and perhaps even turn his attention to his most dangerous enemy, Great Britain. However, the brief campaign to conquer Russia proved to be Napoleon Bonaparte's undoing, causing the destruction of his massive army, and the first step toward his eventual downfall and exile.

It is important to note why Napoleon chose to invade his then-ally at the time. The war with Russia had its ultimate underpinnings in Napoleon's inability to take over England. Having failed to defeat the Royal Navy at the battle of Trafalgar in 1805, and lacking the necessary land force to mount an invasion of the island nation, Napoleon turned to economic warfare, enacting the Continental System and issuing decrees that prohibited practically every country on the European continent, all either conquered by or allied with the emperor, from trading with Great Britain.

Although the restrictions did hurt England's trade, which was becoming a manufacturing powerhouse that could supply weapons and other goods to anyone opposing Napoleon, the Continental System ended up injuring the mainland countries of Europe more. Some, like Portugal, refused to abide by the decree, leading Napoleon to try to conquer the country in 1808, and to the Peninsular War with Great Britain. Others, like Russia, simply defied the ruling by secretly trading with England, as they desperately needed to export their natural resources without paying the stiff tariffs imposed by France on trade between members of his empire.

There was also friction between Alexander and Napoleon concerning the Little Emperor's reorganization of nations and territories in his burgeoning empire. Napoleon had long been planning for the nation of Poland, then a French satellite, to serve as a buffer between France and Russia, and his incorporation of Galicia, ceded by Austria in the Treaty of Schönbrunn, into that territory didn't help matters. When Napoleon disregarded the Treaty of Tilsit and annexed the Grand Duchy of Oldenburg, a holding of Alexander's brother-in-law, the Czar had had enough, and formally severed his ties with the French Empire on December 31st, 1810, knowing full well it would mean war with his superior foe.

However, what on paper looked like an overwhelming, lopsided mismatch proved to be much different in reality. For starters, Napoleon had grown—well, fat and sassy would be a good description. The hard-charging general of a few years earlier had been replaced by an overweight, sedentary family man. After his divorce of Josephine to provide an heir for his empire, Napoleon swiftly wed the archduchess of Austria, Marie-Louise, who just as quickly bore him a son, Napoleon Francis Joseph Charles, whom his father had titled "the King of Rome." Two years of easy living in Paris, dining on rich food, heavy on the cream, had expanded Napoleon's waistline, and diminished his aggressive nature.

Also, there was increasing evidence that Napoleon, never one with a small ego, had become even more enamored of his own infallibility than usual. Since 1808, he had been overseeing the campaign to subjugate Spain, his first step to install his brother, Joseph, on the throne. However, the Spanish viewed the French Revolution with deep suspicion, since the new government had stripped the Catholic Church of much of its power. For the Spanish citizens, with their identity deeply rooted in their religious heritage, the possibility of this happening in their country was unacceptable. Soon the peasants were in revolt against their occupiers, aided by the British, who naturally saw the unrest as a chance to gain a foothold on the continent, and destabilize their long-term enemy France even more—a win-win for them. Against all military logic, Napoleon was convinced that not only could his campaign to finish conquering Spain and Portugal be handled without him directly overseeing it, but he also planned to open a second front far to the east.

Many of Napoleon's advisors, both civilian, such as Armand de Caulaincourt, the former French ambassador to Russia, and military were against this campaign, citing the difficulties of managing it along with the ongoing trouble in Spain, but the emperor waved them off and pressed forward. He signed alliance treaties with Austria and Prussia in the early months of 1812, further alarming Russia, which demanded that France remove its Prussian garrison and its forces from the Silesian fortresses. The stage was now set for Napoleon's invasion.

And when he planned to take Russia, he was going to do it in a big way. Napoleon's military genius lay not in the development of new tactics and doctrine, but in the skillful application of existing ones. He was always a champion of victory through not only superior force, but an overwhelming one, and as such, he set out to create the greatest army Europe had ever seen, not only to force Russia to the treaty table, but also as a pointed expression of France's—and his own—military might.

With his Grande Armée split in two due to the ongoing business in Spain, Napoleon had to bolster his invasion force with conscripts from his allies. However, this was soon accomplished, and by June of 1812, he commanded a field army of 612,000 men,

with 2,000 cannons and 250,000 horses. Bringing up the rear in
Germany and the French Rhineland was another 130,000 troops,
for a force of more than 740,000 able-bodied soldiers. Of them,
only 300,000 were actually French, the rest were assembled from
across Europe—Dutch, German, Swiss, Italians, Poles, Lithuanians—
all fighting under the French flag.

Napoleon's plan was to split his army into three groups, a main
force of 250,000 men, led by himself, a southern wing of 80,000
men, commanded by his brother Jérôme, and another army of
80,000 men in between the two, led by Eugène de Beauharnais.
Upon entering the country, he would engage and defeat the standing Russian army, most likely at Smolensk, and force Alexander to
negotiate for peace. He expected to accomplish all of this in only
a few months, hoping to be back in Paris before winter, in time to
quell the constant political intrigue fomenting against him.

Czar Alexander's forces were vastly outmatched. At no time did
he have more than 450,000 troops to call on, and his commanders
were never able to mass more than 180,000 for battle at any one
time. The Russian commanders, Prince Mikhail Barclay de Tolly,
head of the main force of 130,000 men, and Prince Peter Bagration
to his south, with another 50,000, knew they had been assigned
what was virtually a suicide mission. Although 40,000 more men
were south of the Pripet Marshes, they could not reach what would
be the front in time, and neither could the rest of the Russian army,
which was being mobilized in the rear. During the first few weeks
of the campaign, it looked as though Barclay's force would somehow have to fend off the massive Grande Armée by itself. When
the inevitable battle came, it should have been a slaughter.

Instead, it was a slow, agonizing demise—but of the Grande
Armée, not the Russian forces. The campaign began well enough,
with Napoleon's gigantic army presenting an awesome sight as it
entered Russia on June 24, 1812. Four days later, it reached Vilna, the
capital of Lithuania, which had been deserted by both the enemy
army and its citizens. Napoleon had hoped to engage at least one
or both of the Russian forces here and defeat them, but the two
opposing units had wisely already retreated, evincing Russia's only

hope of victory—to draw Napoleon farther into the country, and let the inertia of his huge, unwieldy army destroy itself. This was not necessarily a planned tactic of Barclay and Bagration, but more a blunder toward eventual victory, dictated by the simple desire to survive.

At Vilna, Napoleon made his first mistake—he halted his army and waited there for eighteen days, expecting Alexander either to fight or negotiate. Although there was good reason to rest his forces—the hot summer was proving to be just as dangerous as the oncoming winter would be to his troops—an army at rest is an army in decline. Disease ran rampant, with many soldiers suffering from dysentery. Since the invasion had begun in spring, before planting, horses were fed with green oats, killing hundreds. The fighting had barely begun, and already Napoleon had had to abandon 100 guns and 500 ammunition wagons before he left.

Meanwhile, his first corps, led by Marshal Louis-Nicolas Davout, arrived at Minsk on July 8, but still were not able to engage Bagration's forces, which kept eluding them. At this time, the two Russian armies were still separated, giving Napoleon's forces the best chance to defeat one, then the other. However, Napoleon's delay in Vilna, compounded by Jérôme's hesitation and ineptitude at forcing a decisive battle, led to the Russian armies joining together. Frustrated by what he saw as Jérôme's dithering, Napoleon promoted Davout to commander of the entire right flank guard. Insulted, Jérôme left the army completely, returning to Westphalia, and causing more delays while Davout assumed complete command of the force. Unfortunately, although he was an excellent leader in most respects, the cavalry officer pushed his men too hard in pursuit of the enemy, killing horses by the hundreds, and reducing his forces due to hunger and exhaustion.

Historians have made much of the supposed "scorched earth" policy the Russians were said to have employed to further weaken Napoleon's forces, but the emperor was already aware he would have to bring everything he would need for the invasion, even though that meant nightmarish record-keeping and extended supply lines. The fact is that with fields under cultivation, and most stores gone to feed the population during the previous winter, there simply wasn't anything to forage for. Also, many villages were too far away from the army's route to allow for effective food gathering, so everything had to be brought along, a logistical nightmare. Just trying to feed 612,000 men for one day requires dozens of tons of food, and if that supply was cut off, the army's decline would be swift and practically irreversible.

With the Russian still not even close to giving the Grande Armée a stand-up fight, Napoleon brought his forces together and pressed on, taking the city of Vitebsk on July 28th after heavy fighting, but nothing that put the Russian army in danger. Here he stopped his army again for fifteen days. Advisors tried to get him to halt the campaign, but Napoleon knew he must continue if he were to have any hope of victory before winter. By this time a full one-third of his army was missing or incapacitated, the problem compounded by his having to leave garrisons in the towns along the way to prevent supply lines from being cut. If he messed around in the country much longer, Napoleon soon wouldn't have an army left to command.

On August 13th, the Grande Armée was on the move again, heading toward Smolensk. Along the way, Napoleon learned that the two Russian armies had come together again. After two days of skirmishing in the suburbs, Bagration disobeyed orders and withdrew again, leaving Barclay's army alone. Instead of taking advantage of the split, by the time Napoleon found out about it, Barclay had been able to withdraw from the city as well.

Having lost yet another chance to defeat his enemy, Napoleon faced hard choices now—hole up in Smolensk until spring to continue the campaign, risking the political intrigues in Paris exploding in revolution while he was gone; march on Moscow, hoping that Alexander would negotiate; or head straight for the capital city of St. Petersburg and force Alexander to capitulate. The Russian army was heading toward Moscow, 240 miles away, which made Napoleon's mind up for him. Rousing his exhausted, hungry army, which now numbered only about 150,000 men, Napoleon gave chase on August 20th, with Murat keeping up the grueling pace.

The forced march to Moscow decimated the French army even more, with 18,000 more men incapacitated, and often slaughtered by the Cossacks when left behind along the way. But soon Napoleon would finally get his wish for a stand-up battle.

After the narrow escape at Smolensk, alarmed at the uncooperativeness of Bagration and Barclay, Alexander put Marshal Mikhail Kutúzov, a 67-year-old officer so fat it took several men to hoist him on his horse, in charge. Kutúzov was clever but lethargic, although he agreed with the czar that Moscow should be defended—the Russian citizens would not stand for another city to be deserted and taken by the invaders. They would make their stand outside a town called Borodino, seventy-five miles west of Moscow. His army of 120,000 was ragged and hungry, but in better overall shape than the French. It was the best chance they would have of stopping the invasion once and for all.

On September 1st, receiving the news that the Russians were preparing for battle, Napoleon was overjoyed. At last, the fight he had been wanting since he had entered the country in June was about to happen. He stopped the army for three days, giving the ammunition wagons time to catch up, and on September 4th, gave the order to advance on the Russians.

Kutúzov had had several days to fortify his position, and he had taken full advantage of it, concentrating his forces on a ridge overlooking the right bank of the Kolocha, a tributary of the Moskvá River, and reinforcing it with several earthen redoubts. His left flank, unprotected by the water, was on a detached knoll, known as the Shevárdino redoubt. After the long march, the two armies were roughly equally matched, with Napoleon's 133,000 men and 600 cannon against Kutúzov's 120,000, with the same number of guns.

Fighting began on September 5th, with Davout capturing the Shevárdino redoubt by nightfall. Napoleon had his scouts review the enemy line, and prepared his men for a frontal assault on September 7th. One group, led by Davout and Marshal Ney, would attack up the middle while another group on the right, led by Marshal Joseph-Antoine Poniatowski, would try and break their opponent's left flank. The plan appeared relatively simple, but would have one crucial difference from Napoleon's previous campaigns: the general would not be personally overseeing it. The stress of the march and the weather had finally gotten to the emperor, and on the morning of the battle he was quite ill with a feverish cold. After dispatching his initial orders from his camp on the Shevárdino redoubt, he did little in terms of administration for the rest of the day.

At 6 a.m. on September 7th, following heavy bombardment of the Russian positions by French artillery, the attack began. The two elements of Napoleon's army performed well under hellish conditions, with heavy fighting all along the line. The flanking effort proved ineffective, although Bagration was killed in the fighting. In the end, the battle was reduced to a blood-soaked series of French charges up the center.

By sheer weight of numbers, and after several devastating charges into a hail of Russian grapeshot and musket fire, the French succeeded in taking the hills. It is here where many historians believe Napoleon made his second great mistake of the campaign. Marshals Ney and Poniatowski had driven the Russians from their redoubts, but hadn't broken them yet. Ney went to Napoleon and requested he send out the rested, 18,000-strong Imperial Guard to ensure victory. But Napoleon's gambling spirit failed him during this crucial decision. He chose to play it safe instead, feeling if he committed all of his troops, then had to fight a battle the next day, he would lose everything. He refused the request, sending out only a single division of the Young Guard in the event of a Russian counterattack.

While this seemed to be the prudent decision, it also prevented what was ostensibly a French victory, albeit a bloody one, from becoming a rout of the enemy, and an end to the campaign. Instead, Kutúzov broke camp and left for Mozháysk the next day, leaving a strong rear guard to deter pursuit.

The final losses on both sides were horrendous. Although the Russians lost more men, about 45,000, the French had lost around 30,000 men, almost a quarter of the remaining army. Even worse was the death of sixteen French generals, including Auguste de

Caulaincourt—Armand's brother—and thirty-one wounded. Even worse, the French victory was meaningless—the Russian army had been able to leave the area, and Napoleon was no closer to bringing Alexander to the armistice table than before. He wandered the blood-soaked battlefield several times, almost unable to come to terms with what had happened—"I have beaten them. I have beaten them. It means nothing?" he asked of his generals, none of whom had a satisfactory answer. Where his past victories had brought his enemies to the negotiating table, this costly victory, bought at almost too high a price, had gained Napoleon nothing. His enemy was still in the field, and Russia had still not been brought to heel.

On September 14th, Napoleon's army entered Moscow, which had also been deserted by the Russians and was now inhabited primarily by a large contingent of criminals who had been released by the retreating Russian army to roam the streets. Again, Napoleon faced the choice of whether to stay or go. Although much of Moscow had been put to the torch by the remaining Russians, there was still enough food for his army to weather the season, and continue the campaign in spring, although at a tremendous cost in both time and money. There was still the chance that his enemies might be able to mobilize enough of a resistance to him back in Paris. Still, he borrowed a page from his brother Jérôme, and dithered in Moscow for a month, hoping that Alexander would seek terms.

But to Alexander, things were progressing as he had hoped. As early as 1811, he had told Caulaincourt, "Your Frenchman is brave, but long privations and a bad climate wear him down and discourage him. Our climate, our winter, will fight on our side." And that is exactly what happened.

The French were slow to seize and protect the food stockpiles in Moscow, and soon exhausted them. Although Napoleon opened the markets in Moscow and sent out foraging parties, both efforts led to naught, and soon the French army, including the cavalry, were slaughtering their horses to survive. As many as 20,000 horses died or were killed in Moscow during the month-long stay alone.

Napoleon seemed to have every intention of staying through the winter, but bad news from two fronts made his departure a necessity. First, in Spain, Wellington defeated Marmont at Salamanca, and had entered Madrid. Second, and more ominous, Kutúzov, who had rested and reorganized his 100,000-strong army, launched a swift attack on Murat at Tarútino, forcing him to retire with a loss of men and guns. But even worse than this setback was the steadily worsening weather. Napoleon had already planned to move back to Smolensk to shorten his supply lines; with Murat's defeat, that option moved from a possibility to a necessity. The first snow fell on October 13th, and six days later, the tattered, battered, exhausted, hungry remains of the Grande Armée, reduced to only 70,000 men, began their long retreat from Moscow.

But, much like the rest of the campaign, this trip was beset with bad luck and trouble. Napoleon had planned to return to Paris by a more direct, southerly route, but the concern that Kutúzov's army would be waiting for them forced Napoleon to retrace his steps along the same route he had used to enter Russia—a route that had already been stripped bare by both the Russian citizens and the French army during their first march. The ultimate irony of this was that the southern route was clear, and could have been traveled without difficulty. If this had been done, the subsequent horrors of the march out could have been minimized.

Instead, Napoleon headed southwest to aid Murat. With the offensive advantage, Kutúzov attacked again at Malo-Yaroslávets, killing 5,000 French soldiers. He might have defeated the French army then and there, but the general broke off his attack and withdrew to the west, where he was still able to threaten Napoleon's line of retreat, and forced him to travel northwest to reach Smolensk. The trip was a grueling nightmare, the French skirmishing with harassing Cossacks the entire way, and abandoning the booty they had looted from Moscow, along with their wounded, whom Napoleon would not leave in Moscow. Marshal Ney's rear guard was set upon at Vyázma on November 3rd, with his unit of 6,000 reduced to a mere 1,000 men when the fighting was done.

Some historians claim that the Russian winter should not have received as much credit as it does for helping to destroy what was left of the French army, pointing to records that indicate the winter was milder than usual. The fact remains that no army even tries to move in winter weather unless there is no other choice, and the results for the Grande Armée were as dismal as the results would be for another great and terrible army that would try the same invasion—with similar horrible results—130 years later.

Upon reaching Smolensk on November 9th with only 50,000 men, Napoleon received even more bad news. First, the stores of food in the city were gone, devoured by the relief columns. Even more disheartening was the message that General Malet, who had been committed to an asylum in France, had escaped and made a bid to seize the French throne, convincing several high government officials that Napoleon had been killed in Russia. His plan nearly succeeded before he was captured and executed. But even worse, when the rumor of Napoleon's death had reached the populace, not one person had moved to proclaim his son, whom Napoleon had named "King of Rome," as the hereditary emperor. Clearly, Napoleon had to return to France and put his own house in order.

But there was one more obstacle to overcome: the Berezina River. After leaving Smolensk on November 14th, the advance guard encountered Kutúzov's army at Krásnoye, which barred their retreat. Pitched fighting took place, and Napoleon, perhaps finally realizing the precariousness of his situation, moved the Imperial Guard and Davout's forces up to the front. Once again Ney's rear guard was attacked and cut off from the main group; once again his force of 6,000 was smashed to pieces, with only 800 surviving this time, earning him the sobriquet "the bravest of the brave," which should also have applied to any soldier following him, given their abbreviated life expectancy.

Napoleon had planned to head to Minsk, but abandoned that plan after learning it had fallen to the enemy. Forced to travel to Vilna, his army would have to cross the Berezina, a tributary of the Dnieper River. Expecting the river to be frozen—although hundreds of French horses had already died, since their hooves were not shod with frost-nails, and suffered broken legs every time the officers tried to cross a frozen body of water—Napoleon had left his pontoon bridge-making equipment behind two days ago. But the capricious Russian winter had one more surprise in store for him—a sudden thaw, which broke the ice and flooded the river, making it even more treacherous than usual. Russian forces had already destroyed the only bridge in the area, and were closing in for the kill, seeing the demoralized, starving French as easy prey, trapped between the anvil of the river, and the heavy hammer of the Russian forces.

But Napoleon was not to be daunted so easily. He reorganized his men, and ordered two bridges built. Once again, Marshal Ney was instrumental in holding off the Russians, buying time for the construction at the cost of his men's lives. Even so, the crossing was a chaotic mess of men, horses, and equipment. At least 25,000 men and 30,000 noncombatants died during the three-day affair. Yet the casualties might have been even higher if not for Napoleon's cool overseeing of the operation—something that many probably wished he had done a few months earlier.

After the Berezina crossing, the Grande Armée was shattered, its 50,000 effective soldiers and another 50,000 stragglers from other units barely able to function as a unit, much less fight. At this point, Napoleon left his remaining soldiers and traveled with all due speed back to Paris to clean up the messes that had grown considerably larger during his absence.

While there are several obvious reasons for the failure of Napoleon's campaign into Russia—the sheer insanity of opening another front on the other side of the continent when Spain was anything but pacified, the difficulty of maintaining such a large force in a hostile land, the interminable delays during the campaign, the inability to gain a clear strategic advantage either militarily or by negotiation—all contributed to its demise. But after reviewing all the evidence, two main facts come to light that doomed Napoleon's invasion from the start.

First, Napoleon really didn't want to fight this war. He *needed* to, for Alexander had betrayed him by pulling out of the Continental System, and if that wasn't rectified, other nations would have done the same, eroding Napoleon's hold over the continent. But the fact remains that he was an unwilling invader, with neither his heart nor his head fully committed to the fight, thereby ensuring that he would not be as tactically ruthless as necessary to achieve victory. Military strategists from Sun Tzu ("And so if I wish to do battle, the enemy cannot but do battle with me") and von Clausewitz, who fought on the side of the Russians at Borodino, and who later wrote in his classic treatise *On War*:

> *The military power must be destroyed, that is, reduced to such a state as to not be able to prosecute the war. . . . The country must be conquered. But even when both these things are done, still the war . . . cannot be considered at an end as long as the will of the enemy is not subdued also, that is, its government and its allies must be forced into signing a peace, or the people forced into submission. . . .*

It is obvious that Napoleon's heart wasn't in the war—he stayed in the rear, he didn't mingle with his men, except to hold endless, pointless parade reviews—and therefore did not act like the commander of an invading army, whose point was to conquer the target country in the most efficient way possible.

Napoleon's Grande Armée could be considered the largest military bluff in history—he hoped his massive force would make his enemy roll over and surrender rather than risk battling such an overwhelming force. But when that didn't happen, and he was forced to fight, he seemed hesitant and unsure of himself and his forces. He wanted to give Alexander every chance for peace, and by doing so undermined his position of strength from the moment he entered the country in June. Once there, he let the defenders set the nature of the conflict, chasing them around the country instead of identifying the key strategic targets in the country, whether that would have been Moscow or St. Petersburg, and making for them. Instead of plodding along in fits and starts, letting exhaustion and disease whittle away his mighty force to nothing, a decisive thrust into Russia to capture either capital might have gained him the results he had to achieve, but didn't really want to do.

The second crucial mistake Napoleon made, quite simply, is that he didn't *lead* his men. Again, as Sun Tzu wrote in *The Art of War* about a leader commanding his troops:

> *And so one skilled at employing the military*
> *Takes them by the hand as if leading a single person.*
> *They cannot hold back.*

And:

> *He looks upon the troops as his children.*
> *Thus they can venture into deep river valleys with him.*
> *He looks upon the troops as his beloved sons.*
> *Thus they can die together with him.*

More than likely Napoleon would have preferred that his men die *for* him, and for their country, but the fact remains that his legendary leadership skills were absent during this campaign. During the entire time he was aloof and distant from his soldiers, traveling in his huge private caravan, surrounded by his private guard. He did not walk among the men at night as he used to. He did not converse with the infantry as he had in years past, nor did he lead at the front as he used to—at the major battle of the entire war, he sat out the fighting with a severe cold. Napoleon is famous for boasting that he "was worth one hundred thousand men" in terms of morale, but when his soldiers needed him most in the inhospitable terrain of Russia, he wasn't there for them.

Even then, Napoleon might have pulled off his conquest if his position back in France had been secure. However, by the time of the Russian invasion, he was probably the most hated man in Europe, making it impossible to secure his hold over the Continent, when all of his allies had to be subjugated by force or the threat thereof, including elements of the political factions in his homeland. When the opportunity to move against their absent dictator presented itself, the forces arrayed against him did their best. Napoleon knew his enemies were plotting, which forced his campaign onto an artificial timetable for success, and if it didn't happen, he would be in trouble not only on two fronts, but on three, if one includes Paris. Once things began to unravel in Russia, the snowball of trouble swiftly became an avalanche that swept over Napoleon, carrying him all the way back to Paris, and to his eventual defeat at the hands of the Wellington and the Anglo-Prussian army at Waterloo.

*There is an irony about the final battles lost by Napoleon
and how he lost what was perhaps the first World War
ever fought. After all there were battles in India,
the Pacific coasts, Africa, and the Americas during this period.
Where the irony comes in is that, at the start of this section
on Napoleon and his enemies the opposing allies,
particularly the Prussians, failed to adjust their strategies
to a new way of fighting a war. Now the "same old way"
is the province of Napoleon, not his opponents.*

THE LION TRAPPED

Napoleon's Fight for France, 1813–1814

JOHN HELFERS

After the disastrous Russian campaign, Napoleon Bonaparte returned home to find his nation beset by enemies from both outside and within. Czar Alexander, emboldened by the destruction
of the Grande Armée and their embarrassing retreat, continued his
advance on the fragmenting French Empire, sending an army into
the Grand Duchy of Warsaw. While Napoleon could have created a
natural buffer between France and Russia by promising the Polish
their freedom in exchange for fighting against the Russians during
his own invasion, he was unwilling to take that step, fearing what
might happen if he wasn't in control of Poland, and so there was no
one to oppose the Czar's incursion. By March of 1813, Prussia threw
its lot in with Russia, declaring war on France as well.

On the surface, things weren't quite as black as they appeared.

While Napoleon's army had been crushed on the Russian steppes, only about 100,000 of the original number of 612,000 surviving the campaign, only about half of those soldiers had been French—the rest were conscripts from his allied nations. Napoleon immediately called up the French cadet classes of 1814 and 1815, as well as whatever able-bodied men were left from the classes of 1809 through 1812, and his army quickly swelled back to more than 450,000 men. True, many were untested in battle, and the officer ranks had been severely depleted during the Russian campaign, but with Napoleon leading them, he was certain of triumph—his overconfidence again leading him into an untenable situation. However, the one thing that Napoleon could not replace, and which would play a pivotal role in his eventual defeat, was the loss of more than 200,000 trained horses, greatly limiting both the effectiveness of his cavalry and his ability to reconnoiter enemy movement.

On the diplomatic side, Napoleon still had his alliance with Austria, sealed by his marriage to Marie-Louise, who had also borne his son. Surely Francis I would not declare war on his own daughter and grandson. Napoleon tried to strengthen his hand further by confirming Marie-Louise as Regent of France while he was on campaign, and also named his son as the official heir to the throne. Unfortunately, Charles Maurice de Talleyrand, a French diplomat and politician who had been a thorn in Napoleon's side for fifteen years, often working more for his own interests than the emperor's or cutting private deals with enemy leaders, was quietly mounting an opposition movement among the elite of Paris, intending to restore the Bourbon monarchy. Instead of a united Paris and a united France behind him, Napoleon's own country was divided, weak, and unable to support him to their fullest extent.

But the only way the Russians would be driven back was by combat, and after three months of reorganization, Napoleon had moved a total of 300,000 men into Germany when he personally led his new 85,000-man Army of the Main, along with the 60,000-man Army of the Elbe, led by his stepson, Prince Eugène, against his enemies to drive them out of Germany and Saxony in late April 1813.

For all of their recent success in harrying the French out of Russia, the czar's forces were in disarray. Field Marshal Kutúzov had died in March, and had been replaced by Count Wittgenstein, who realized that Napoleon was moving to take Leipzig and met his advance at Lützen on May 2nd. After an afternoon of bloody fighting that stretched into the night, the French won, although their casualties were high, losing 10,000 men to the Allies' 20,000. Napoleon had acquitted himself well in the battle, leading his men personally, as he had done years ago during his successful earlier campaigns. He was overjoyed at the victory, feeling that he was "again the Master of Europe." Unfortunately, this would not remain the case.

Napoleon's army marched into Dresden on May 8th, where he restored Frederick Augustus to the Saxon throne. The Allies reset their positions with 85,000 men on the upper Spree River at the town of Bautzen, 35 miles east of Dresden, leaving Berlin relatively undefended. Rather than march on the capital, Napoleon decided to try and defeat the army in one stroke, sending four corps to attack head on while Marshal Ney would cross the river upstream and cut off the Allies' retreat. Battle was joined on the morning of May 20th, and after two days of heavy fighting, the Grande Armée took Bautzen, although at a high cost, with at least 17,000 men lost. Also, the Allied army was allowed to leave when Ney's force was spotted while he approached their rear, but he did not engage them.

The battle was a victory for the French, but produced no real tactical advantage—Napoleon had not routed the enemy army, and now found himself in a precarious position deep in hostile territory, with little ammunition and large numbers of sick and wounded soldiers. The fighting had also come very close to the Austrian border, and that country was making aggressive overtures against France, Napoleon's marriage alliance notwithstanding. Also in June, the emperor received the news that his war against Spain was lost, with Joseph Bonaparte defeated by Wellington at Vitoria, practically insuring that the British would follow up with an invasion of France. Once again, Napoleon's ludicrous plan to carry out two separate wars on both sides of the continent came back to haunt him.

The only plus from the recent battles was that the Allied army was in a similar condition to Napoleon's, having lost roughly 40,000 men in the last two major battles, but a campaign of attrition worked against the French army more severely than its enemies. Both sides agreed to an armistice until August 17th, a break that also worked more to his enemies' advantage. Francis offered his foreign minister to try and mediate a solution to the conflict, which Napoleon agreed to, only finding out later that the plan was a sham, with the minister, Prince Clemens Lothar Wenceslas Metternich, requiring that Napoleon give up practically everything he had gained since becoming First Consul in 1799, reducing the empire to its boundary lines of 1798. Agreement would have meant the end of the empire, which Napoleon could not and would not accept. On August 12th, Austria declared war on France.

This was a serious problem for the emperor; not only did he lose one of his strongest allies, but Austria joining the war meant that Napoleon's front was now vulnerable from the south from an army marching through Bohemia. In fact, that was part of the Allies' plan, with a 230,000-strong Army of Bohemia, led by Field Marshal Carl Philipp Schwarzenberg, marching from Prague to attack from the south. At the same time, the 95,000-man Army of Silesia, led by Field Marshal Gebhard Lebrecht Blücher, would tie up the French right flank, and a third army, the 110,000-man Army of the North, commanded by former Marshal Jean-Baptiste Jules Bernadotte, Napoleon's timid brother-in-law who had become Crown Prince of Sweden, would both protect Berlin and menace the French garrisons near the lower Elbe. The total might of the Allies was 435,000 men, enough of an advantage to make the difference in the upcoming war. The overall strategy of the Allies was called the Trachtenberg Plan; it called for avoiding combat with forces led by Napoleon himself, and concentrating on his subordinates, who, as will be shown later, often did not fight effectively when given their own initiative.

Napoleon was in a good position when the actual campaign began. Most of his force of 375,000 men was concentrated behind the Elbe, and he had also fortified Dresden into a secure encampment to serve as an operational headquarters. The logical plan would have been to engage and crush the Army of Silesia with his superior numbers, then battle the Army of Bohemia as it came out of the mountain passes, dividing and conquering the overall force as he had done in previous campaigns. The younger Napoleon would have done just that, but the older one waited for the enemy to come to him—a decision that would ultimately lead to his defeat.

Napoleon also split his army into three groups—never a wise move when facing a superior force, unless the intended targets are fairly close together—sending 72,000 men, led by Marshal Charles Nicolas Oudinot, to capture Berlin, and another group of 102,000, under Marshal Etienne Jacques Macdonald, to engage Blücher's army. Unfortunately, the commanders of both armies were less than stellar leaders when given their own initiative, and both gambits failed. Oudinot marched to within 12 miles of his goal, but was pushed back by determined Prussian defenders, and retreated on August 23rd after losing 3,000 men and 23 guns. Macdonald fared far worse, being completely routed by Blücher on August 26th, losing 20,000 men and 103 guns. Not only had Napoleon reduced his main force by almost 175,000 men, but the two missions had failed utterly, wasting men, horses, and equipment he could not afford to lose.

At the same time, Schwarzenberg's large army, now outnumbering the French defenders, came out of the mountains and prepared to attack Dresden. On the 26th, he launched an initial attack against the city's defenses, but the assault wasn't coordinated among the various units, and they were repulsed. Napoleon took the offensive the next day, and inflicted considerable damage in a pitched fight, killing 38,000 of the enemy while losing only 10,000 men. The following day, however, the Allies followed the Trachtenberg Plan and retreated. If he had pursued, Napoleon might have been able to finish the Army of Bohemia, but he chose not to, squandering another opportunity to garner a desperately needed decisive victory.

The ill-chosen tactical blunders continued. On August 30th, 30,000 of Napoleon's men, led by General Dominique Vandamme, who had been ordered to march into Bohemia and attack Schwarzenberg's right flank, were trapped and destroyed, losing half of their force, their commander, who was captured, and all of their guns and equipment. The Trachtenberg Plan was succeeding; without direct orders from their emperor, his marshals were ineffective on their own, and could be fought and defeated.

Again Napoleon faced a difficult choice. With his green army depleted by the recent fighting and errors, he could either move against Prague or try to take Berlin. Prague posed many tactical and logistical problems; it was a fortified town, making prolonged fighting necessary, and it would stretch his supply lines very thin, meaning if the Allied armies broke them at any point, he would be cut off. On the other hand, Berlin held several advantages for him, not the least of which would be that Napoleon would be centrally placed and able to go to anywhere he would be most needed in five days. He would also be able to protect his front line from Hamburg to Dresden, and there was the additional bonus of plenty of food in the capital city.

This shift in tactical thinking, planning in terms of capturing cities instead of seeking out and crushing the enemy army, reveals a marked shift in Napoleon's military goals. Instead of aggressively moving to defeat the enemy forces, the emperor was now focused on taking and holding territory. The previous lessons of the wars he had waged—keep all forces concentrated, march in columns within mutual supporting distance, pursue the enemy relentlessly—had all been discarded. The bold, decisive Napoleon of past campaigns had been gradually replaced by a cautious, tentative commander, who would see opportunities for victory slip through his fingers again and again.

Ney, who had been promoted to lead Oudinot's forces, took on a Prussian army at the village of Dennewitz on September 6th, and fared no better than his counterparts. His force was completely routed, losing 24,000 men (to the Allies' 6,000 casualties) and 600 guns.

Aware that the momentum of the war was turning against him, and uncertain how to proceed, Napoleon did the worst thing possible under the circumstances—nothing. Throughout most of September, 1813, he waited and watched the enemy army, which was doing the same to him. Although he made plans for several offensives, he abandoned all of them as he came to the realization he faced the same situation that he had in Russia the previous year. Fall was coming, and with it would come Russian reinforcements. His army's morale, particularly that of his generals, was low, and food and supplies were lacking, especially in the region east of Dresden, where his forces were already subsisting on reduced rations. On top of it all, there was the constant threat of insurrection back in Paris. On September 17th, Napoleon took all of these factors into account and made plans to retreat to Leipzig. However, he did not leave, but instead stayed in Dresden, trying to raise his troops' morale, which was ebbing fast due to the lack of positive action.

At the same time, the Allies were doing exactly the opposite of Napoleon, preparing to mount their largest offensive of the war. Convinced the time had come to destroy the French army once and for all, Blücher persuaded the leaders of Russia, Prussia, and Austria to back his play. He would personally lead 65,000 men northwest, paralleling the Elbe River, cross near Wittenberg, then turn south to Leipzig. His right flank would be led by Bernadotte, who would cross the river near Dessau and move south, while the left part, led by Schwarzenberg, would form the other half of the pincer movement to trap the Grande Armée, and would advance on Leipzig from the southeast. It was a tactically sound plan, worthy of Napoleon himself, and its execution began on September 26th. Blücher crossed the Elbe on October 3rd and defeated Bertrand's men at Wartenburg. Bernadotte's army also crossed the river as planned, encountering no opposition. By early October, Schwarzenberg had also brought his 130,000 men across the Elbe. The pincer was forming around the Grande Armée.

Receiving some hint that the Allies were on the move, but unsure of their ultimate intent, Napoleon dispatched strong reconnaissance teams, and also ordered more fortifications to be constructed, too little, too late. Once again, his delays would cost him and the forces under his command dearly. By October 6th, Napoleon tried to concentrate his forces at Meissen, but realized too late that he was slowly but surely being surrounded. Although he made bold promises not to leave Dresden, by October 8th he had moved his headquarters to Wurzen, on the road to Leipzig. Harried and confused, he continued to retreat in the face of the closing Allied ring, ending up at a small village two miles north of Leipzig, where he would make his final stand.

The stage was now set for a winner-take-all battle, and the French army was in serious trouble before the fighting even began. Exhausted and hungry, the 190,000 men of the Grande Armée were hemmed into a low area by 300,000 Allied troops. Of the seven roads around the city, six were held by the Allies, with only one route to the south still open, crossing a marsh by way of a single stone bridge.

The Battle of the Nations began on the cold, rainy day of October 16th, with the Allies pressing from the south and the north. Of paramount importance was the exit to the southwest, which was heavily guarded by the French. The fighting raged back and forth all day, ending in a draw, with casualties reaching 20,000 men on both sides. The next day, Napoleon sent a courier with a request to discuss peace terms, but it went unanswered by the Allies, who were in no mood to give the dictator any quarter. However, they were also in no hurry to resume the fight, as 100,000 reinforcements were approaching, 40,000 fresh Russian soldiers, and the ever-hesitant Bernadotte was finally deploying his 60,000 men to the northeast, further strengthening the ring around the French army.

Fighting resumed on the 18th, and was just as bloody. The sheer weight of the Allied army, now numbering almost 400,000 men, forced Napoleon's army of 170,000 to slowly give ground, retreating into the outskirts of Leipzig by the end of the day. Casualties were heavy again, with each side losing about 25,000 men. That evening, Napoleon accepted the futility of his position. He might have been able to defeat the various Allied armies had he engaged them separately, but against their combined mass, there could only be one outcome. That night—the first anniversary of his retreat from Moscow—he ordered a general evacuation to the southwest.

However, this time there would be no brilliant retreat plan as in Russia. The Allies swarmed in, with the French rear guard holding them off while the withdrawal began. The lone road to the bridge across the marsh was crowded with men, horses, supply wagons, and what was left of the artillery, all of them harassed by former German allies. However, at 1:00 p.m., a corporal destroyed the bridge prematurely, trapping four corps on the far side of the marsh. In the ensuing confusion, Prince Josef Anton Poniatowski of Poland, one of Napoleon's staunchest allies, having just been promoted to Marshal of France two days earlier, drowned, and 33,000 men and 260 guns were captured by the Allies. If Schwarzenberg had moved more troops to the area, he would have captured Napoleon and his entire army in one fell swoop. As it was, Napoleon left Germany relatively unopposed, fighting only one more battle against 40,000 Bavarian troops, which he blasted apart with artillery. Upon reaching Mainz on November 2nd, he left three corps as a rear guard, and left for Paris on the 7th.

On November 8th, the Allies proposed an armistice that would reduce France to the natural borders of the Alps and the Rhine River in exchange for peace. This would greatly strengthen Czar Alexander's foothold in Europe—he had already established himself as king of Poland, and he wouldn't give that up without a hard fight, and had cemented a firm alliance with the king of Prussia, to whom he had promised all of Saxony. He even had a plan to install a puppet ruler on the French throne, allowing him a foothold to bring more of Europe under his control. Obviously, Napoleon could not accept such an offer, and the Allies drew up plans to invade France on December 1st.

Now Napoleon was in true dire straits, faced with defending his homeland against a unified army of his enemies, and having returned with only 56,000 beaten and exhausted men. He was still fighting a war on two fronts, as 100,000 men were still struggling against Wellington's British army in Gascony. Another 100,000 troops had been left to man garrisons in Germany, which were now coming under siege by the Allies. The invading enemy army would number at least 400,000, although it would be some months before they could be properly organized and dispatched. However, Schwarzenberg was already leading his army of 210,000 across the Rhine in late December, following up Blücher's force of 110,000. Bernadotte's army of 100,000 would come to France through the Netherlands, but late enough not to make much difference.

Napoleon used the time he had to its fullest advantage. He rounded up every able-bodied soldier he could find, from the regimental depots to the cadet class of 1815, and fielded an army of 120,000 by January, 1814, with 12,000 cavalry. However, the public and governmental pressure against yet another war was growing; the treasury was empty, and the legislature was reluctant to throw more funds into another bloody, depleting conflict. The French citizens were sick of the fighting as well, and after having squandered their support on the Russian campaign, Napoleon had to exert all of his charisma and skill to convince them to continue the struggle, even for their homeland.

Yet if his countrymen were finding it difficult to rouse themselves, Napoleon himself was another matter. With his army outnumbered three-to-one, he knew the only viable strategy would be to divide and conquer, taking on and defeating each army by itself. Not only was he fighting for his country, but for his very political life, and the master tactician in him reawakened. On January 25th, he left Paris to take command of his troops personally.

The Allied army had not been idle either. Schwarzenberg had taken advantage of the nonexistent French defenses, and had penetrated as far as Chaumont, Langres, and Châtillion-sur-Seine, with the scant resistance melting away before his advance. The first real encounter between the two sides occurred on February 1st, when Blücher and Schwarzenberg's armies, which had joined together, defeated Napoleon's forces at Brienne-le-Château, each side losing about 5,000 men. Perhaps made overconfident by their victory and numbers, the two commanders then separated; Blücher was to march directly for Paris to the northwest, while Schwarzenberg would march west to the Seine valley, and then on to the capital.

It was exactly the chance Napoleon had hoped for, and he took full advantage of it. Assessing Blücher's army as the more immediate threat, he struck at it first, and from February 10th–14th, dealt the Prussian general four successive defeats, showing the mastery of tactics and logistics that had made him the preeminent military mind of the age. Blücher's corps were poorly organized and strung out along their advance route, and Napoleon fell upon the piecemeal units and destroyed them in a series of brilliantly executed movements. It would be the last successful series of battles in his career.

However, in the south, things weren't going as well. Napoleon had assigned 32,000 men, under Oudinot and Marshal Claude Victor, to defend the Rhine crossings against Schwarzenberg's army. But a column of the enemy had driven Victor's men off the bridge at Bray-sur-Seine, leaving the road open to Paris. Again, Napoleon had to take command himself to save the situation, traveling to the area and turning back the enemy advance on February 17th and 18th. Flush with his series of victories and thinking he had his enemies on the run, Napoleon turned down a request to discuss peace terms with Schwarzenberg, against the advice of his foreign ambassadors. He ignored the fact that his army was exhausted, and that at each battle he had been forced to commit his Imperial Guard, with the attendant casualties and wear. If he had had an army as large as the ones under his command even two years earlier, he could have afforded to whittle away his enemies until he could rout them decisively. But now, time worked against him.

The Allies received fresh reinforcements, and Blücher pushed toward Paris again by way of a roundabout withdrawal and approach from the north. He and his army of 100,000 escaped a confrontation with Napoleon by blowing up a bridge across the Marne at La Ferté, delaying the French army for 36 hours. He continued withdrawing north, apparently to draw Napoleon away from the capital and leave the way open for the southern army. At Laon, a town with an excellent elevated position that dominates the surrounding countryside, Blücher dug in and waited for his foe. He concentrated his main force at the Chemin des Dames, a large ridge that runs parallel to the Aisne River. The French attacked there in force on March 7th, with Ney's men coming up the middle in a frontal assault against Blücher's attached Russian troops. Fighting was fierce all day, and Napoleon again had to commit his Guard and their artillery to force the enemy off the ridge, but all they did was fall back to an equally defended position at Laon itself. Each side suffered the loss of 7,000 men, and again Napoleon failed to secure victory.

The next day, Napoleon marched on Laon, hoping to defeat Blücher's army once and for all. Unfortunately, he now made the same mistake his enemies had; he divided his army into two groups to attack from both sides. The two wings could not communicate with each other, as the land between them was held by Cossack patrols.

Both actions met with failure. Ney's right force was held up even before they could commit to their attack on Laon, while Marmont's forces were completely routed in a night assault by the enemy, losing 2,500 men and 45 guns. Napoleon's army was coming apart around him. Also, he received word from the south that Schwarzenberg was on the move again, had beaten Oudinot and Macdonald, and was threatening Paris. Again he was forced to leave one front and rush to the second, where he stopped an advancing Russian corps near Reims on March 13th, but at last, the impossibility of his position sank in. He sent word to his brother Joseph in Paris to make plans to evacuate his wife, the current Regent of France, Marie-Louise, and his son, writing a chilling, pointed message: "I would rather see my son drowned in the Seine than fall into the enemy's hands."

With everything falling apart, the emperor decided on one last gamble, to march south and attack Schwarzenberg's right flank, hoping to disrupt his men and command, much as he had done to Blücher in February. Leaving token forces to harass Blücher, on March 20th he and 21,000 men met the enemy force of 20,000 at Plancy, on the Aube River. The Austrians held their ground, however, and Napoleon was forced to withdraw after losing 4,000 men.

Now the Allies seized their own opportunity; with Napoleon's army divided, the time was right to seize Paris. They immediately marched toward the capital. When Napoleon found out about this, he devised a crazy plan to march east, between the two armies, in hopes of cutting the lines of communication, and drive Schwarzenberg back to the Rhine. The only problem with this was that Marmont and Mortier would be left to defend Paris with 17,000 men, facing Blücher's army of 100,000. Napoleon wrote of his plan to his wife, and the letter was intercepted by the Allies, who continued their dash to Paris. Schwarzenberg's forces met the French defense on March 25th and routed them, killing 9,000 men and capturing 50 guns, while Blücher's force approached from the northeast completely unopposed.

The invading army at the gates of Paris threw the city into a paroxysm of fear. The populace, terrified that the invaders would exact revenge for past wrongs, such as the burning of Moscow, packed up and fled. Joseph had overseen Marie-Louise and Napoleon's son's evacuation on March 29th over her protests, as she thought she could rally the citizens to resist the invasion if she stayed. Napoleon had also left orders that no one was to remain in the city to negotiate with the enemy, but was undone again by Talleyrand, who had been plotting with the Allies to remove the emperor from power, and brokered a deal to allow the enemy into Paris. When Czar Alexander entered the city, he was a guest at Talleyrand's home. On March 30th, Marmont, with no troops left to mount any kind of defense, surrendered to the Allies.

When Napoleon learned what had happened, he realized the critical mistake he had made by leaving Paris so thinly guarded. A forced march through the night brought him to within twelve miles of the capital, where he learned that the city had been officially handed over by his brother Joseph, just a few hours before Napoleon would have arrived at the gates.

Crushed by the news, Napoleon retreated to Fontainebleau, where he planned to take his remaining 60,000 men, including 9,000 of his exhausted Guard, and march on Paris. But at last, his commanders had had enough. His advisor Caulaincourt and his marshals, including Ney, Berthier, Oudinot, Macdonald, Moncey, and Lefebvre, all refused to follow his orders, pointing out that all it would accomplish was a terrible loss of life that France could ill afford. Napoleon might have rallied his troops, for the soldiers still adored him, but he let the calmer heads among his army persuade him to stand down. The revolt of the marshals was the final blow to Napoleon's plan; on April 4th, he abdicated the French throne in favor of his son and Marie-Louise as Regent.

This however never came to pass. Talleyrand had persuaded Marmont to abandon Napoleon, and bring his 11,000 men with him. (His soldiers were not happy to learn they had involuntarily switched sides, but there was nothing they could do about it.) With this treachery accomplished, the Allies' position was strengthened even further, and they called for his unconditional abdication; there would be no Napoleon or his progeny on the throne again. Only banishment awaited him now.

Many of the same faults that plagued Napoleon in Russia came back to haunt him during his defense of France. He had never trained his marshals to operate independently of him, and when he did not personally oversee the battles, they often went very badly. Also, given the destruction of his army in 1812, he was forced to fight a war with inexperienced troops, which can only do so much, even with one of the greatest commanders in history leading them. Also, he never had enough men to adequately challenge the Allied army, and was reduced to fighting a series of increasingly desperate holding actions as their superior forces ground his army to pieces. Add to this the dissipating support of the French government and its citizens, who were perfectly willing to cheer his victories, but less willing to slog along with him to his defeat, and a major aspect of what is needed to win a war, the support and will of the people, was lost. Finally, Napoleon could not adapt his strategy to the Allies' Trachtenberg Plan, which called for their avoidance of him to take on and defeat his marshals instead, slowly weakening his army by degrees, and forcing its inevitable defeat.

It would seem that Napoleon had gambled for the last time. Removed from the throne and shunned by his own government, an ignominious exile and death were all that awaited him at Elba. But the master of war had one more trick up his sleeve, and was prepared to bet everything he had—his allies, his country, his family, in one last desperate bid to regain control of France. But fate would have one, last defeat in store for him—at a place that has grown synonymous with the term "epic defeat"—Waterloo.

LOSING BIG

What follows are wars whose loss changed the course of history and so made our world what it is today. Wars that should have been won by one side, but weren't. Wars that everyone knew the outcome of and where everyone was wrong. These span history, showing once more that incompetent leadership and bad decisions have been part of warfare since our ancestors were using stone axes. In a few cases you will be surprised at how close victories we take for granted today were to being defeats. The success of the allies in WWII, as you will see, was not even slightly inevitable. Many of the conflicts in recent history, were in reality far from foregone conclusions with just the change of one attitude, policy, or procedure making all the difference. So enjoy the combination of why and what might have been.

*Determining what went wrong, and things went very wrong,
for Athens in the fifth century B.C. is like unraveling a very
complicated mystery. The simple fact is that the real problem
was the multitude of bad choices made. Even in short form,
the history of the twenty-seven-year war that ended with
Athens prostrate and defeated is convoluted and full of
misguided plans. You almost lose count of the amazing
number of war-winning plans that came to nothing; ranging
from starting strategies that were fatally flawed on both sides
to final defeat caused more by hubris than any military factor.*

BEWARE OF GREEKS

The Peloponnesian Wars, Greece, 431 B.C.

WILLIAM TERDOSLAVICH

War is easy to start, but harder to end.

This lesson was hard for Athens and Sparta to learn, as they
fought each other to a bloody standoff for much of the Peloponnesian Wars, lasting twenty-seven years. It was a war between equal
unequals. Sparta had the best army in Greece. Athens had the best
and largest navy.

Sparta feared the growth of Athenian power, and for good reason. Athens controlled about 150 city-states in its "Delian League,"
a dues-paying alliance used to finance the Athenian navy. Its original purpose was to forestall another Persian invasion. Athens
fought Persia in 490 B.C., and the Greek city-states banded together
a decade later to stop another Persian invasion. The Persian threat
hardly existed in 431 B.C. as the rich and prosperous empire had no

interest in the relatively poor and hard to conquer Greek cities, but the Athenians did not see that as a reason to disband the Delian League. Athens could not afford to let any member slip the alliance, which would deprive it of tax revenue and undermine the perception of Athenian power. Any city or island that tried to quit got an unwelcome visit from the Athenian navy.

Sparta controlled about 50 city-states in its alliance network. Among them were willing allies like Corinth (second largest navy) and Boeotia (second best army), which bordered Athens and did not want to succumb to an "alliance" with their neighbor. Sparta feared a day would come when Athens would rule Greece at the expense of all, hence the Spartan war aim of "Freedom for the Greeks"—an odd goal for a military police state that kept tens of thousands of Greeks enslaved to feed its small corps of fulltime soldiers.

Why They Fought

War between Athens and Sparta was a question of when, not if.

A fifteen-year war between the two ended inconclusively in 445 B.C. Now the smaller allies of each would drag the two powers to war again. Athenian friction with Corinth heightened tensions. An Athenian embargo against neighboring Spartan ally Megara made things worse. Corcyra (modern Corfu), possessing the third largest navy, sided with Athens against Corinth. Finally, the city-state of Potidaea in northeastern Greece rebelled against the Athenian alliance, siding with Sparta.

As leader of an alliance, Sparta had to lend weight to its allies in their grievances with Athens. Repeated negotiations finally boiled the problem down to a single Spartan ultimatum, perhaps trivial—remove the embargo against Megara, or else. Pericles, the elected first-among-equals in Athens, decided to draw the line right there and rejected Sparta's final threat.

It was 431 B.C..

The war was on.

No one expected the war to drag on for twenty-seven years.

Sparta and Athens would spend the next three decades fighting for
influence over the allies. They were the poker chips of political
power, changing hands by force, adding tax revenue to the winner and taking it away from the loser. Both sides searched for the
strategy that could deliver the quick knockout blow, never finding
it. Victory and defeat were hard to see until the very end. Sparta
did what Sparta always had done—muster its army and invade the
enemy country. By now there were only 4,000 to 5,000 fulltime
soldiers (Spartiates, or Equals) to serve in the line, down from the
8,000 to 9,000 that had marched against Persian invasion in 480–
79 B.C. Sparta could form the unbreakable core of any Greek army,
sure to win any land battle. Heading an army of allies numbering
about 20,000, Spartan king Archidamus II invaded Attica. This hostile horde ravaged the countryside, burned crops, and desecrated
family altars and hearths. In Ancient Greece, these actions were
louder than fighting words. They were sure that Athens must send
out its army to avenge these insults to its honor, to decide the issue in a single day of fair face-to-face battle on a suitable patch of
open ground, to win or lose the war in one fighting day.

But that did not happen.

The farmers sought safety behind Athens' walls.

The Athenian army did nothing.

Why?

Pericles crafted a strategy that played more to Athenian strengths
than Spartan expectations. At war's beginning, Athens could field
an army of 15,000 to 20,000 hoplites. These were pretty good
part-time soldiers, but clearly no match for the Spartans. Pericles
relied instead on three advantages unique to Athens.

First, the city had extended twin walls about seven miles to its
port of Piraeus. Through this impregnable corridor Athens funneled
the food imports that made up for the loss of local crops. Second,
Athens had the best and largest fleet. They were able to secure the
coastal sea lanes from Piraeus to the Black Sea, thus protecting the
grain trade that ran through the straits of the Hellespont to what is
now southern Russia. The third advantage was financial. Athens had
about 6,600 talents in silver and gold in its treasury and enjoyed

an income of 1,000 talents of silver per year. A large treasury paid for a large fleet, given that it took one talent per month to keep a single warship afloat, and Athens managed for much of the war to keep its fleet between 200 and 300 warships. This pile of money was the true foundation of Athenian power, all of it amassed from trade and dues paid to the Delian League. So long as no member of the league changed sides, Athens was financially secure and politically powerful.

Pericles' defensive strategy was a radical departure from the Greek way of war, but his goal was simple: convince the Spartans that Athens was unbeatable, so why fight it?

To some degree, Sparta played sucker to Athenian cleverness.

Every year, Archidamus II led a Spartan/Allied army into Attica to ravage the countryside.

Every year, the Athenians sat tight and did nothing.

The technique of siege warfare was not advanced enough for Sparta to take fortified Athens. And it lacked a navy good enough to defeat the Athenians.

Pericles understood the mechanics of his strategy. To sell it required the politics of persuasion, best done as an appeal to patriotism. For it is the will to fight, not just the means to fight, that propels a nation through a war. The public funeral for those who were first to die in the fighting was the stage for Pericles' Funeral Oration, delivered toward the end of the war's first year.

Athens was worth fighting for because it was so special, he explained. "Let me say that our system of government does not copy the institutions of our neighbors. It is more the case of our being a model to others, than of imitating anyone else. Our constitution is called a democracy because power is not in the hands of a minority but of the whole people. When it is a question of settling private disputes, everyone is equal before the law; when it is a question of putting one person before another in positions of public responsibility, what counts is not membership of a particular class, but the actual ability which the man possesses. No one, so long as he has it in him to be of service to the state, is kept in political obscurity because of poverty. . . . We are free and tolerant in our private lives; but in public affairs we keep to the law. This is because it commands our deep respect."

Pericles reminded the Athenians that their city was "open to the world," without the need to keep military secrets because its secret weapon was the loyalty and courage of its citizens. He noted that the Spartans used hardship to train their soldiers while the Athenians did without the training and were just as ready to face the same dangers. Debate only strengthened courage, Pericles reasoned, as the Athenians always knew what they were getting into, while others began to fear when they began to think. Each Athenian "was the rightful lord and owner of his own person," and ruled their own lives with "exceptional grace and versatility." These qualities found among the people made Athens powerful in the present, he stressed. "This, then, is the kind of city for which these men, who could not bear the thought of losing her, nobly fought and nobly died. It is only natural that every one of us who survive them should be willing to undergo hardship in her service."

Pericles had no idea how bad, or how long, these hardships would be—or that he would soon die and not be available to lead. His speech foreshadowed how well the Athenians would bear the burdens of war, but not how they would fight it.

Battle on Land and Sea

The Greek way of war was based on getting the fight over with in a hurry, as most soldiers were also farmers and needed to get home in time for the harvest. The preference was for a fairly fought battle on a patch of open ground. Heavy infantrymen—the ones who would stand in the main line—were men of means who had to provide their own armor, shield, and spear. They were called hoplites, taking their name from the large, round shield they carried, a *hoplon*.

Hoplites lined up eight ranks deep in a formation called a phalanx. Each one held his shield in his left hand, providing cover for his buddy on his left. (Hoplite lines would drift to the right during battle as each soldier sought cover behind the shield on his right.) In his right hand he grasped his eight-foot-long thrusting spear. The first two or three ranks could bring spears to bear against the enemy. The remaining rankers pushed their shields into the backs of those in front of them. Battle between two phalanxes started as a shoving match, with few wounded or killed. One side would eventually break, and in fleeing, be killed by their pursuers.

Full-time soldiers were the rule in Sparta, a militaristic society that used its small, elite army to maintain a reign of terror over a massive slave population that outnumbered them twenty to one. The enslaved farmers grew the food that fed the warriors, who pursued no trade but soldiering. Those Athenians who were richer than hoplites served in the cavalry, providing their own horses. Greece was mountainous, with few plains or pastures, so horses were never many and always expensive. Poorer men who could not afford hoplite gear became light infantry, armed with javelins or slings. They would pelt the enemy from a distance and withdraw to avoid close-in fighting. Lacking armor and spears, they would have been chopped up easily in a face-to-face fight against heavy infantry.

In much of Greece, each citizen purchased his own arms. But in Athens in particular, the poorest of the poor, known as *thetes*, went to war with nothing more than a seat cushion and an oar. They were the foundation of the navy, rowing the trireme, a sleek and narrow galley with three banks of oars, requiring a crew of about 200, of which 170 were rowers. It weighed about 25 tons, was about 125 feet long and 13 feet wide at the hull (18 feet wide when measuring the outrigger for the top bank of oars), built low to the water to allow easy reach by the 14-foot oars. Like the merchant ships of the day, triremes usually did not sail beyond sight of land and didn't handle well in stormy seas. They had to land every night to allow the crew to eat and sleep. These wooden warships could travel about 50 miles a day, given these constraints. They also had to be taken out of water periodically to clean and repair the hulls.

The bow of a trireme sloped downward and forward into the water, ending in a stout ram below the water line. This was the trireme's main weapon. It took a well-trained crew to row the ship, as anyone who was out of synch with the stroking rhythm could immobilize the vessel. Tactics were limited to line abreast (*periplus*), where the goal was to outflank the enemy, or line ahead (*diekplus*), to sheer off the oars of the enemy ship and punch a hole in his fleet's line. In restricted waters, maneuver became useless. Ships would then grapple enemy vessels and send boarders over to fight on deck. Boarding was the preferred tactic of those lesser navies that could not match Athenian seamanship. Almost always in open water, an Athenian fleet would outmaneuver its enemy with well-practiced ease.

The limitations of armies and navies, once coupled with geography, played a strong role in dictating strategy for Athens and Sparta. Much of the Peloponnesus—the peninsula south of Corinth—was aligned with Sparta. Corinth sat on the narrow neck of land connecting the Peloponnesus to Greece, which along with nearby Megara maintained the land link to Boeotia, a broad, flat land north of Attica containing an alliance of ten cities, led by Thebes. Sparta and its allies had to keep this land bridge open so that troops could transit, unthreatened by the Athenian navy, as well as to invade Attica itself.

For Athens, naval control of coastal Greece going to the northwest and northeast was vital. Uninterrupted stretches of coastal waters leading back to Attica made up the trade routes that kept Athens fed with grain imports and financed through trade. Any coastal city that defected to Sparta gave it the naval base needed to cut those links, as well as deprive the Athenian navy of needed bases. The coast of northwestern Greece led to Corcyra (Corfu), the jumping-off point for naval fleets and merchant ships bound for Greek cities in southern Italy and Sicily. Northeastern Greece led to the Hellespont, the narrow waterway connecting the Greek-controlled Aegean with the Black Sea, where Athens traded olive oil for wheat to feed its people. Many Greek-populated islands and cities dotted what is now the Turkish west coast, with many paying dues to the Delian League. Athens needed to control these cities and islands for income.

The First Moves

Athens dispatched 70 triremes and 3,500 hoplites to Potidea to besiege the recalcitrant city. The only way this could be done was by blockade. The fleet kept cargo from coming in. The army surrounded the city with a wall to make sure no food was brought in and no people came out. Eventually the people would starve and submit. But the blockading forces have to be supplied and paid for the blockade to have an effect. It took two years to take Potidaea. Athens spent 2,000 talents to accomplish this, and it blew a hole in the budget far beyond expectations. The Periclean strategy was to be easily financed for three years from an existing pool of wealth and income totaling about 6,600 talents. This still not touching an emergency reserve of 1,000 talents. But that would be the case only if there were no more sieges like Potidaea.

Athens guaranteed its naval superiority shortly after the war's start when its admiral Phormio, though gravely outnumbered, bested Corinthian and Spartan naval squadrons in the Gulf of Corinth. The Athenian triremes literally rowed rings around their enemies.

But this time the enemy that changed Pericles' plan was not the Spartans. Unbeatable at sea and avoiding combat on land, Athens was invulnerable to all, but could not defend against a far humbler enemy: germs. As the result of overcrowding plague broke out in Athens in 430–29 B.C., carrying away a big chunk of the population, Pericles included. From this time on, Athens would be constrained from fielding large armies and fleets. By the third year of the war, Athens' loss of military-aged citizens, coupled with the expense of retaking Potidea, constrained them for most larger military operations.

New Leaders, New Strategies

It was inevitable that once new leaders replaced Pericles, new strategies would follow. There rose a feeling that something had to be better than watching the annual Spartan invasion, or going broke waiting for the Spartans to give up. Athens' strategy had to include keeping its allied cities in the fold while Sparta tried to suborn or conquer them, thus threatening the trade routes. Without them the lone city would quickly go broke. One plan was for Athens to use its fleet to take the war to the underdefended Spartan coast.

Primary among those who came after Pericles in the 420s were the hotheaded demagogue Cleon and the more sober-minded Nicias. Cleon wanted to police the alliances harshly by wiping out those smaller cities who had defected. Nicias came to the fore later in the 420s, when it came time to broker a temporary peace with Sparta, and was more moderate.

The 420s saw Athens dispatching warships to Lesbos to keep the island from changing sides, taking its main city, Mitylene, by siege. Cleon wanted to put the population to the sword to set an example that no one messes with Athens. He was outvoted in the assembly, and word of the change barely got to Mitylene in time, just as the general on the scene was preparing to kill everyone. (Compare this to Potidaea, where the population was allowed to leave the city once it surrendered.)

The Athenian budget saw its reserves dwindle to about 1,000 talents. Athens upped its dues for the "members" of the Delian League, not too subtly sending twelve warships out to collect the money. It also directly taxed its own citizens, a rare event, to cough up another two hundred talents.

Another modest force of twenty triremes was dispatched to Sicily to aid an ally and increase Athenian influence on the island, a venture which failed to achieve its goal. Sparta was also busy probing Athenian allies throughout the region, looking to foment changes in government—and alliances—but their intrigues also came to naught.

In 425 B.C., Athens took the war to Sparta. A relief force of forty triremes, bound for Sicily, doubled back when it got word that the twenty-ship force there had accomplished nothing. Demosthenes persuaded his co-commanders that they land at Pylos, a small island off Sparta's shore, and build a fort. Five ships and a small garrison were left behind. The Athenian presence at Pylos enticed

Spartan slaves to escape. This was a serious threat to Sparta's very existence. Without enough slave farmers, Sparta's full-time soldier-citizens would starve.

Sparta could not let the Athenians stay on Pylos. They dispatched 420 troops, all heavy infantry, to build their own fort on Sphacteria, a small island just south of Pylos. The plan was to shuttle them over, fresh after a short trip, and defeat the Athenians left behind. This became moot when the Spartans next lost a naval battle to a returning Athenian war fleet. Now the Spartan garrison was stranded on Sphacteria and could not afford to lose 420 of its best hoplites. Sparta offered peace terms, but these were rejected by the Athenians, since Sparta would not recognize the futility of fighting Athens.

Cleon commanded the Athenian reinforcements to take Sphacteria, after losing a dare in the Assembly from Nicias to "put up or shut up." He was assisted by co-commander Demosthenes. The relief force would reinforce Demosthenes' tiny garrison with 800 hoplites, 800 archers, 2,000 light infantry and 8,000 lightly armed rowers. Upon reaching Sphacteria, the Athenians used their light infantry to fight not mano a mano in a tight formation, but in a manner that was considered unfair under the formal standards of Greek warfare, pelting the Spartan hoplites with arrows and javelins from the high ground as they faced the Athenian hoplites. The armored Spartans took hits. Unable to close with their tormentors, they retreated to their fort, only to find themselves cut off by still more light troops. With 120 dead and the rest starving for lack of supplies, the remaining Spartans surrendered.

Surrendered?

In 480 B.C., a force of 300 Spartans fought and died to the last man to stop the Persians from advancing through the pass at Thermopylae.

Now Spartans were surrendering to a bunch of low-life light infantry?

Unthinkable!

Shameful!

What happened to "come home with your shield or on it"?

Were those just empty words?

Some slogan!

The destruction of the myth of Spartan hoplite invincibility was much more significant and far outweighed in importance both the loss of the city and the casualties incurred. Many of the captives were from Sparta's best families, and together represented about ten percent of the Spartan battle line. Sparta could not afford to lose these men, and the Athenians knew it. Back to Athens the prisoners were sent, with the threat of death hanging over them if Sparta did not come to terms.

By now, Athens had antagonized just about every one of the major states that opposed it. While holding Spartan hostages forced a separate peace with Sparta, this peace only separated the Peloponnesian superpower from its alliance with Megara, Corinth, and Boeotia. Those places remained at war with Athens, knowing that, had they surrendered, they would inevitably become little more than vassal states.

So the war went on and Athens next decided that taking Megara would cut off Boeotia from the rest of the Peloponnese, split its opponents, and finally win the war. Athens was intrigued with the democratic faction in Megara and sent a 5,000-man force to pressure the city and exploit any change in government. They were thwarted by Spartan General Brasidas, who was nearby with a mixed force of 6,000, including 2,200 Theban hoplites and 600 cavalry. The Athenians declined battle. The pro-Athenian Megarians were found and killed. The venture came to naught. Another chance to win the entire war was lost.

Swinging north in 424 B.C., Athens sent a large army of 17,000, of which 7,000 were Athenian hoplites, into Boeotia. This army was experienced and well-practiced. The Athenians once more saw a chance to end the war successfully by knocking out one of its main enemies. Unfortunately for Athens, this was not to be the case. Boeotia had the second-best army in Greece. For good reason: the lands around Boeotia were known as "the dance floor of war" to the Greeks. Its broad plains provided many places to have a good fight and many wars had been settled there. This meant that the Athenians were facing a tough opponent on home ground that ideally suited their hoplite armies to the disadvantage of the light infantry. The Boeotian confederation, led by Thebes, fielded an army that had no trouble trouncing the Athenians at Delium, throwing them into a panic when a small squadron of Theban cavalry appeared behind their hoplite line. The philosopher Socrates was nearly killed fleeing this battle.

Now Amphipolis in northeastern Greece decided to buck the Delian League, bolting for Sparta in 424 B.C. Athens dispatched another fleet and army to take care of the defecting ally, but the Athenian general Thucydides was outsmarted by the locals and failed to retake the city. For this he was cashiered from service. With his career in ruins, Thucydides turned his attention to writing a history of the war he was in, explaining the worst catastrophe ever suffered by the Greeks. "My work is not a piece of writing designed to meet the taste of an immediate public, but was done to last forever." It has, so far, and is considered one of the great classics of military history. Writing this with his pen, Thucydides accomplished more than he ever did with his spear.

The ubiquitous Brasidas led a small force of freed Spartan serfs and lesser citizens to assist Amphipolis. This was a force Sparta wanted to station as far as possible from Sparta lest the other serfs get uppity. Cleon led the Athenian reinforcements. Both leaders fell in battle as Athens recovered Amphipolis. This was their only victory after two major defeats. With both of her recent forays against Sparta's allies unsuccessful, the Athenian mood shifted to peace.

With strategic stalemate and Spartan hostages providing an incentive for both sides, Nicias proposed to end the war in 421 B.C. with all alliances and deployments in their present positions. The Spartan hostages would be exchanged with any Athenian prisoners. Sparta and Athens would enter into a fifty-year alliance. Both sides were exhausted, running out of money, and had suffered serious losses. So it was agreed.

Just because Athens and Sparta could not fight each other did not prohibit either side from scheming. Corinth tried to forge a stand-alone alliance against Athens, but with Sparta out of the game, the intrigue got no takers. Athens did see an opportunity to undermine Sparta indirectly, as a peace treaty between Sparta and Argos was due to expire. Argos was one of the few democracies in the Peloponnesus. Athens sent Alcibiades, who concocted the plan, with a small force to aid their new ally.

In 418 B.C., young Spartan King Agis led a large allied army centered on Spartan Hoplites against Argos. The two armies clashed at Mantinea, where 9,000 Peloponnesian hoplites (including the entire Spartan army) defeated the 8,000 hoplites fielded by Argos, its allies, and Athens. Even then, the formalities were observed as the Spartans wisely chose not to directly fight the 1,000-strong Athenian contingent in order to preserve the peace. The major outcome from the battle was restoration of Sparta's military reputation after the humiliation at Sphacteria.

Athens was not at war with Sparta, but still had to police the Delian League. Melos, a Spartan colony that chose neutrality in the war, refused to join. In 425 B.C. the Melians had fought off Athens. Seven years later Athens sent 30 triremes, 1,200 hoplites, and 300 archers to pay an unfriendly visit to Melos, which could only muster eight warships and 1,500 hoplites in its defense. The Athenians tried to use reason to persuade the Melians to surrender, which Thucydides wrote down as "The Melian Dialogue" and which the quotes are taken from.

Here the Athenians would lay out the cold logic of raw power, quite at variance with the city's admirable virtues outlined by Pericles in his Funeral Oration. Tiny Melos threatened Athenian power because its non-alignment would incite other islands and cities to quit the Delian League, and in turn weaken Athenian power. This hazard was greater than risking conquest by Sparta, the Athenians explained. Submitting to Athenian power would spare the lives of the Melians. "If we surrender, then all our hope is lost at once, whereas so long as we remain in action, there is still a hope that we may stand upright," the Melians replied, noting that their ties with Sparta would compel it to aid Melos for honor's sake. Pointing to their command of the sea, the Athenians considered it unlikely that Sparta could save Melos from defeat.

"Our opinion of the gods and our knowledge of men lead us to conclude that it is a general and necessary law of nature to rule whatever one can," the Athenians replied. "That is not a law we made ourselves, nor were we the first to act upon it when it was made. We found it already in existence, and we will leave it to exist forever among those who come after us. We are merely acting in accordance with it, and we know that you or anybody else with the same power as ours would be acting in precisely the same way."

The Melians refused to see Athenian reason and resisted. The Athenians blockaded Melos, eventually forcing it to surrender. This time the Athenian Assembly voted to have all the men killed and all the women and children sold into slavery. The mercy that spared civilians in previous sieges was now gone.

Athens Agonistes

While the peace wore on, Athens continued its search for a strategy that would eclipse Spartan power in one stroke.

Alcibiades, who emerged at this time as the most ambitious and self-serving Athenian, pitched a strategy to conquer Sicily. Syracuse, the island's main city, was equal in size to Athens and possessed a good, if smallish, army and war fleet. Sicily was populous, could provide allies, major tax revenues, and grain exports. Alcibiades urged Athenians to boldly go forth to conquer Sicily, as this would make Athens the master of Greece and avoid slow rot from mounting a passive defense. Nicias counseled caution. Sicily was cowed from joining Sparta so long as Athens remained powerful, but invading Sicily and failing would put the island squarely on Sparta's side, he warned, perhaps breaking Athenian strength for good.

It just looked too risky.

Once Alcibiades swayed sentiment to favor the expedition, proposing to use about 60 warships and several thousand infantry,

Nicias thought he could kill the proposal by upping the ante to 100 triremes, 5,000 hoplites, and a similar number of light infantry. The Assembly agreed, much to Nicias' chagrin. Worse, no one proposed attaching sufficient cavalry to the small army to protect its flanks in the expected battles. Nicias, Alcibiades, and Lamachus, another experienced general, were appointed as leaders of the Sicilian Expedition.

Shortly before the war fleet put to sea in 415 B.C., sacrilege struck Athens. In the dead of night, vandals desecrated the Hermae, little statues of the Greek god Hermes that stood like little lawn gnomes by each Athenian doorway. To the religious and superstitious Athenians, this was not propitious.

Athens mustered 134 war galleys, 60 of which were Athenian; another 5,100 hoplites (1,500 Athenian); 1,300 light troops, 700 rowers serving as marines, and only 30 horsemen, followed by 30 cargo ships with all the craftsmen needed to support this city on the move. They left Athens in political turmoil as a witch hunt was launched to find the blasphemous Hermae hackers.

A cloud hung over the fleet as it sailed off to glory . . . or doom. The Athenians forgot their lines from the Melian Dialogue: "The standard of justice depends on the equality of power to compel and that in fact the strong do what they have the power to do and the weak accept what they have to accept." Democratic Athens was looking to take democratic Syracuse, a city of similar size, not puny Melos.

The previous Sicilian Expedition of 427–24 B.C. was only launched to aid an ally and try to extend Athenian influence in Sicily. This current expedition was huge, and its size created its own problems. City-states along the sailing route refused alliance and provisions, demanding that the fleet move on. They saw it correctly as an expedition of conquest.

Once in Sicilian waters, the Athenian fleet sought a base, only to see many Greek cities keeping their gates shut. Rhegium, on Italy's toe, was out. Messina, just across the straits, stayed shut. Anti-Syracusan Naxos allowed the Athenians to beach their ships, but the city was too far north of Syracuse to make a convenient base. A naval squadron reconnoitered Syracuse's harbor and met no resistance, yet no coup-de-main was mounted to take Syracuse in one sudden blow from the harbor. Finally the Athenians were able to take Catana by trickery. It was just twenty miles north of Syracuse—half a day's trip by trireme.

At this point, a fast trireme arrived from Athens with a recall notice for Alcibiades, who was now blamed with his gang for vandalizing the Hermae. Knowing he stood a good chance of being found guilty regardless of the evidence, Alcibiades jumped ship in southern Italy and hightailed it for Sparta, where he could sell his advice in exchange for sanctuary.

Cautious Nicias was now in charge, never taking a direct course of action to lick a problem. The Athenian fleet sailed north, away from Syracuse, to campaign along Sicily's northern coast, gaining no allies. Despite Nicias' lack of strategic direction, the Athenians were able to refocus on Syracuse upon their return to Catana. A ruse lured the Syracusan army to Catana, allowing the Athenian fleet and army to slip southward to Syracuse, building a stockade on the beach on the north shore of the Great Harbor to protect the triremes.

The Syracusan army hustled back and lined up just to the north of the Athenian stockade, which lay just a mile south of the city. The Athenians lined up on good ground, their flanks protected from the superior Syracusan cavalry by a river on one end and marshes on the other. Though outnumbered by the Syracusans, the Athenians managed to break the enemy line, but could not pursue and destroy retreating remnants. The Syracusan cavalry covered their retreat. If Athens had sent enough cavalry, its army could have finished the war with Syracuse that day. But the lack of horsemen compromised operations. Nicias sent back to Athens for more cavalry to make up for this oversight.

The Syracusans were not idle during the following winter. Hermocrates rallied the populace, reformed the army, issued spears and armor to the poorer men so they too could join the line as hoplites. They extended their walls and fortified outposts to hinder Athenian movements. Syracusan envoys made damn sure the

Athenians did not suborn any other Greek city-states in Sicily, artfully arguing that the Athenians came to conquer, and not to "make nice."

More important, diplomats were sent to Corinth and Sparta to ask for aid. The Syracusan appeal got some support from the traitor Alcibiades. He outlined the Athenian imperialist agenda to take over Sicily, then Italy, then Carthage, then Iberia, becoming an unstoppable force in the region. The threat was exaggerated. (Okay, maybe it wasn't too crazy, since Rome accomplished these conquests two centuries later.) The Spartans decided not to match the Athenian expedition with one of its own. Instead they would send just one general—Gylippus—a lesser citizen and thus expendable. But it would take a while for him to get to Syracuse.

As the spring of 414 B.C. approached, the Athenians readied themselves to lay siege to Syracuse, which promised to be lengthy and expensive. They had the fleet to blockade the city by sea. To seal off the city by land, they needed to build a wall across the Epipolae, the heights overlooking Syracuse. It would have to run about three miles, starting from Syracuse's Great Harbor northward to Trogilus, which is on the northern shore of the peninsula where Syracuse sits.

There were two ways the Syracusans could stop the Athenians. One was to vanquish their fleet in battle, a tall order indeed as Athens had the best navy in the Greek world. The alternative was to build counter-walls running east to west to cut off the Athenian wall that was to run south to north, thus maintaining a supply route into the Sicilian interior.

Athens made the first move, constructing a fortified base for its supplies at Labdalum, on the north side of the Epipolae. A circular fort was built on the south side of the heights. The recent arrival of horses brought Athenian cavalry strength up to 650—still not matching Syracuse's horsemen in number, but enough to protect the infantry building the blockade wall from Syracusan raids. Sorties by the Syracusan army were brief. The Athenians had no trouble checking the Syracusan counter-walls being built south of the Epipolae.

Fortune then shifted against the Athenians. Nicias became bedridden with a kidney ailment and could no longer command from the front. Lamachus was killed in a small skirmish with Syracusan infantry. The Syracusans assaulted the Circle Fort, but were driven away by a fire set by Nicias' troops. Still, the raid demolished the Athenian wall running south from the Circle Fort to the harbor.

Despite these vexing setbacks, Nicias still held the upper hand. He knew that Gylippus was on his way. He knew the Syracusans were discussing surrender. But he did not press home his advantages, either by enticing surrender, quickly finishing the blockade wall to cut off Syracuse, or beefing up naval patrols to keep Gylippus from arriving.

The Spartan general managed to get into Syracuse uncontested—by land, through the unguarded Euryalus pass near the Epipolae. This "army of one" would outnumber all of Nicias' ships, horses, and men. Being lax in planning and execution, Nicias would now unknowingly aid his enemy by making mistakes. Meanwhile, his peace with the Spartans would fall apart, as Athens resumed raiding Spartan lands to help Argos.

Sicilian Stalingrad

Gylippus started the struggle against his enemy with chutzpah. He offered a truce to the Athenians if they left within five days. Nicias ignored the offer. The Syracusans were impressed with Gylippus' nerve and took heart. But when the Syracusans lined up to fight the Athenians outside Syracuse, Gylippus was appalled at their confusion and disorder. He wisely ordered them to return to Syracuse.

Nicias did not pounce on the retreating Syracusans, letting them get away. He did not adequately garrison his fort at Labdalum, allowing Gylippus to seize the Athenian supply depot and treasury in a quick raid. He neglected to finish the blockade wall across the Epipolae, instead diverting Athenian effort to complete a double wall from the Circle Fort back to the beach stockade. Gylippus now started an east-west counter-wall to head off the Athenian blockade wall. The sick and hesitant Nicias could not press home any direct effort to win. Now he made things worse, shifting his naval base to the south shore of Syracuse's Great Harbor to Plemmyrium, which offered little water or firewood. It was about two miles across the harbor from the troops trying to take the Epipolae.

The Athenians fought another battle on those heights, this time beating the Syracusans. Gylippus had kept the Syracusan cavalry out of the fight. Morale was the only resource the Syracusans had in abundance, and now it was threatened. Gylippus made good by accepting blame for the defeat. This impressed the Syracusans, who rallied to his leadership.

Despite all the Athenian errors, the blockade wall was now nearing Trogilus.

If the Athenians finished the wall, Syracuse would be finished, too.

The Syracusans had to stop the wall's progress, or eventually lose all.

Once more, the armies lined up near Trogilus. Now the fight was on open ground, Gylippus put the cavalry into play. They crushed the Athenian left flank, foolishly left uncovered by light troops or cavalry. The Athenian line collapsed. Hoplites fled for the safety of the Circle Fort, escaping destruction by their pursuers. With that victory in pocket, the Syracusans laid the last stone in their counter-wall, cutting off the Athenian wall. Gylippus then built several outposts on the Epipolae, making sure the garrisoned high ground would stay safe for his side.

With their attention turned to the land battle, the Athenians missed the arrival of a Corinthian war fleet in Syracuse's harbor. The Athenian blockaders would now be blockaded.

Hope now drove the Syracusan rowers to train hard.

They were going to beat the best fleet in the Greek world.

Nicias took note of the forces growing against him. The smart thing to do would be to order the expedition to board ships and go home. At least Athens would have an army and a fleet ready to fight again another day. If Nicias did this, he would surely be tried for losing the campaign. The Athenian assembly always rewarded failed commanders with trial and conviction. He wrote back to Athens, asking the assembly to recall the expedition or send reinforcements, and relieve him of command due to illness.

The Athenians instead voted to send reinforcements and more money. Demosthenes, an experienced warrior/leader with victories at Pylos and Eurymedon, along with two co-leaders, sailed with the second force of 73 triremes, 5,000 hoplites, more light troops and supplies. Perhaps in 413 B.C. Syracuse could still be taken.

It was going to be a double or nothing bet.

Gylippus was aware that Athenian reinforcements were probably on the way. Syracuse was bankrolling 7,000 foreign fighters to aid its army. It was also splurging on a fleet with little in the treasury to pay for it. If the Athenians were not defeated soon, Syracuse could go broke.

To press the Athenians, Gylippus launched an attack by land to take the forts guarding Plemmyrium. But he needed a diversion. He ordered the Syracusan fleet to row out and threaten the Athenian anchorage. The Athenians launched ships. As their troops watched the Syracusans lose the naval battle, Gylippus led his force to take the forts, with their stockpiles of food and supplies. Gylippus followed up with yet another naval battle. Hope lay to open sea for the Athenians, but they were fought to a bloody draw by the Syracusans.

Things were looking grave when Demosthenes arrived with his relief force. It was all or nothing now. Demosthenes proposed to take the Epipolae in a night attack and tear down the Syracusan counter-wall, thus restoring the land blockade while the reinforced Athenian fleet kept up a still-effective sea blockade.

At first, the night assault was successful, taking a Syracusan fort on the western edge of the Epipolae. The Athenian infantry ran uphill, smack into a phalanx of Boeotian hoplites, and were routed. Confusion then set in when the Athenians could not tell each other apart from their foes in the dimly moonlit night. The Athenians fell back in fear and panic as the enemy shouted war cries and false orders in the dark.

As bad as things became, the Athenian fleet could still have

busted out of the harbor and made it home, Demosthenes proposed. He was outvoted in council of war by Nicias and the two
"assistant generals" that had arrived with reinforcements.

Then came the lunar eclipse.

Remember that the Ancient Greeks were religious and superstitious. The eclipse of the moon that late August was an ill
omen. While specialists in the occult at that time disagreed on the
meaning of the event, the soothsayer whom Nicias checked with
recommended that the Athenians wait "thrice nine days" before
pulling out. Nicias ordered the expedition to stay put. The Syracusans used the downtime to train some more and force yet another
naval battle in the harbor.

The Athenians still outnumbered the Syracusans, eighty-six to
seventy-six triremes. Some Athenian ships broke through on the
left. The Corinthian commander Pythen, who suffered the pierc-
ing of his line, could have chased the fleeing Athenians, but chose
instead to turn and ram the other Athenian triremes, now locked
in combat with Syracuse's ships. The Athenians lost eighteen ships.
Worse, much of the Athenian fleet was forced to beach outside of
the stockade at Plemmyrium. Crews were slaughtered as they fled
from their ships.

The Syracusans now anchored their warships in line abreast at
the harbor's mouth, tying them to each other with iron chains
and bridging the gaps between the vessels. To see home again, the
Athenians had to break out of the harbor. The Syracusans left one
gap between their ship line and shore to allow the remainder of
their fleet to come and go.

The Athenians had to exploit this gap to break free. Rowing to
battle, they detailed some triremes to engage the anchored ships
to cut the chains and widen the gap. Yet even this force was badly
pressed by the remainder of the Syracusan fleet, which relied on
boarding tactics to fight a land battle on the decks of the tangled
ships, thus negating Athenian advantages in maneuverability and
seamanship. Unable to break out, the Athenians disengaged and
returned to their stockade. They still had more ships than the Syracusans. Demosthenes urged another breakout, but the rowers and

troops saw failure instead of a second chance, and would not answer the call to oars.

Nicias ordered an overland retreat to Catana, still an Athenian
base. The ships were abandoned. Forty thousand men—about half
of them combatants—divided into two divisions, one led by Nicias,
the other by Demosthenes—to march west, then northward toward
Catana and safety. But all they found in the Sicilian interior was
more Syracusan troops. Every pass, every road was blocked by the
enemy. Every attempt to fight through only delayed the Athenians
while the Syracusans were reinforced. They were able to prevent
the two Athenian divisions from supporting each other. Cut off,
surrounded and taking many casualties, Demosthenes surrendered
his division in return for a promise that the prisoners would not
be killed. Of the 20,000 men he commanded, only 6,000 were
still alive.

The Syracusans then brought word of Demosthenes' surrender
to Nicias, demanding that he do the same. Nicias chose to fight his
way through another river crossing, but his force was surrounded
and destroyed. Only 1,000 survived to be taken prisoner.

Demosthenes and Nicias were later put to death by their cap-
tors. Of the 7,000 Athenians captured, only a tenth ever saw their
home city again. The rest died while being held captive in several
rock quarries, sustained by little food, given no shelter from the
elements.

No Margin for Defeat

Athens should have lost the war in 413 B.C. Losses from the Sicilian
expedition were grievous. Three thousand Athenian hoplites were
dead out of a force pool of about 9,000. Another 9,000 rowers
were also lost, with perhaps around 11,000 left. Fleet losses were
scary—160 triremes gone, with only about 100 left, not all seaworthy. The heavy losses of Athens' allies made up the balance of the
dead. Only 500 talents remained in the treasury, a scant twelfth
of the rich pile Athens had at war's start. The Spartan fort at Decelea stood as sanctuary for slaves fleeing the nearby Athenian silver

mine at Laurinum (this strategy was "sold" to Sparta by Alcibiades). All the experienced generals were dead or in exile.

Both sides needed resources.

Sparta tried to build up a new war fleet with its allies, but fell short of the numbers needed to defeat Athens.

Both sides wooed the Persian Empire, but it was the Spartans who got the alliance in exchange for allowing Persia to retake the Greek city states and islands that lay along what is now Turkey's Aegean coast. For a nation fighting for "freedom for the Greeks," it was bitter irony to hand them back to the Persians. The Spartans applied themselves to prying Athenian allies from the Delian League, depriving Athens of much-needed tax revenue and securing new naval bases to threaten the Athenian food lifeline to the Hellespont. First to go over was the island of Chios. Sparta made plays for Samos, Lesbos, and Miletus. Athens sent out its last fleet, spending the next several years sparring with the Spartans, and intriguing for the return of lost cities and islands to the Delian League. But the cruelest stroke came in 411 B.C., when Sparta captured Abydos and had a naval presence in the Hellespont.

With defeat near, Athens abandoned democracy for oligarchy. Alcibiades, who had fled Sparta for Persia after cuckolding one of Sparta's kings, now fled Persia for the Athenian side, arriving at its distant base in Samos. Athenian fortunes turned when one of its "rookie" admirals, Thrasybulus, thrashed the Spartan fleet in the Hellespont at Cynossema. Had Thrasybulus been defeated, Athens would have lost the war then and there.

Now there was hope.

Athens could stay alive if it won every battle.

Sparta only had to win once.

Cynossema was followed up by another Athenian victory at Abydos, this time with Alcibiades in command. The winning streak continued in 410 B.C., when Alcibiades and Thrasybulus divided their naval forces in the face of a Spartan fleet at Cyzicus, surrounding and destroying it. This snuffed the Spartan naval threat in the Hellespont, keeping the grain supply route under Athenian control. These three victories together sank or captured between 135 and 155 warships belonging to Sparta and its allies. The loss almost equaled the one Athens suffered in the Sicilian Expedition.

The Spartans now had a choice—either approach the Persians for more gold to rebuild the war fleet, or offer peace terms to Athens.

They chose the latter course, but the seemingly easy terms made the Athenians think twice. Sparta promised to take down its fort in Decelea if Athens promised to do the same at Pylos. Prisoners would be exchanged. Any cities held by either side when the war ended would stay that way. That would leave Sparta in control of Chios, Rhodes, Miletus, Ephesus, Thasos, Euboea, a portion of the Thracian coast astride Athenian trade routes, their last outpost in the Hellespont at Abydos, and control of the other end of the straits at the Bosporus. Accepting these terms would allow the Spartans to re-start the war in an excellent strategic position to either threaten Athens' grain routes or to pry additional members from the Delian League.

The Athenians turned down the peace offer.

The Spartans built another war fleet, paid for by Persia.

The war was back on.

Athens ousted its oligarchs, returning to democracy. They were now reaching deep into empty pockets to pay for the war. In 409 B.C., the city outfitted 50 triremes and dispatched another 1,000 hoplites to return to the Aegean. The price tag for this would run 30 talents a month, and even then, the rowers were being underpaid. The fleet did not accomplish much that year. Additional campaigns in 408 and 407 did little to eliminate the Spartan presence in the narrow sea between the Hellespont and Bosporus.

Both sides turned to new leaders to deliver victory.

Alcibiades finally returned to Athens, securing a command of 100 ships and 1,500 hoplites. On him the city pinned its hopes.

Sparta also dispatched a new commander, the low-born and expendable Lysander, to meet with the Persians. Now Cyrus, the younger son of Emperor Darius II, took direct control of what is now western Turkey to work directly with the Spartans and finance the rebuilding of their war fleet.

The Persian-Spartan treaty limited rowers' pay to three *obols* a day—the same pay rate as the Athenian navy. Lysander's master-stroke was simple: pay the Spartan rowers four *obols* a day. By offering better pay, Lysander deepened his hiring pool for rowers while draining the same for Athens.

Lysander's second stroke was offering the leading Greek citizens of the Ionian cities the promise of Spartan backing for pro-Persian oligarchies if they supported his cause with gold. Obtaining payments became much easier.

Alcibiades moved the Athenian fleet to Notium, near Ephesus. While he was away on a secondary mission, the fleet suffered a defeat at the hands of Lysander, losing twenty-two ships. Alcibiades returned with thirty triremes and the unified fleet still outnumbered Lysander's. But the Spartan wisely chose to decline battle. Alcibiades suffered blame for the lack of results. That, coupled with his reputation for discordant politics, made his falling out with the Athenian Assembly inevitable. Alcibiades went into exile again to avoid trial, conviction, and disgrace in Athens. Conon took over command of the fleet.

Lysander's four-*obol* pay scheme now sucked rowers out of the Athenian navy faster than a Spartan naval victory. In 406 B.C., Conon could only man 70 of his 100 triremes. Lysander's "tour of duty" ended and he handed command over to Callicratidas, along with 140 triremes. Callicratidas caught Conon en route to Lesbos, taking 30 of his galleys and blockading the rest at Mitylene.

Crisis gripped Athens—again!

There were only 40 ships left in the navy. Athens managed to raise its fleet to 110 within a month. This required melting down sacred statues and digging into sacred treasuries to come up with 2,000 talents to pay for the new ships.

Experienced rowers were hard to find.

Farmers were trained to stroke.

Slaves were offered citizenship to entice them to the thwarts.

Anyone who could fog a mirror was given an oar.

With help from remaining allies, Athens sent 155 warships under eight "admirals" to smash the Spartans. At Arginusae, the Spartan Callicratidas fought outnumbered and outflanked, losing 77 ships out of 120, as well as his life. It was a staggering defeat. In the rush to relieve Conon, Athenian survivors of stricken triremes were overlooked and not rescued promptly. For this, Athens cashiered all eight admirals. Lysander returned to rebuild the Spartan fleet.

In 405 B.C., Sparta offered terms again, willing to cede Decelea without asking for an Athenian concession in return. All possessions held by both sides would stay that way, only now Sparta no longer held the Bosporus and allied Ionian cities were fewer. Again the Athenians turned down the offer, knowing that Sparta could renew the war with Persian aid.

Lysander took his rebuilt fleet back to the Hellespont, using his small embarked army to take Lampsacus for a naval base. The Athenian fleet followed, now commanded by six inexperienced leaders. They beached the fleet at Aegospotami, far from a good water source and a market. Daily, the fleet would row to Lampsacus to challenge the Spartans. Daily, Lysander refused battle. Then the fleet would return to the beach, and the rowers would disperse to scrounge their daily meals.

Command rotated daily among the six Athenian leaders. Philocles decided to bait the Spartans by taking only a portion of the fleet to Lampsacus. Seeing an opportunity to destroy the Athenians in detail, the Spartan fleet rushed to sea, pursuing the Athenians all the way back to their base. There the Spartans found the last fleet of Athens beached, the crews dispersed in their quest for food, water, and firewood. There was no fight. The Athenian fleet was captured. A small Spartan land force simultaneously captured the shore camp. Of the 180 triremes in the Athenian fleet, 170 were captured. Between three and four thousand Athenian rowers were executed immediately.

Athens tried to negotiate a peace with Sparta after hearing the bad news. But no terms were acceptable so long as the Long Walls connected Piraeus with Athens. Thebes was even more adamant— the city's leaders wanted Athens razed and turned into a sheep pasture. The Spartans imposed a "kinder, gentler peace"—the Long Walls had to come down, Athens would be allowed to have a 12-ship navy and cede control of its foreign policy to Sparta. All exiles could return, resulting in a flood of people more sympathetic to oligarchy than democracy. Athens had to abandon control of all foreign cities, but could rule over Attica.

On this note, the Peloponnesian War ended in a whimper, with Athens having done more to lose the war than win it.

Looking back, the defeat in Sicily broke Athenian strength. From that point, Athens would make desperate war when nearly bankrupt, never to be as powerful again. What fleet remained could provide survival only so long as no defeat was suffered. The Athenians started the war with tremendous financial strength and finished it broke. The advantage in gold shifted to Sparta once it secured a Persian alliance.

Sparta could afford to fight to the last Persian gold piece, rebuilding the fleet every time it lost a battle.

Persia could afford to fight to the last Spartan, if that meant hobbling Athens.

Into those desperate straits rowed the Athenians. They had to win every battle just to live.

The Spartans only needed to win one battle to win the war.

Hubris, religious fanaticism, and that "failure to communicate" here set up one of the great upsets in history. Spain had ten times the wealth and five times the population of England, not to mention the greatest infantry of its day. But Philip II still managed to lose his ultimate fleet and usher in the era of English domination of the seas that did not end until WWII.

THE COLLAPSE OF THE SPANISH ARMADA

Venit, Vidit, Fugit:
England, 1588

JAKI DEMAREST

Venit, *Vidit, Fugit.* "He came, he saw, he fled," was the inscription on one of the more irreverently funny victory medals struck by the English after their surprise defeat of the seemingly invincible Spanish Armada in 1588. Other victory medals were more subdued, giving the credit to God for coming down quite so spectacularly on the side of Elizabeth of England. "He blew with His winds, and they were scattered." "God breathed, and they were scattered."[1]

In other words, *Non nobis, Domine.*

Elizabeth's father, Henry VIII, would surely have committed judicial murder to have had such a victory to his credit, for all that it owed to God's blowing and scattering. And it may well have been the ultimate vindication for Elizabeth's mother, Anne Boleyn, who had been one of Henry's innumerable judicial murders when Elizabeth was three. Both at home and abroad, the devastation of the Spanish Armada established for Elizabeth a prestige bordering on the semi-divine, while Philip II of Spain was humiliated, the illusion of Spanish invincibility forever smashed.

Of the 130 ships that had set sail from Lisbon, Portugal, in May, 1588, bearing 30,493 men, according to Spanish records (numerically the greatest naval fleet of its age), half those ships and less than 10,000 men straggled home to Corunna and Santander in mid-September, exhausted and starving, to tell the tale.[2]

It was said that every noble family in Spain lost at least one son in the Enterprise of England.

Amor Vincit Omnia

The enmity between Philip II and Elizabeth I, and thus Spain and England, may well have begun with love. Elizabeth certainly boasted often enough that it had been so. When Philip and Elizabeth met, he was King Consort of England, married to Elizabeth's half-sister, Mary I, better known to history as Bloody Mary. Philip was also, as Mary's Spanish, Catholic husband, intensely unpopular in an insular, largely Protestant England. Mary's attempts to drag England back into the Catholic fold with a steady course of religious persecution didn't help England to warm to Philip or Spain in the least.

With cold English dislike pouring down on him from all sides, lonely and isolated, and tethered to a bitter and fanatical woman ten years older than himself, Philip must have been easy prey for Elizabeth, twenty-two, brilliant, reputedly pretty, with much of her mother's glittering style and Melusine fascination. After their first meeting, on April 30, 1555, at Hampton Court, they appeared to have reached an agreement, and a truce. Elizabeth was released from her imprisonment at Mary's hands, and reinstated at court. She and Philip hunted, hawked, and danced together through that spring and summer, until he left for Spain again in August, and while Mary seemed to have taken Elizabeth back into the royal bosom, it was evident to such impartial observers as the Venetian ambassador that Mary hated Elizabeth.[3]

Certainly Simeon Renard, the Spanish ambassador, had cautioned Philip that "the Princess Elizabeth is greatly to be feared, she has a spirit full of incantations."[4] But Philip apparently disregarded that excellent warning; years afterward, "Philip was heard to reproach himself because he had allowed himself to entertain a passion for his sister-in-law."[5]

When Mary died, three years later, Philip supported Elizabeth's claim to the English throne, and sent a proposal of marriage through his new ambassador, the Count de Feria.

It wasn't a popular prospective match in either England or Spain, and needed to be pursued with caution on both sides. It took several months and four separate meetings to resolve the issue, months in which Elizabeth scrambled to consolidate herself on the throne. After the first meeting, de Feria confidently told his master that "if she decides to marry out of the country, she will at once fix her eyes on your majesty."[6] That confidence gave Philip a bit of his own, and the luxury of painting himself as a Catholic martyr in the situation. "I have decided to encounter the difficulty, to sacrifice my private inclination in the service of our Lord and to marry the Queen of England."[7]

To quote Monty Python's *Holy Grail*, "Let me face the peril!"

Philip also tellingly instructed de Feria "not to expose him to a refusal which would make his condescension ridiculous." That last was the most important of all. The prickly dignity of the Spanish king must not be offended by a woman, and an Englishwoman of dubious birth, faith, and reputation, at that.

Elizabeth strung both de Feria and Philip along for months, playing the "maybe so, maybe no" game she would continue to play so effectively for the rest of her life. And when she finally felt secure enough on her throne, with a French embassy safely on its way and ready to open negotiations of its own, she called de Feria again and delivered the death blow to any hope of the marriage. She told him, laughing, that she could not marry Philip because she was "a heretic." De Feria left England shortly afterward, furious and dispirited, declaring that "this country . . . has fallen into the hands of a woman who is a Daughter of the Devil. . . . We have lost a kingdom, body and soul."[8]

And so they had. For her part, Elizabeth taunted Philip for decades afterward with cynical sallies that made him a laughingstock in Europe: "My enmity and his having begun with love, you must not think we could not get along together whenever I choose."

England went on its way as a Protestant power, lost to Catholicism, and over the course of the next thirty years, relations between the two countries deteriorated steadily. English privateers attacked Spanish shipping and raided Spanish holdings in the Americas, carrying home booty from the New World. And while Elizabeth put up token protests of their terrible behavior, she also quietly took shares of each new haul, building up a lean but barely sufficient war chest. Those naval skirmishes steadily seasoned England's commanders, honing their tactics and capabilities.

While Mary, Queen of Scots, was alive, and the heir presumptive to Elizabeth's throne, Philip held his peace, unwilling to see the Dowager Queen of France sit on the English throne and alter the balance of power in Europe. But in quiet anticipation of Mary's death, and a clearer claim for himself to the English crown as former King Consort, he bided his time.

He began planning the invasion of England as early as August, 1583, with the sort of exquisite and loving detail only a desk-bound fanatic could bring to such a project. He worked in the greatest secrecy and largely alone, believing that God would take up the slack for any flaw in his Great Enterprise.

And, oh, what flaws there were.

The actual building and outfitting of the Armada began in 1584, also in secrecy. That secrecy didn't last long; Sir Francis Walsingham had built for England what could be described as the world's first secret service, a superb international network of spies and informants. Elizabeth was clearly aware of the danger when she had the Queen of Scots executed, and that knowledge must surely have added its own weight to the months of tortured hesitation and indecision before Elizabeth struck the final blow.

When Mary, Queen of Scots, was executed on February 8, 1587, Philip's timetable for the Armada kicked into overdrive. The last reason for Spanish restraint ostensibly gone, it was time to return England to the Catholic fold by force and do away with the heretic queen who'd humiliated Philip in the eyes of the world.

England's timetable for resisting invasion clearly kicked into the same overdrive. On April 12, barely a month after Mary's execution, Elizabeth and her government sent Francis Drake sailing out of Plymouth to attack Spanish shipping in the harbor of Cadiz. It was a bold move for the habitually cautious Elizabeth. She sent another set of orders after he'd sailed, countermanding the attack, but these were almost certainly a diplomatic C.Y.A. rather than a serious rethinking of the "best defense is a good offense" strategy.

It had always been her style to prevaricate gracefully, to keep up for the world the façade of a "weak and feeble woman" whose privateers were continually acting against her wishes and orders. The fact that their letters of marque to do exactly what they were doing came from her in the first place, and the lion's share of the booty was quietly collected by her, escaped no one with the eyes (or spies) to see it. But the fiction was flattering to the masculine pride of anyone who could not abide "the monstrous regiment of women," and a diplomatic master stroke.

At the least, Elizabeth's countermanding orders went out too late to stop Francis Drake.

He sailed boldly into the harbor at Cadiz on April 29th, 1587, sending the unprepared Spanish naval and land forces into a panic. For two days, Drake plundered and burned ships in the harbor without encountering much in the way of resistance, destroying thirty-seven naval and merchant vessels. For the next month, he kept up a relentless course of attacks between Lisbon and Cape St. Vincent, capturing ships and destroying supplies intended for the Spanish Armada.

Every bit as critical as the ships he denied the Armada, he destroyed "barrel staves to the quantity of 1,600 to 1,700 tons, according to Drake's own estimate, sufficient to make barrels for 25,000 to 30,000 tons of provisions and water."[9] This might not sound like much initially, but the Armada was plagued by rotten provisions, stores of food that rotted before the Armada ever left Lisbon. Water barrels made with green lumber that leaked. Badly pickled food rotting in the hogsheads. Drake did more than buy the English another badly needed year to prepare for the attack. His raids ensured that when Philip pushed to send his Armada out of Lisbon the next year, it was so badly provisioned that its failure was virtually guaranteed.

Buying that extra year bought the English something else. The man originally slated to command the Armada was Don Álvaro de Bazán, Marquis of Santa Cruz, Commander of León, Member of the Military Order of Santiago, Captain General of the Navy of the Ocean Sea, a highly seasoned, highly talented naval commander with five decades of successful campaigns under his belt. He had, in fact, decisively beaten a combined force of Dutch, English, Portuguese, and French privateers in the Battle of Ponta Delgada in 1582, and that despite the fact that he was outnumbered more than two to one.

Santa Cruz at the head of the Great Armada could have been dangerous indeed.

On his death, however, Santa Cruz was replaced, not by either of his most seasoned admirals, Miguel de Oquendo y Segura or Juan Martinez de Recalde, but by the Duke of Medina Sidonia, Don Alonso de Guzmán El Bueno. Medina Sidonia had no naval or military experience to recommend him to the post, making him roughly as qualified as your average George W. Bush political appointee. But he was, by reputation, a good Christian, humble and self-effacing, of high rank and ancient family, and absolutely obedient to his micromanaging king.

Philip's orders for Medina Sidonia's appointment were, intriguingly enough, dated three days before the death of Santa Cruz. It is probable that the too-independent Santa Cruz was slated to be replaced by a more malleable commander, and his living or dying made no difference to that decision.

Poor Medina Sidonia immediately wrote a letter to Philip, begging him to reconsider his appointment, bringing up the genuinely excellent points that the duke lacked military experience of any kind, knew nothing of sailing or strategy, and suffered from poor health and seasickness. But Philip reacted badly to anything he perceived as criticism, and he surrounded himself with secretaries who were afraid to give him any. Medina Sidonia's letter never reached Philip.

He did as well in the post as anyone with no experience of strategy or the sea was going to do. Medina Sidonia was a reasonably talented administrator. He established good relations with his senior officers, and worked hard to organize the chaos of military provisioning. The Armada still went out with rotten stores of food, leaking barrels of water, and guns and ammunition insufficient to the purpose, but if Medina Sidonia hadn't at least *tried* to get a handle on the situation, it would have been worse. The fact that he could get the whole operation pointed in one direction and sailing at all is a testament to his administrative skills.

Venit

Once the Armada left Lisbon on May 28, 1588, too late to take England by surprise and too early to be adequately provisioned, it limped along the Iberian coast at around 2.5 knots a day. The galleons were floating castles, tall, cumbersome, and slow. They were designed for boarding actions, bristling with marines, with gunbanks that were meant to fire a single broadside before a boarding action. The Armada was only as fast as its slowest ships, and it took three weeks to sail the 300 miles from Lisbon to Cape Finisterre. Disease, hunger, and thirst were already beginning to set in.[10]

When the Armada reached Corunna, Medina Sidonia grappled with his first command decision: to anchor and re-supply, or press on and keep what momentum they had. He hesitated, long enough for a severe storm to set in before they could anchor anywhere. Ships of the line were blown as far off course as the Scilly Isles. Several ships ran aground on the French coast, including three of the four galleys.[11] Medina Sidonia's decision was finally made for him, if belatedly; he anchored the fleet in Corunna for a month, re-supplying, while his pinnaces rounded up strays scattered across the Bay of Biscay. It was an inauspicious beginning.

During his stay in Corunna, Medina Sidonia wrote Philip another letter, warning him that the Armada was already encountering serious difficulties, and might not be up to the job Philip had carved out for it. Philip, monomaniacal once he'd fixed on a course of action, proved incapable of reconsidering its wisdom, and ignored Medina Sidonia's doubts and complaints. The Armada would sail. God would guide it.

On the English side, Lord Admiral Charles Howard of Effingham, in charge of the English fleet and acting on the impulsive advice of Francis Drake, moved his fleet into the Bay of Biscay, hoping to catch the Spaniards with their proverbial pants down in Corunna. But the tactics that had covered Drake in glory the previous year didn't take into account that the same strong southerly wind, currently keeping the Armada from progressing northward, might just blow the entire English fleet past the Armada, leaving the English coastline undefended. Once out in the Bay of Biscay and feeling the effects of that wind for themselves, the English thought better of their position and retreated to Plymouth, to harbor there and wait for the Spanish in English waters.

On the 19th of July, the Armada finally succeeded in crossing the Bay of Biscay, and was spotted off the Scilly Isles by the *Golden Hinde*, captained by Thomas Fleming. The *Hinde* raced for Plymouth with the news, only to find that Francis Drake was inclined to take it with a sangfroid bordering on apparent indifference; he insisted on finishing his game of bowls before going anywhere.

In perfect truth, there was nowhere he could have gone. The English fleet was harbored, the tide was against them.

Here, Medina Sidonia's hesitation cost him the game. The Spanish commanders hastily convened a council of war and advised him to press his advantage, sail into Plymouth Harbor on the tide and trap the English at anchor. While it is seriously doubtful that Medina Sidonia's 18,000 soldiers could have taken and held England without reinforcements from Philip's nephew, Alexander Farnese, the Duke of Parma, in the Netherlands, the Armada could have decimated England's naval resistance right there in a perfect reversal of Cadiz. And England was nothing without her fleet. She had no standing army, nothing but a hastily cobbled and ragtag band of 4,000 recruits stationed at Tilbury.

Medina Sidonia declined to act on the advice of his officers, let the opportunity go by, and the English fleet slipped the net on the next two tides.

The news raced to London and around the English coast by way of a series of beacons, *Lord of the Rings* style. The lighting of one led to the lighting of the next, and the next, announcing that the long, suspenseful wait was over, and the Armada was in the English Channel. For better or worse, the battle was on.

The faster English ships tacked upwind of the Armada initially, taking the weather gauge from the Spanish and slowing the Armada further. It was a significant advantage, but it wasn't enough to give either side a decisive initial victory in the first week's engagements. The Armada inched its way up the channel, its goal being to ferry the Duke of Parma and 16,000 of his crack Spanish troops from somewhere along the Flemish or French coast across the Channel to England.

Therein lay the really, really bad part of the plan. The two commanders had never managed to finalize arrangements on where, how, and when to meet. The Armada had set sail without those assurances. Philip had apparently trusted to God to get it all sorted out. And without Parma's reinforcements, the Armada's complement of 18,000 soldiers was hardly going to be enough to mount a successful invasion of England.

The ability of an army of 34,000 to take and hold England was also questionable, despite the lack of a standing English army, and the Duke of Parma, the best of Philip's military commanders, apparently thought so, too. He appears to have made no serious effort to meet the Armada anywhere. Spain was already fighting one bloody difficult war against the extremely tenacious and well-organized Dutch resistance; Philip could not have chosen a worse time to divide his focus and fight that war on two fronts. And Parma, who was seeing firsthand exactly what a determined resistance movement could cost an empire, had to be leery of his chances of fighting two of them.

Medina Sidonia sent letter after letter to Parma's headquarters in Ghent, in fast pinnace after fast pinnace, trying to arrange to meet him and his men somewhere, anywhere, and ferry them over. And while Parma never came out and said "no," he never said "yes," either. He made no reply at all.

Wherever they met, it would have to be a deep water port, one Parma wouldn't have to fight to hold, and one at which the Dutch ships wouldn't harry the Armada at anchor. All those competing factors left them with no realistic options.

The first several days' worth of naval engagements were indecisive at best. Medina Sidonia kept the Armada in a tight crescent formation, with his strongest warships on the flanks and his more vulnerable merchant vessels cradled in the center. Anything trying to break that formation by attacking that weak center was going to have to face Spanish gunfire on two sides to do it.

The English began by trying to take advantage of their superior mobility and the longer range of their gunnery. It was effective only to a point; at distance, the 17-pound shot of the English culverins proved better at taking down (repairable) riggings than doing damage below the waterline.

In the inconclusive engagements off Eddystone and the Isle of Portland, the Armada's shorter shot did no appreciable damage to the English ships, nor could they close without breaking their rigid but defensible crescent formation. The English managed to pick off two Spanish galleons, the *Nuestra Señora del Rosario*, which suffered collision damage in that tightly packed crescent, a harbinger of things to come, and the *San Salvador*, incapacitated by an explosion in the powder store.

Both ships were captured and taken in tow by the English. But the English fleet and Spanish Armada were running into similar problems, making their early engagements a toe-to-toe slugfest.

Spanish naval tactics were old school; they depended heavily on boarding actions, which meant they had to be able to get close enough to board. A single close-quarters shot from their guns was all they anticipated needing, as the next phase of the action was always boarding and hand-to-hand fighting. Spanish marines were deadly there, and the Armada was naturally packed with them.

The problem was that the English weren't playing by the old school rules. Their gunners had trained in the art of rapid fire and reload. The English ships were built for speed, not ferrying power. The Spanish couldn't match English speed or firepower, and couldn't get near enough for a boarding action, but the English shot wasn't powerful enough to do much damage at a distance. They were going to have to get closer to the Spanish ships, possibly close enough to risk the boarding actions the Spanish were counting on.

After a final action off the Isle of Wight, in which the Armada came off worst and had to abandon the temporary harbor it had made there, Medina Sidonia was forced to make for the continent, still having heard nothing from the Duke of Parma.

With what must have been a growing sense of desperation, Medina Sidonia headed for Calais, hoping to arrange to pick up Parma and his forces off the Flanders coast. It was obvious by now that the confrontation was by no means one-sided, and was increasingly favoring the English as their more mobile sense of naval tactics adapted from engagement to engagement.

The Armada was already well outside the scope of Philip's lovingly, if imperfectly, concocted plan. It hadn't survived contact with either his enemies or his relatives, and the Spanish were being increasingly forced to improvise in enemy territory.

The English weren't idle, while the Armada was making its slow and ponderous way to the continent. Howard of Effingham pursued them doggedly up the Channel until July 23rd, when they reached Portland Bill and the wind veered to the northeast, giving the temporary advantage back to the Spanish. The Armada turned and attacked, giving yet another furious, confused, and inconclusive battle.

It did have one intriguing feature, in the form of a line-ahead attack ordered by Howard, in which the *Victory*, *Golden Lion*, *Elizabeth*, *Mary Rose*, *Dreadnought*, and *Swallow* took part. They were ordered to reserve fire until they had achieved close quarters, both to preserve their dwindling ammunition and to inflict more damage with the shot they had. The line-ahead attack, with each ship following behind, rather than beside as was normal, may not have been enough to decide the battle one way or the other, but it was clear proof that Howard was learning, and adapting his strategies faster than the Spanish were.

The problem of distance and ammunition continued to beleaguer both sides. The English ships were going to have to get closer to inflict any real damage, and the Spanish ships couldn't get close enough to inflict any particular damage at all. The shot they'd been provided with was ill-made, badly fired and brittle, and tended to bounce off the hulls of the English ships without effect.

It is estimated that the Spanish fired over 100,000 cannonballs over the summer's engagements with the English, without sinking a single English ship. Either they were precursors to the stormtroopers of *Star Wars* fame, or the shot they were firing was so badly made that it was more dangerous to their own gun crews than to the English ships.

Vidit

On the 27th of July, the Armada took the risk of anchoring off Calais. It made the Spanish officers nervous. (Believe it or not, they weren't idiots; they'd simply been assigned a bloody impossible task with wholly inadequate provisions. Anyone who works in a modern-day office can undoubtedly identify.) At Calais, they were a sitting collection of painted wooden ducks and they knew it, but there were a few advantages. The possibility of re-supply, for a few ships at least. Plus, the greater chance of getting someone through to the Duke of Parma. More urgent messages were immediately dispatched to him by multiple couriers, and for the first time, Parma sent back a reply.

He wasn't ready.

He wasn't going to be ready for at least another six days.

It would take, he estimated, a minimum of six days to assemble his army in port, in Dunkirk. A week, while the Armada waited at anchor. Better still, Dunkirk was currently blockaded by a small Dutch fleet under the redoubtable Justin of Nassau. Parma wanted the Armada's swift, light ships dispatched to Dunkirk to drive off the Dutch, but Medina Sidonia refused, fearing, not incorrectly, that the Armada would be a defenseless collection of lumbering hulks without the petaches' speed.

The Armada anchored in the same tight-knit crescent formation they'd held to since Corunna. It gave them reasonable protection from being picked off singly at the edges by Howard, who hadn't let up the chase. It also left them vulnerable to the most devastating attack any fleet had evinced since the days of Greek fire: hellburners.

Hellburners were the new and vastly more deadly generation of fireships, remarkably modern in their conception, with a delayed fuse and a sophisticated clockwork and flintlock mechanism, filled with charges of around 7,000 pounds of gunpowder mixed with stones and iron filings, encased in oak and sealed in lead, to intensify the explosion.

As if it needed it. After 7,000 pounds of gunpowder with iron filings, anything else strikes one as overkill.

Hellburners were the vicious brainchild of Italian engineer Federigo Giambelli, working on Elizabeth's payroll to support the Dutch rebels. Two hellburners had been used to devastating effect in the Siege of Antwerp in 1585, dark harbingers of a new age in warfare, killing over a thousand soldiers at a time in massive explosions.[12] Every military mind in Europe sat up and took notice.

Three years later, the senior officers of the Spanish Armada knew just how vulnerable they were to hellburners. It was that knowledge, and that fear, that was their ultimate undoing.

At midnight on the 28th of July, eight English fireships, manned by skeleton crews and filled with those combustible materials that could be spared by a fleet already running dangerously short on ammunition, sailed into the Armada where it lay at anchor off Calais.

The Spanish, who had been watching and waiting for just such an attack, responded by sending out picket vessels to intercept the fireships and tow them to shore to burn out harmlessly there. The pickets only managed to catch and tow one of the eight vessels that way, and the other seven plowed into the Armada's tightly packed crescent formation.

It was then that panic set in. These were simple fireships, not the vastly more dangerous hellburners, but the Spaniards had no way of knowing that. While the principal warships held the line, others cut and ran, quite literally, cutting their cables and main anchors and scattering in confusion, some colliding in their haste to escape. The crescent formation was broken, the Armada was in chaos. The English closed in for the kill.

Medina Sidonia made one last desperate attempt to regroup the Armada off nearby Gravelines, a safely Spanish-controlled port in Flanders. He was out of time and out of luck. After days of intense but indecisive engagements, Howard and his senior officers had continued to adapt their strategies and had managed to hit on the right answer: they were going to have to close to within a hundred meters of the Spanish galleons to penetrate those thick oak hulls.

They did, firing relentless and repeated broadsides, finally doing damage below the Spanish waterlines. Their superior mobility kept the galleons from closing for boarding actions, and the Spanish guns and shot proved, once again, woefully inadequate to the task.

Only two Spanish ships were lost in the actual battle, but casualties among the Armada crews were phenomenally high, and a number of ships were so badly damaged that they ran aground a day or two later. Blood was seen pouring from the scuppers of Bertendona's carrack, her battery guns silent.[13] The galleons had had to bear the brunt of the defense, sailing individually against groups of English ships worrying at them in concert, in the nautical equivalent of bear baiting. The *San Lorenzo* ran aground and was taken by Howard, after a ferocious fight. *La Maria Juan* was sunk. The *San Mateo* and *San Felipe* managed to limp away from the battle, but were so damaged that they ran aground on the isle of Walcheren, to be captured by England's Dutch allies. Other, smaller carracks foundered and ran aground as well. In the midst of it all, the *San Martino*, Medina Sidonia's flagship, fought valiantly, plunging into the fray to rescue besieged Spanish ships at least twice.[14]

The damage taken by the Armada's ships was so substantial that most of them were no longer seaworthy, let alone battle ready, by the time the remainder limped out into the North Sea.

Fugit

The wind had backed southerly the day after the battle, and Howard was continuing to dog the Armada up the Channel, nearly exhausted though his own ammunition was. There was no way, damaged as they were, for the Spanish to fight both wind and enemy fleet, and press directly for safe harbor in Corunna. They continued to head north, harried by the English all the way.

Medina Sidonia had no good options for refit and re-supply. He could attempt to turn around and meet Parma at Dunkirk, fighting difficult winds, the English fleet, and their Dutch allies in his already-weakened state. The safely Spanish-held port of Gravelines had similar difficulties. To the north of those ports, every other major port was held by the Dutch resistance or by Protestant nations unlikely to be sympathetic to the great Catholic crusade to depose Europe's primary Protestant leader.

Charles Fair suggested in his 1971 *From the Jaws of Victory* that Medina Sidonia could have put in at Hamburg or the Firth of Forth, "where he might have been well received," but neither seems likely. James VI of Scotland, later James I of England, was an ally of Elizabeth's in spite of the recent execution of his mother, Mary, Queen of Scots. Had a strong Armada capable of beating the English set in for re-supply, it is entirely possible that James would have switched sides, but as the Spanish ships were clearly disintegrating by that point, their battle already lost, it would have defied pragmatism for him to offer them aid. And Hamburg, not a deep water port of the kind the Armada would need, rather far inland and Lutheran since 1529, seems even less likely as a possible pit stop for the Spanish.

For better or for worse, and it was definitely for worse, the Armada had little choice but to try to limp home without a refit and re-supply on the continent.

Howard was forced to break off his pursuit of the Armada when they reached the Firth of Forth; his shot lockers were very nearly empty, and the English had done, for the moment, all the damage they could. The rest was in God's hands, and for several nervous weeks, the English stayed on the alert, preparing for the possibility of a second wave of attacks from a refurbished and re-supplied Armada.

The attack never came. Medina Sidonia took his battered ships around the west coast of Ireland, hoping to be able to re-supply in a Catholic country friendly to their cause. It was their last hope, and it was to prove the greatest disaster of all.

The Spanish ships had to try to pilot that rocky and difficult coast without charts, in North Atlantic storms of freak severity, most of the ships having cut their heavy anchors at Calais to escape the fireships. The lack of those heavy anchors meant that ship after ship ran aground on the coast of Ireland, unable to keep from being driven onto the rocks.

Unusually severe North Atlantic storms and the rocky Irish coast did more damage to the Armada than the English had. Spanish crews that landed in Ireland, voluntarily or otherwise, were hanged more often than not by the local English authorities, in the command of the ruthlessly pragmatic Sir William Fitzwilliam, Lord Deputy of Ireland. Fitzwilliam was responsible for the executions of more than 2,000 Spanish soldiers and sailors, sparing only those of extremely high rank.

Harsh as his methods were, they did prevent the Spanish from strengthening the Irish rebellion.

By the time the broken remains of the Armada limped back to Corunna on the 11th of September, 65 ships were all that remained to it, and of those 65, a number were too badly damaged to be salvaged, and had to be scuttled in port. Less than 10,000 men survived, and of those 10,000, many more were taken by disease after the Armada had reached safe harbor. More than 20,000 men had died over the course of Philip's misadventure, of starvation, disease, wounds in battle, execution in Ireland.

The Duke of Medina Sidonia was among the survivors, unfortunately for him. He had to be carried home in a litter, in secrecy, because the blame for the failure of the Enterprise was being laid entirely at his door. Tales of his cowardice and ineptitude traveled far and wide, including one to the effect that he'd hidden in a specially reinforced room in the *San Martino* while battle raged around them. He lived on for a number of years, occupying various administrative posts in the Spanish government, but no one ever even *thought* of giving the poor bastard another military assignment.

As for Philip, seeing the wreck of years' worth of plans and dreams, unable to explain why God had apparently turned against his great crusade in quite so terrible a fashion, his reaction was complex. On the one hand, he was gracious enough to forgive Medina Sidonia with the moral equivalent of a shrug: "I sent my ships to fight against the English, not against the elements." All things considered, it was probably the best vindication Medina Sidonia could have expected, and the best he would receive, at least until the critical historical examinations of the twentieth century would find him neither cowardly nor a fool, whatever his mistakes in leadership.

On the other hand, Philip's *ex post facto*, King Lear-style challenge savors of blind arrogance: "Great thanks do I render to Almighty God, by whose hand I am gifted with such power that I could easily, if I chose, place another fleet upon the sea. Nor is it of very great importance that a running stream should be sometimes intercepted, so long as the fountain from which it flows remains inexhaustible."[15]

Philip's was the characteristic hubris of a world power sliding into decline, scrambling inelegantly to stay on top against the delicate but inexorable working of the clockwork machinery of innovation, economics, and history.

*How the British Empire lost the War of Independence to an
army of backcountry farmers, merchants, and leg-breakers.
The American colonies should not have won,
and certainly the army and navy that would soon defeat
Napoleon should not have lost. But they did.*

LOBSTER STEW

1775–1783

PAUL A. THOMSEN

At the 1763 conclusion of the Seven Years' War/French and
Indian War, the British Empire maintained hegemony over much of
the known world. Their navy dominated the seven seas. Their business agents were found in nearly every major port and city across
the globe. The mere sight of their red-clad British Regulars, deri-
sively called "lobsters" by American colonials, instilled fear in colonial friend and imperial foe alike.[16] Indeed, most sane individuals
of the eighteenth century considered challenging the British to be
an act tantamount to suicide, but only a few years later, the empire
fought and yielded a civil war in North America to a small band of
ill-equipped, untrained, and heavily fragmented rebels.

While some have argued alternatively that republicanism, strategic genius, destiny, or even divine light allowed the Patriots
of the American Revolution to drive off the British military, the
historical record between 1775 and 1783 reveals an entirely different story.

They did not realize they were fighting an evolving enemy at each stage of the conflict until it was far too late to fully utilize the knowledge.

They fought a conventional war based on centuries of European experience of wars fought within a code of honor, against very unconventional opponents utilizing asymmetrical tactics, who saw victory at any cost as far superior to honor.

They squabbled among themselves over tactics and strategies and, worst of all, they alienated their own colonial and imperial supporters by engaging in brutal practices over protracted periods, with little to show for the imperial cost.

Ironically, the longer this civil war dragged on and the more reinforcements were sent to America, the more rapidly the British Empire cooked itself, but they had never lost such a fight, and hence, refused to surrender their preconceptions.

Consequently, on October 19, 1781, at Yorktown, Virginia, the imperial crustaceans, finally very obligingly crawled into their now-boiling colonial pot and zealously sealed the lid shut atop themselves and their imperial designs on the thirteen North American colonies.

The origins of this British civil-war-gone-horribly-wrong can be traced back to the way the empire managed their 1760s British colonial policies. With the treasury severely depleted by protracted warfare and a major Native American uprising against the North American colonies, the British government attempted to remedy their security and economic troubles by prohibiting colonial settlement west of the Appalachian Mountains, levying taxes on traded luxury items (including sugar, molasses, and tea), and quartering troops in settlers' houses when barracks were unavailable. Almost paradoxically, in making North America secure from exterior threats, British imperial policies actually created a political, social, and economic environment that destabilized the entire regional colonial infrastructure, starting with the colonial radical fringe and culminating in the trader elite and landed gentry.

In response to these perceived slights, the colonial radicals, leg-breakers, merchants, farmers, and backcountry vigilantes joined together in mob justice and political action, threatening to shove their rallying cry of "No taxation without representation" down the throats of British imperial governance throughout Atlantic coastal towns and cities.[17] Some humiliated prominent loyalists in hanged effigies and, sometimes, by liberal use of tar and feathers. Others burned the houses of imperial officials to the ground. Still others hurled insults, snow, ice, rocks, and even garbage at passing British Regulars, daring them to open fire on the assemblage. Yet, instead of rising to the challenge as they would have in *any* of their conquered territories, the British humored the protestors as adults might colicky children. They entreated the fractious rabble as a whole unit with tailored policies of informal appeasement to gain a "just" return on their investments, humoring the populace and hoping the radicals would just go away. They did not. As a result, of these perceived colonial victories, the American colonial radicals grew still more brazen, took arms, and drew more moderate citizens to their cause without any fear of reprisal.

When these increasingly organized acts of protest finally erupted in open warfare on April 19th, 1775, in a veritable hailstorm of colonial musket fire at British Regulars tasked with searching Concord and Lexington, Massachusetts, for weapons, the British sowed the seeds of their own military destruction.

They could not have been more wrong in their intelligence, strategy, or applied tactics.

Failing to find success with novel military action, they responded to the crisis in accordance with centuries of ingrained European military tradition. Instead of returning in force to the region, the British, believing they were vastly outnumbered, chose to protect that which they considered most valuable to the empire, the colonial cities, and waited for reinforcements.

They could not have been more wrong in intelligence, strategy, or action. First, while British military forces in North America were limited, the initial casualties suffered by the Regulars were largely incurred due to surprise and lack of coordinated planning, and not their ability to project power. Second, the colonial radicals only became a serious and organized threat to the British *after* the June 14, 1775, creation of a Continental Army by the Continental Congress, agreeing that "An Attack on One Colony Is an Attack on All."[18] Third, as Massachusetts Military Governor and British North American army commander General Thomas "Honest Tom" Gage later learned, neither he nor his men nor the urban populace were safe from the rebellious mainland inside the peninsula harbor-bordered city of Boston. Instead of holding the high ground around the city, they abrogated the shoreline to every armed radical, recalcitrant, and disaffected farmer in the region, looking to bag themselves a "lobster" and indirectly granting the Patriots exactly what they needed: time to wear down the garrison through siege warfare, await the arrival of heavy cannons, and, eventually, opportunity to bombard the city into submission.

On June 17, 1775, the British compounded their errors further by dually creating another British tactical nightmare and simultaneously whetting the appetites of the rebels. The British commanders ordered the bulk of their forces to take the distant hills overlooking the city from the rebels. Three times the British Regulars braved sustained rebel fire uphill against withering fire before they were finally able to retake the high ground. At the end of the day, the death toll was at least forty percent of their Boston garrisoned complement, 1,150 casualties. Yet, only after the herculean feat had been accomplished against the now-concentrated and numerically superior enemy did British General Gage realize, "The loss we have sustained is greater than we can bear."[19] Having foolishly spent the bulk of their in-country assets in a pyrrhic victory, the British could no longer protect the port city from being overrun by a rebel band they failed to fathom.

"These people shew a spirit and conduct against us they never shewed against the French," wrote General Thomas Gage on June 26, 1775, to Lord Barrington, Secretary of State for War, "and every body [sic] has judged of them from their formed appearance and behaviour when joined with the Kings forces in the last war; which has led many into great mistakes.

"They are now spirited up by a rage and enthousiasm [sic] as great as every people were possessed of, and you must proceed in earnest or give the business up. A small body acting in one spot will not avail. You must have large armys [sic], making divertions [sic] on different sides, to divide their force. . . .

"We are here, to use a common expression, taking the bull by the horns, attacking the enemy in their strong parts. I wish this cursed place was burned."[20]

Rather than throw away still more seasoned veterans to fruitless forays inland, the British military abandoned their 1775 self-created Boston nightmare for safer ground and ample reinforcements, leaving the city and her few loyal Tory citizens to the privations of their rebel enemy. Sadly for General Gage's replacement, General Lord William Howe, "Honest Tom's" mistakes were rapidly re-crafted by General Howe as his own. Instead of retaking Boston, the British military followed a more civil and conventional course: they tracked the rebel Continental Army to New York and attempted to save the general populace from the patriot movement.

In the summer of 1776, the largest fleet ever assembled arrived at the mouth of the New York Colony's Brooklyn Harbor. As one witness to the arrival of Howe's fleet of reinforcements later remarked, "I can't believe my eyes. It's like a forest of pine trees are moving in out there. In ten minutes the whole bay is full of ships. It looks like all London is afloat here."[21]

And if it didn't work the first time, where was the harm in trying again?

As the 22,000 British soldiers and Hessian mercenaries prepared to invade and crush General Washington's 10,000 Continental Army soldiers and militia, encamped in Brooklyn, it seemed that the Patriots had finally met their match. Yet, instead of meeting force with force, the British once more followed conventional protocol, first entreating the colonials to surrender through diplomacy, then failing that, landing troops in Brooklyn on August 22. Then failing to kill the rebel army, he landed his men again on Manhattan Island on September 15, 1776. Finally, throughout October and November, he lagged behind the retreating main element of the Continental Army into Westchester and New Jersey.[22] Not once did they suspect rebel duplicity. Not once did they expect their enemy to refuse to stand and fight. And not once did they catch the enemy army and kill it.

Moreover, rather than punish their errant children, the British military called a time-out.

Each time the British military had brought the ragtag band of rebels to the brink of annihilation, but just when final victory seemed at hand, General Howe simply gave up the initiative in favor of prudence and integrity. After decimating the Continental Army at the Battle of Long Island, he allowed General George Washington, backed up against the East River and flanked on three sides by vastly superior numbers, time to either offer a formal and honorable surrender or make a final peace with his maker before dying the next morning. General Washington had other plans. Instead of lying down to die, overnight a fog covered Brooklyn—and the ignoble escape of the Continental Army in "appropriated" watercraft to Manhattan Island. Days later, Howe's men were slowed by the seizure of New York City and narrowly missed the flight of the bulk of their enemy northward and off Manhattan Island. Weeks later, again the British Army were stunned by their enemy, who seemed to know only two actions, which have since come to be the founding principles of asymmetrical warfare: fire and flee. Finally, even when General Charles Cornwallis closed to within an hour of the enemy running across New Jersey in December, 1776 (and secretly planning to attack the town of Trenton), he was ordered to break off the pursuit, halt his advance at Brunswick, and await further instructions.[23]

As if rooting out a now-mercurial colonial insurgency was not enough, the British field commanders, likewise, refused to fight on the same page.

The British commanders repeatedly refused to lead their armies to function in a directed manner that would allow for the opportunity of victory. Had those December, 1776 orders not arrived, General Cornwallis would likely have annihilated General Washington's army and the organized resistance to British rule. Worse, as the British became mired by these tactical victories and sank into an ever-deepening countryside morass, they were also losing internal military cohesion both on message and within the ranks. Over the course of the war, the British military simply did not evolve a major strategy to end the war. Every British commander from Generals Gage to Howe to Clinton to Cornwallis began their expeditions with traditional measures, failed to learn from their contemporaries' failures, and fell into the same traps. If they survived those traps, they simply pressed forward with increased determination. As a result, the British military were consistently strategically a chapter or three behind their enemy and growing more weary with each step taken.

When compelled to adapt, the British military begrudgingly learned one set of colonial dance steps, but they refused to learn any more. After all, who dances to more than one tune?

Moreover, the British conventional mentality and the actions of their unconventional foes forced the British Empire to expend their limited reserves beyond the established goal of hunting and killing the Continental Army. Every plan was predicated on short-term problem solving and conventional gains made against a shifting, fluid, and strategically amorphous enemy, acting to consistently replace solved problems with still more conundrums. General Thomas Gage had suffered from a bunker mentality. It had alienated the British military from the Massachusetts populace and had eventually cost him the entire colony. When General Lord Howe attempted to shield the colonial urban Tory populace from privation, he simultaneously forfeited the greater threat of an evolving organized wilderness campaign. British General Henry Clinton followed suit, but by 1778, with little to show for their efforts but disasters, the British military was wearing out their welcome with their local Tory supporters. General Cornwallis, languishing in a rear echelon position with army rivals, at one point wrote his superior, "I must beg that your lordship will be so kind as to lay my most humble request before his Majesty, that he will be graciously pleased to permit me to return to England."[24] He was refused his leave and, shortly thereafter, was granted a position of authority in the south, where he was tied down by conventional forces, guerilla bands, bloodthirsty loyalists, and in the final stages of the war, the health of runaway slaves.

Well, if the colonials were so smitten with running around the countryside, where was the harm in just standing by and waiting for them to attack?

Ironically, when the British military finally learned that denial of ground and the waging of a war of attrition were the necessary tools that they had been lacking to grind down the rebels in the Northern and now Middle Colonies, they had very little to fight with and that which they had was rapidly succumbing to entropy. Due to the political divisions in Parliament and the already strained fiscal state of the empire, the British military in America was forced to make do with what they had. When reinforcements could be managed, they would be sent, but by 1779, they were few and far between. Worse, everything the British had liberated they had to protect for fear of enemy predation. Still worse, when they kept their men on high alert for weeks on end, as the British had placed their Hessian mercenaries occupying the New Jersey town of Trenton in December, 1776 (as rapid response teams to meet any emerging threats), the troops could, would, and did burn out. Once ordered to stand down, the enemy invariably received word of the orders and thus the loyal British citizens were, according to one period writer, "exposed to cruel oppression of the enemy" and the Tory volunteers would then leave "the army in disgust, and disaffection spread rapidly through the whole province."[25]

Instead of taking the direct approach, the scenic route offered so much more to see and do.

Denial of resources also had other unforeseen consequences. When the British military closed traffic to a suspected Patriot enclave or in anticipation of a patriot attack, as was often the duty of Colonel John Simcoe and the Queen's Rangers, they starved the very colonial commerce the empire needed to pay the bills. When they bolstered their ranks with mercenaries or Tories to project power throughout a wider area, as exemplified by the exploits of British General John "Gentleman Johnny" Burgoyne's march on Albany, the British polarized public opinion against their actions by alienating the local populace with the presence of foreigners' severely limited English-speaking capabilities. Inevitably, as they pursued the rebels in their organized campaigns, as exemplified again by General Burgoyne's 1777 campaign, and later General Cornwallis' 1780 and 1781 campaigns against General Horatio Gates' and General Nathaniel Greene's southern Continental Army elements, respectively, the British military also often found their own supply lines besieged by small roving rebel bands, and their forces worn down in the wilderness between settlements with nothing to show but wagons of wounded.

If their colonials were so good, then the Tories must have been better!

As the war continued to drag on with no end in sight, British military commanders were repeatedly stunned by new outbreaks of rebellion in regions made safe and secure (largely the southern colonies) by the application of extreme measures. When the British managed to annihilate a component of the Continental Army at the August 1780 Battle of Camden, their belated application of terror and subjugation, in the form of bayoneting prisoners, drew northern ire and steadied the wearing resolve of the few fugitive Continental Army leaders to have escaped the fall of the south; the actions of a handful of officers were limited without an army to direct. Ironically the British, once more underestimating the situation, indirectly gave the rebels a new army and fresh targets by acceding to months of colonial Tory petitions to aid the British army in prosecuting the war and provisioned the militias with British supplies and weapons. Within a few weeks, the southern urban landscape bathed in the blood of old Tory enemies that had little to do with the current conflict.

"On most of the plantations," recalled one resident, "every house was burnt to the ground, the negroes were carried off, the inhabitants plundered, the stock, especially sheep, wantonly killed; and all the provisions, which could be come at, destroyed. Fortunately the corn was not generally housed, and much of that was saved."[26]

Within a few months, the now-organized Tories were visiting similar carnage upon the countryside with even greater relish, and driving both former Patriots and most neutrals into the arms of the Patriot cause in the hopes of ending this new reign of terror. "In the summer of 1780," recalled William James, a former member of Francis Marion's southern guerilla forces, regarding the viciousness of the roving bands of armed Tories, "Col. Ferguson, of the British 71st, had undertaken to visit the tory [sic] settlements in the upper country, and train up the young men to arms. Among these several unprincipled people had joined him, and acted with their usual propensity for rapine and murder. Many Americans, fleeing before them, passed over into the state of Tennessee, then beginning to be settled. By their warm representations, they roused the spirit of the people of that country, which has since become so often conspicuous. Although safe from any enemy but the savages of their cane brakes, they left their families, and generously marched to the assistance of their friends. Nine hundred of them mounted, under the command of Col. Campbell, poured down from the Allegany, like the torrents from its summit. Armed with rifles, sure to the white speck on the target, at the distance of one hundred paces, or to decapitate the wild turkey on the top of the tallest pine—these were indeed a formidable band. . . . Eleven hundred of the enemy were killed, wounded or taken, of which one hundred were British."[27]

For the British, there was nothing like taking their work home with them.

By 1781, the British military succumbed to the rising temperature of the North American colonial population. Although the British military was able to gain a few public relations successes (for example, the turning of Patriot Benedict Arnold, the hero of the Saratoga Campaign, into a loyal British officer), they were short-lived, few, and were seldom exploited to effectively win back waning colonial-imperial interest and, as throughout history, the wear and tear of British armies of occupation eventually became too much for most colonial cities. Food was scarce. Public streets were patrolled by armed British Regulars not knowing whom to trust and wary of potential threats coming from disguised Patriots or their sympathizers. New arrivals waited outside of barracks and houses, anxiously waiting to be transported into the war zone. British soldiers were seen destroying property, stealing, and committing acts of unprovoked public violence. Consequently, urban street life was becoming as dangerous as the war in the backcountry.

Rather than make their own homes near the action, they made a little action of their own in others' homes.

In regard to British military, actions in off-hour high society circles were little different. Previously forgivable actions of a liberating army became far more noticeable symbols of Patriot propaganda when the tastes of certain British officers, such as General Lord William Howe, ran to colonial women of single and married status (most frequently affluent Tory women). Tory commoners, too, had much about which to worry. The British armies of occupation demanded entertainment. In response, certain establishments were opened to service the troops, much to the chagrin of their more religious Tory neighbors. Many Philadelphian members of the Society of Friends, once grateful to be liberated from the rebels, grew increasingly alarmed as the months passed and their purported saviors continued to engage increasingly grand acts of debauchery, including the reopening of the theater district, public drunkenness of troops, and the opening of Houses of Ill Repute to service the desires of the British infantry.

If one did not like the accommodations, they were always changed.

Before long, even the most ardent of Tory holdouts were growing frustrated with the new threats of their now long-overstayed guests. In other times, petitions to close the more boisterous establishments would have been considered due course for urban governance, but under military rule, such lobbying efforts were suspect of being misconstrued as sedition.

Numerous dilapidated prison ships, stationed along the shorelines of several major cities, served as a constant reminder for city residents of the price they might pay in crossing the British military authority. The vessels leaked, were lice-ridden, and served as a breeding ground for smallpox. Prisoners, some taken as early as 1776, were fed one meal a day, were forced to remain below decks in rags with little room to move, and were granted only brief glimpses of the sun at the start of every day, when they were ordered to pass up the bodies of their comrades who had died the night before for discarding over the side of the vessel, along with the contents of the Patriots' chamber pots. While the vessels had originally been commissioned to hold enemy soldiers, over time some Patriot-sympathizing families followed. When the Continental Army could not convince the British to improve the quality of the prisons, a few Tory residents attempted to follow their religious convictions to ease the suffering of their enemies. Yet, when they tried to offer food and other humanitarian aid, the British commanders became increasingly rigid. Aid in any form to the prisoners by even the most liberal Tory could be considered seditious. Hence, by 1780, even the more liberal-minded Tories were backing away from their former protectors as anxiously as they could.

Denial wasn't just a military goal. It was also a state of mind.

In 1781, Lord Cornwallis' army, driven out of the country of the Carolinas, had attempted one last-ditch effort to kill the Continental Army. Propelled northward, they moved to protect the Virginia coastal town of York. Now cornered on three sides by the Continental Army and their newly arrived French soldiers (acting under the geopolitical calculation that "the enemy of my enemy is my friend") and hemmed in by a French naval fleet, the might of the British Empire was forced to face the folly of their military actions.

There was nothing capable of being won and everything to be lost. With the entrance of the French into the war, the stagnation of the war in the north, the middle colonies showing discontent, the south now in flames, and the defeat of General Cornwallis, the British simply gave up. The British military were stalled in the same place they had been at the start of the war. They still did not understand the enemy they had created, nor could they compel the Patriots to fight a conventional war. Politically and militarily, therefore, the civil war could drag on indefinitely, swallowing men and material in a vain attempt to subdue a group of barely profitable backcountry recalcitrant colonies. The British treasury was far lower than ever before and the French were attacking British holdings throughout the world. It had repeatedly bludgeoned itself

against walls of its own ideological construction, against empty
ground once occupied by fleet-footed enemies, and outwore the
welcome of even their most ardent colonial supporters by acts of
indifference and desperation for seven years. Rather than continue
to fight a war without end, like the lobsters the colonists had occasionally called them, the British accepted that they had defeated
themselves and shut the lid on the pot they had set and boiled for
themselves.

One of the great What Ifs of history is the question:
Could the South have "won" the American Civil War?
Here the eminent scholar and author of many books
on that war William R. Forstchen answers that
question and explains why they lost.

THE CONFEDERACY

North America, 1861–1865

WILLIAM FORSTCHEN

It was the greatest tragedy in our nation's history, and its traumatic memory lingers, as Lincoln once said, "unto the latest generation." It is the most studied, debated, and passionately argued event in American history. In those debates two big questions always seem to be the focus for those interested in our Civil War: what was it all about, and could the South have indeed won?

To answer the second question, perhaps a brief review of the first question. The causes need to be looked at. For those with Yankee leanings, slavery is usually the first issue cited, the idea that if not for slavery and the moral imperative to honor the opening paragraph of our Declaration of Independence, there never would have been the great debates about States' Rights versus Federal authority, and thus no war. For Southerners, States' Rights is first and foremost the central issue involved. Given modern sensibilities and moral values, of course the question of slavery is painful to raise, and its mere presence makes any who are pro-Confederate cringe, but the argument in response is that the "peculiar institution" as it was then called, was about to disappear anyhow. If the South had been left to their own devices, slavery would have ended without the cost of six hundred thousand lives and, afterward, the hateful legacy of racism and Jim Crowism.

We'll return to this issue of slavery later, for it might very well be the central core of how a nation lost a war.

It was a war that Winston Churchill described as one of the most inevitable in history, that "these" United States prior to 1861 "were" a union that contained several fatal flaws. The compromises the Founding Fathers made were done out of necessity in order to forge together a Constitution that all would agree to, and like most compromises, left all parties with a certain degree of dissatisfaction. By 1850, the flaws were increasingly evident. It was not just about States' Rights versus Slavery, North versus South, but beyond that there is merit to the thesis of Grady McWhiney, in his fascinating book *Cracker Culture*, that there was a fundamental cultural divide in America. The North was oriented toward legalism and mercantilism, emerging out of an English Puritan culture. The South was an entirely separate entity, evolving primarily from pre-Revolutionary War Scot-Irish heritage that placed its emphasis on family name, honor, ownership of property. Fiercely independent, they abhorred the values of the North. There is a validation of this when you read how each side stereotyped the other at the onset of the war.

Yankees were money hungry, a nation of shopkeepers "slaving" for pasty-faced merchants hiding behind lawyers. The Yankees were grasping and had no sense of personal honor while moving to usurp power by increasing federal control.

To the North, the South was illiterate, ignorant, obsessed with dueling and ridiculous antiquated concepts of personal, family, and regional honor. The infamous Sumner-Brooke incident, where a Southern congressman caned a northern senator on the floor of Congress, was seen by Northerners as a cowardly attack, while Southerners in general applauded, saying that Brooke was defending his family's honor after Sumner had issued a personal insult to one of Brooke's relatives, and he therefore deserved the fractured skull dealt out in reply.

On the eve of war, for the South, it was seen as a conflict about personal honor, the honor of their state and region, after unrelenting insults and moral double dealing by Yankees, who had now elected one of their lawyers (forget about Lincoln's log cabin and Southern origins, at this stage he was a highly successful corporate lawyer—imagine a litigation expert, after making millions, running for office today), who would twist the Constitution to his own purposes.

Herein will lie some of the roots of how to lose a war.

Could the South ever have won? It is worth looking at what many believe in today as possible turning points of the conflict before looking at the root cause of how they did indeed lose a war.

There might indeed have been one main chance, but it was not during the time period of 1861–65, but instead was ten years earlier. If ever there was a time for the South to leave the Union, they should have pulled it off in 1850, rather than 1861. This was the year of the great debates, where the nation did totter toward disintegration until Congress hammered out what is called the Great Compromise of 1850. This again, like most compromises, left all parties dissatisfied. Its end result was simply to postpone the inevitable for another decade.

If the South had walked in 1850, the military situation would have been profoundly different, based upon one key factor: railroads. In 1850, there was less than 8,000 miles of track in the entire nation; by 1861, it would be nearly 30,000 miles. Why would this be important? Logistics. As Helmuth von Moltke, the Prussian Chief of Staff during the Franco-Prussian War supposedly declared: "The amateur studies tactics, the professional—logistics."

The landmass of the eleven states that would comprise the Confederacy is greater than all of western Europe. Remember that forty years earlier, not even the great Napoleon could conquer and hold that much territory. If one follows the campaigns of the Civil War, both armies were dependent on one of two methods of maintaining supplies, either rivers or rail. In 1850, there was precious little rail in the South, and in the North, the vast complex web that would support the war effort in the 1860s was not yet linked together. The factory systems of the North, so efficient in the 1860s, were just beginning to emerge in 1850, and even the population ratio, not yet fully flooded by the vast wave of immigration in the 1850s, presented better odds for the South. And finally, the tactical nature of the fighting would have been profoundly different. Rifled weapons were not yet the norm, the famed (or infamous) "minie ball" had yet to be invented, and the average range of shoulder weapons was under a hundred yards. Ideal range for shoulder weapons when facing the wild, gallant charges that so typified Southern arms in the 1860s, and which generated mass slaughter for their side when dug-in troops could shred such charges at three hundred yards. In 1850, those same charges, more often than not, would have carried the battlefield.

If the South had decided to walk in 1850, the ability of the North to field an army of more than a million men to "suppress the rebellion," to put that army into action, and to sustain it on far-flung fronts a thousand miles apart, would have been gravely compromised. An aroused South, with short logistical lines in their home territory, could have undoubtedly blocked whatever efforts the North made, and thus sustained the war until the will of the North collapsed. Always realize that, above all else, this was a war of political will. The South merely needed to defend. The North had to maintain an aggressive war long enough to finally move vast armies literally from the Mississippi, across Tennessee, and then from Atlanta to the sea, and present before the next presidential election the vision of a victory near at hand. Sherman's seizing of Atlanta in September, 1864, assured Lincoln's reelection, a Union political victory which then assured a final victory in the field. Prior to that, Lincoln himself doubted that he would win. In 1850, Atlanta had no military significance whatsoever; the rail net that made it a focal point in 1861 did not even exist. An 1850 Sherman moving an army of the size necessary from Chattanooga (another rail nexus point that did not yet exist in 1850) to Atlanta and then to Savannah would have been a logistical impossibility.

The South would have been able to hold out long enough until a presidential election put forth a candidate, most likely in 1852, who would have been forced to say "the hell with it," concede the fight, and then try to focus Northern efforts on Westward expansion.

It is just a fantasy scenario of course. No one in South Carolina in 1850 could look fifteen years into the future and announce "We better do it now before the railroads are built and rifled weapons change the entire nature of warfare."

And so the war came in 1861, and the next question is, were there indeed pivotal moments when the South might have won, the theory being that one decisive battle might have decided the issue.

Weigley, in his studies of the concept of the "battle of decision," or single decisive battle, points out there was a time, militarily, when one battle did indeed decide the issue in a day. There is a long list of these single days, often just an hour or two, that decided all: Marathon, Actium, and Hastings, among them. Once the opposing army was not just defeated, but driven to near extinction, its leader killed, the only logical conclusion was for the losers to concede. But the new realities of industrialized warfare made this "battle of decision" increasingly doubtful. An army could be annihilated, but as long as the losing side maintained its political will, and its industrial base was not yet overrun, within weeks, months at most, factories could replace the lost equipment, replace a hundred thousand rifles and two hundred cannons. And with the population explosion of the nineteenth century, they could draft a hundred thousand more men—as long as the political will was maintained. Also, gone were the days when a king or warlord was on the front line. Increasingly he was back at the capital, instead of lying dead on the field, as at Hastings, and thus shattering the rally point of resistance. Yes, there would be single battles of decision in the nineteenth century, such as the brief Six Weeks' War between Prussia and Austria in 1866, or at Sedan when the Prussians triumphed over the French in 1870 (and did capture the emperor, Napoleon III), but in both of those cases, the will of the losing side was already badly shaken and they were about ready to concede the game.

During the American Civil War there were, perhaps, three battles, all in the East, that might have fit the criteria of a "battle of decision," with the supposed potential of ending the war in a day with a Confederate victory.

The first was Bull Run (or Manassas, as the victors called it). At the end of the day of battle, three months after the war started, the Union army was in disorganized rout, leaderless, demoralized, flooding back into Washington crying that the rebels were on their heels.

Could the South have won the war that night?

Thomas "Stonewall" Jackson urged the two commanders, Beauregard and Johnston, to launch an aggressive pursuit and by the following dawn they would be before the doors of the White House and the Capitol with Southern independence won.

Doubtful.

No matter how tough Southerners claimed to be when compared to the "pasty face, shopkeeper Yankees," put on thirty pounds of gear over a heavy wool uniform, and run about for eight hours in ninety-five-degree heat for a day while people are trying to kill you, and see how you feel at the end of it. Southern armies of 1861 were just as naïve, ill trained, poorly organized, and no tougher than their Yankee counterparts.

Jackson would claim that if given but a division, or just a brigade, he could have taken Washington that night. Such a move would have required force-marching five to ten thousand already exhausted, dehydrated men twenty miles, then seizing one of the bridges across the Potomac by storm, followed by a vicious street fight from the swampy edge of the Potomac on up to Capitol Hill.

Not all the troops in the District of Columbia that night were demoralized and beaten ninety-day volunteers. There was a hard cadre of professional regular infantry who had covered the retreat of the panic-stricken volunteers. There was the "old guard" of professional, leatherneck marines at the nearby Naval Yard, several gunboats at that yard, and the serious tactical problem of trying to seize a bridge intact by frontal assault before the days of airborne assault against the opposite shore.

Based on other battles, it is likely that even with the panic-stricken survivors of First Manassas, if backs were pushed to the wall, the bulk of them would have turned and fought with a vengeance.

Yes, the flag of the Confederacy did briefly fly above Arlington Heights (the home of a then obscure officer named Robert E. Lee), but to believe Jackson's fantasy that Manassas was already the battle of decision is absurd. Hard driver that he was, he might have arrived at Iron Bridge on the Potomac, but he would have done so almost alone, or at best with several thousand blown, exhausted troops, as ready to collapse as their opponents.

First Manassas was not the potential decisive battle that could have brought a speedy Confederate victory.

Fourteen months later came the Antietam Campaign. Harry Turtledove, the well-known and highly respected master of alternate history, built an entire series around the speculation that here might have been the moment of Southern victory.

The story behind the events leading up to the Battle of Antietam is well known to any devotee of Civil War history. After his triumph at a second battle fought near Manassas, General Robert E. Lee, now in command of the valiant Army of Northern Virginia, ventured an invasion into Maryland. He had hopes of perhaps even driving into Pennsylvania, and to thus lure their famed rivals, the Army of the Potomac, into a battle of decision, far beyond the safety zone of the fortifications around Washington, which Union forces could always retreat to in the past, if defeated.

General Lee initiated a daring, masterful plan. While the Union forces were still reeling from their defeat at Manassas, he would divide his army into four separate units, which for a time would be out of range of mutual support of each other; they would envelop the Union garrison at Harper's Ferry, capture it, along with its vast stockpile of supplies (again logistics), while half of his army under his trusted corps commander James "Pete" Longstreet would position for a move into Pennsylvania.

This gutsy plan unraveled by pure chance. Lee sent out a circular to his division commanders, "General Order 191," outlining the details of this plan, with marching orders for each division.

Just outside of Frederick, Maryland, on September 13, 1862, an Indiana regiment, advance guard of the cautiously moving Army of the Potomac, under the command again of General George McClellan, took a break from their march. A soldier noticed three cigars lying in the grass by the side of the road, with a piece of paper wrapped around them. Far more interested in the cigars than the paper, he picked up his find, passed two of the treasured cigars to comrades and then, like so many of us—eating breakfast, lounging on the porch, or engaged in various other activities—who are readers at heart, he opened the note to read it . . . and in less than an hour that note was in the hands of McClellan. It was an exact copy of General Lee's "Order 191," the complete details of the disposition of all Confederate forces in Northern Virginia and Maryland, their routes of march—and just how vulnerable those forces were, spread out across several thousand square miles. Who dropped those orders by accident on the side of the road outside Frederick will never be known. A courier, perhaps even one of the generals who received it. An investigation was launched by Lee, but never followed up aggressively and it remains a mystery to this day. Regardless of who was at fault, it is as if on June 4, 1944, the Germans somehow had obtained every detail of the Allies' plans for the invasion of Normandy.

Harry Turtledove creates a very compelling series on the "what-ifs" regarding those orders—if they had not been found. It is good alternate history, but not real history. In real history the orders were found, and the normally slow General McClellan did show a tad more aggressiveness in moving his army over the Catoctin and South Mountain ranges, to the west of Frederick, forcing Lee to abandon most of his plans and instead concentrate on the banks of Antietam Creek, where on September 17, 1862, the Army of the Potomac met the Army of Northern Virginia, the two gallant foes fighting each other to a bloody standoff in which twenty-three thousand young men became casualties in little more than ten hours.

There was never a chance for a battle of decision here for the Southern cause. Whether it had taken place at Antietam, or elsewhere, the simple fact of the number of troops under arms for the South was the key issue. In fact, it should have been a battle of decision for the North, with General Lee's army pinned against the north shore of the Potomac and wiped out. But General Mc-Clellan, paralyzed by faulty intelligence and his own fears that Lee somehow outnumbered him two to one (in reality, his army of 75,000 nearly outnumbered Lee's little more than 40,000 by two to one), did not push more violently for that battle of decision. Never was Antietam the moment where the South could have won the war, rather it was a moment when the North might have ended the tragic conflict and in so doing, spared the nation nearly three more years and a million more casualties.

Gettysburg has always been the focal point of the Southern dream that, if ever there was a moment when Southern arms could have carried the day and gained the Confederacy its independence, it was there at a crossroads town in Pennsylvania, obscure before July 1, 1863, and forever after, a single word that shall echo as long as this Republic endures: Gettysburg.

Could Lee and his noble Army of Northern Virginia have won this battle and in so doing, won the war?

There is endless speculation that Lee threw away two golden moments, which could be known as the Ewell Thesis and the Longstreet Thesis. The former argues that General "Dick" Ewell, corps commander on the left flank of the Confederate Army, on the afternoon of July 1, 1863, threw away the golden opportunity of that day when, after crushing the Army of the Potomac's XI corps north of the town of Gettysburg, he failed to aggressively advance and seize the now-legendary high ground south of Gettysburg—Cemetery Hill.

The Longstreet thesis, upon which Shaara builds his Pulitzer Prize winning novel *Killer Angels*, maintains that on the evening of July 1, 1863, General Longstreet urged Lee to disengage from continued frontal assaults and instead, "move around their left," meaning outflanking the Union Army, in the classic style which the Army of Northern Virginia had demonstrated at Second Manassas and again just two months earlier at Chancellorsville.

Lee demurred, according to the novel, and only ordered a limited flanking attempt, which on the afternoon of the second day of battle, resulted in the bloody and futile attempt to take the anchor point of the Union left flank at Little Round Top. And then on the third day, again ignoring Longstreet's advice, Lee sent three divisions of his army in a frontal assault against the center of the Yankee line—Pickett's Charge.

These "alternate" views have been the center of debate by amateur and professional historians for nearly 140 years.

Both arguments, no matter how seductive they are to Southerners who wish to believe that during those crucial three days all things "were still possible," ignore certain realities.

Regarding the Ewell thesis, several crucial elements are ignored. First, that Dick Ewell's troops had, on average, force-marched anywhere from twelve to nearly twenty miles during the morning and early afternoon of July 1st, in nearly ninety-degree heat, to reach the battle and then engage. By the time the last of the Yankees had been driven back to Cemetery Hill, his troops were exhausted, thirsty, and mixed together, as is typical of any units, throughout history that had just fought a hard running battle for several hours. They needed time to form backup, at least rest briefly, find fresh water, and prepare for the next stage of the attack. During this time, a full brigade of Union troops, wisely left behind on that hill by General Howard, had been furiously digging in, and by late afternoon, the very capable Union artillery officer, Henry Hunt, had positioned over forty guns in revetments. Hunt later boasted, with good reason, that he wished the Confederates had indeed made a full-scale attempt, for he would have shredded them, as he had done exactly one year earlier at Malvern Hill on July 1, 1862. Civil War infantry, charging up a slope, across a third of a mile of open ground, against two battalions of dug-in artillery, was an exercise in slaughter and futility. And finally, Ewell did have reason to exercise caution. There was no such thing as recon birds or satellite photos to tell him what was lurking behind that hill. He had some intelligence that an entire fresh corps, the tough men of the Army of the Potomac's XII corps, were indeed moving up. Even if he had taken the crest, at bloody cost, could he have held it until the following morning? Doubtful.

The Longstreet thesis is the one that draws far more attention, again thanks to Shaara's well-written novel. The problem is that the novel, across the thirty-five years since its publication, has taken on the aura of fact. A careful study of the historiography of the debate around the Longstreet thesis reveals one all so crucial point: in reality there is not a shred of documentation, dated from the time of the battle, that Longstreet ever did offer such advice. It was not until half a dozen years afterward that the debate started, based upon "he said" versus "no he did not say" arguments among the survivors after Lee was dead. For any historian, it is primary documents, written at the time of the event, that matter most, not recollections made years, and then finally decades after that event.

Whether Lee was advised by Longstreet or not, the reality is that flanking attack on July 2, 1863, was a bloody disaster. The road to move Longstreet's corps into place for the attack was not properly scouted out, and after moving halfway to their jump-off point, it was discovered that their route of march exposed them to observation from the Union lines. It required a doubling back for half a dozen miles of the entire corps, and rather than kicking off the attack late in the morning, it was not until late in the afternoon that the assault on Little Round Top began. The troops attacking were exhausted after a march twice as long as anticipated, again without water, in nearly ninety-degree heat, and though famed as one of the great "what-ifs" of the war, it was an attack doomed when facing determined and equally gallant troops, who now saw this fight as defending their home territory.

As for July 3rd? That was doomed before it even started.

But in the spirit of speculation, given that Gettysburg is seen as the great turning point of the war (though no one actually said so at the time), let us consider for a moment what might have happened if Lee had not just won at Gettysburg, but had indeed fought a great "battle of decision" that had destroyed or captured most of the Army of the Potomac.

This author might have a better stab at the subject than most,

considering that I wrote three books, in co-authorship with former Speaker of the House of Representatives Newt Gingrich, on
this exact topic—a speculation of how Lee might have won the
Battle of Gettysburg and the results deriving from that victory.

Even if Lee had triumphed in a Gettysburg campaign and smashed
the Army of the Potomac—then what? In a speculation on alternate
history, one can play with many factors, but the laws of nature
should still be adhered to. Through the first week and a half of July,
1863, the region was soaked by intense storms. In fact in the real
history of that campaign, the Potomac River flooded and washed
away Lee's pontoon bridge over that river, leaving him stranded
and ripe for capture, and if not for the ridiculously slow advance of
General Meade, Lee should have indeed been pinned and captured
at Falling Waters, Maryland, the week after Gettysburg.

The roads between Gettysburg and Washington were rivers of
mud. If Lee had been able to crush the Army of the Potomac near
Gettysburg, and brushed aside the remains—then what? Advance
on Harrisburg to gain the political prestige of seizing a state capital of the North? Impossible, for he had attempted that the week
before, but it proved impossible when Union militia burned the
bridges spanning the Susquehanna River. So that road was closed.

Like Hannibal after Cannae, for Lee, ultimately there was only
one road that should have been taken, and that was straight at the
enemy's capital, be it Rome or Washington, D.C.

But like Hannibal, Lee would have found himself confronting
a nearly insurmountable barrier: the fortifications and the troops
still behind them.

Even while Meade sallied forth to challenge Lee in Pennsylvania,
well over twenty thousand well-armed troops had stayed behind
to guard Washington. In the two years since the start of the war,
thousands of men had been continually digging WWI-type fortifications, and in July 1863, Washington was the most heavily fortified
city in the world. Earthen works surrounded the city, and along all
likely approaches, those fortifications were in depth, looking very
much like a WWI battlefield. Earthen ramparts twenty feet high,
capped by artillery capable of firing hundred-pound shells, backed

up by thirty-pounders and heavy mortars ringed the city. If, after a triumph at Gettysburg, which even in the best of circumstances would have cost him ten to fifteen thousand casualties, Lee's army had floundered through the mud on a forced march of at least four to five days, they still would have had to storm those works.

The chances of success? Well, given that this author has co-authored three books on this exact subject, we'll leave that to those books, but I suspect you can guess the results, based upon realities that authors, such as McKinley Kantor, ignored when he wrote *If the South had Won the Civil War*.

This author concludes that a mythical, singular victory by Confederate arms, in the field, in a battle of decision, could never have overthrown the Union cause, regardless of the fanciful dreams of those who even today speak of the "Lost Cause," and how close it came to winning.

How to lose a war, though, is the key question of this series, and this author sees where the South could indeed have won the war, done so easily, but it would have required a profound step. A profound step, however that in so doing, would have eliminated the key underlying cause of the conflict, and forever altered the social structure of the South.

Directly put the answer is simple: free the slaves.

Southern apologists today, in presenting the argument that slavery was not the cause, eagerly roll forth documentation that at least thirty thousand men of color fought under the banners of the South. They have a difficult but interesting position to maintain.

They do correctly point out a glaring hypocrisy of the North throughout the war when, with the Emancipation Proclamation, Abraham Lincoln proclaimed to the Northern cause that this was a war of liberation, and in so doing forever seized the moral high ground.

But there are a few points to the Emancipation Proclamation that are forgotten. First, that the Proclamation itself was only part of a broader package. It was the stick, and the carrot is forgotten. While issuing the Proclamation, Lincoln also offered to the South generous terms. That if prior to January 1, 1863, the various

Confederate armies agreed to demobilize, representatives from the various states in rebellion could return their representatives to Washington, as long as such representatives and their constituents reaffirmed their oath of allegiance to the Constitution. If this was done, slavery would remain in place. Lincoln's detractors are quick to point out his comment from this time, that his goal was first and foremost to preserve the Union, and that if this meant that slavery was to stay in place where it already existed, so be it.

The Emancipation Proclamation was "the stick." If the offer of reconciliation was not taken, only then, as of January 1, 1863, would all slaves still behind Confederate lines be set free. In short, Lincoln with this Proclamation freed only those slaves not yet back under the jurisdiction of the Federal government. Exempt from this Proclamation were those regions in the South, such as New Orleans, the western half of Tennessee, and northwestern Virginia, that were already occupied. And most definitely, nothing was said about those slave states, Missouri, Kentucky, Maryland, and Delaware, which were still in the Union and supplying troops to the Northern cause.

Here is the moment of how to lose a war. If the South had been willing to face the true military and political reality, Jefferson Davis could have pulled the rug out from under Lincoln, gained the moral high ground, without doubt gained European recognition, and thereby gained independence.

In 1864, two noted citizens of the South, General Patrick Cleburne and Secretary of State Judah Benjamin, would both make this call for Emancipation of slaves in exchange for freedom and full citizenship, and both appeals were rejected by President Jefferson Davis, the Confederate Congress, and bitterly denounced by almost every newspaper editorial in the South. Benjamin's appeal, made at a public gathering in Richmond, almost triggered a riot among the listeners. But then again, that particular audience was well behind the battle lines and not doing the actual dying.

More than a few "pro-Southerners" today maintain that at least thirty thousand men of color did serve in the Confederate forces. There is at least some evidence to validate this, photographs of regimental reunions after the war, some contemporary written accounts, but no official statements to this effect. The uncomfortable issue of mixed race in the South, the policy that but one drop of "negro blood" in a person's veins made them subject to servitude, is a forgotten aspect of the history of slavery, as is the dividing off of people from citizenship if they were mulatto, or the now-forgotten identities of quadroons and octoroons. How many who were one quarter African-American, or one eighth, who served in Confederate ranks is not recorded, or whether they should be counted as black, white, or simply as soldiers of the Confederacy is a difficult topic that few wish to venture near today.

Or, on the other side, that there is clear documentation that at least three thousand men of color owned slaves themselves. The plantation of one, near Camden, South Carolina, is proudly and more than a little ironically pointed out to visitors today, as having been owned by a black man who owned dozens of slaves. Few point out that early in the war in 1861, that two local militia regiments in New Orleans, made up entirely of "men of color," did volunteer to fight in defense of their home city—an offer met with discomfort and silence on the part of Confederate authorities, but then moot after the city fell to Union forces in April, 1862. Those two regiments are considered by some historians to actually be the first black regiments to serve, since shortly after New Orleans was captured, they agreed to serve as local guard and eventually went into the field—against the Confederacy.

The entire issue of race and racism in America, the tragic legacy of that war, still lingers like a wound barely healed, and at times makes open honest discussion and debate a difficult field to move in, regardless of the race of the historian or those who are objectively interested in the subject.

Regardless, when it comes to the historical evidence, a few things do stand clear. With the South's rejection of Abraham Lincoln's peace offer of 1862, the Emancipation, by executive decree, was enforced by advancing Union troops as of January 1, 1863. It was by no means popular at the start; in fact, more than a few Lincoln and Union supporters up to this moment recoiled, declaring that the war was strictly about the interpretation of the Constitution and they would now refuse to fight. Protest meetings were held by some regiments serving in the field, and more than a few declared that if the proclamation was now official policy, they would desert and go home, that the Cause for which they fought, the preservation of the Union and its Constitution, had been corrupted by Lincoln.

Undoubtedly, some did desert. But then again, desertion throughout the war was rampant on both sides, and the proclamation could have just been a convenient excuse. The announcement that black regiments would be officially accepted into the ranks of the Union armies was met by protest on both sides as well. Over 200,000 men deserted the Union colors and at least 104,000 men the Confederates over the course of the war. In reply, President Davis pushed the now-infamous declaration that men of color captured in battle would be immediately sold into slavery, and their white officers executed for inciting servile revolt. Fortunately, it was an order ignored by nearly all generals in the field, General Lee flat out refusing to comply. And when the message was answered by the Lincoln administration that such actions would be met in kind with equal treatment to Confederate POWs, the issue was dropped. The war, already sinking deeper into brutality would indeed have spun out of control into outright barbarism, if such actions had begun on both sides. So, fortunately for this nation today, wiser heads did prevail, at least on this issue and in spite of the massacre at Fort Pillow and the cry of "no prisoners" at the Battle of the Crater (a cry issued by both sides at that disastrous battle). Black soldiers of the North were taken prisoner as were their officers.

As more and more black troops joined the Union cause, a societal change did begin to take place in the North, basically for the most pragmatic of reasons. The early fervor of volunteerism, which had filled the vacant ranks in 1861 and '62, had died out by 1863. We forget today the actual societal impact, on both sides, of this war. There were just under thirty million people, white and black, living in the thirty-four states at the start of the war. Over six hundred thousand would die, close to a million more would be injured or horribly maimed physically or psychologically (the latter, what we today openly accept as post traumatic stress syndrome). It would be the equivalent of America today, with three hundred million citizens, enduring the tragic loss of over six million of its young men dead, ten million or more injured or profoundly impacted psychologically, a million becoming addicted to morphine, millions left homeless, and property damage by today's standards well into the tens of trillions of dollars. In comparison, America, with 120 million citizens in 1941, lost approximately four hundred thousand dead during WWII. Such figures might give us a more realistic sense of just how horrifying the Civil War was. But one more example: by modern standards, the three days of Gettysburg would be equal to nearly six hundred thousand Americans killed, injured, missing, or taken into captivity, in three short days.

And so, on the pragmatic side, the flood of black volunteers to the Union cause, which started in 1863 and was triggered by the Emancipation Proclamation, meant that rather than nearly two hundred thousand whites being forced into the Union armies by the draft, two hundred thousand men of color, instead, eagerly joined the army in what was now a war of liberation for their brothers and sisters in bondage. A popular song of 1864, which today would be seen as beyond the pale of racism, has lyrics where an Irishman, singing in brogue, declares that beneath the skin, a black man's blood was just as red as his, so why not let him fight and stop a bullet instead.

The societal forces set in motion by the mobilization of black troops carried profound implications, as was so brilliantly pointed out by Frederick Douglass, who on July 4, 1863, proudly declared that once a black man wore the uniform of his country, had a rifled musket in his hands, and a cartridge box on his hip stamped U.S., he defied any power on earth to deny that man full and equal citizenship.

So different this war had become in just two short years. It was so clearly stated, when at Gettysburg, Lincoln opened his speech, not harkening back to the Constitution but rather to four score and seven years past, when it was declared that all men were created equal. The nature of the war, the very reason for the war, was shifting from the Constitution to the meaning of the Declaration of Independence.

How to lose a war? It was not on the actual battlefield that the Confederacy lost the war. A battlefield decision might have been the case, if the South had decided for secession in 1850 rather than 1861, when logistically and militarily, the suppression of the rebellion would have been well nigh impossible. Where the South lost the war was on the moral and political front, on January 1, 1863.

Lincoln's Emancipation Proclamation, properly analyzed by Southern leaders, should have revealed the handwriting on the wall. The North was about to seize the moral high ground. Though taunted and rejected by many in the North, nevertheless this proclamation would stay in place as long as Lincoln remained in the White House.

First, it would provide a moral argument to the rest of the world as to the nature of the war. One of the great hopes of the South was that eventually England and France would move to their side, recognize their government, and perhaps even break the blockade. There were more than a few in England who took delight in seeing their rebellious cousins having such a bitter falling out, and looking ahead, saw that a divided America would not be a major economic threat in the future. But in general, the Victorian middle class found slavery to be absolutely repugnant (while ignoring at the same time how so many subjects of the crown were being treated in South Africa and the Raj). As long as the South upheld slavery, there would be no support in Parliament for intervention. As for the emperor of France, locked in a surreal war in Mexico, slavery was an issue sufficient to block him as well. Lincoln, by the proclamation, had checkmated the South as far as foreign intervention went.

Second, as already pointed out, close to 200,000 men of African descent would be in uniform by 1865 on the side of the Union, close to one out of every four soldiers under arms.

And finally, it gave a moral high ground that only a few in the North accepted at first, but would gain strength in the final year of the war, until finally, it was seen as a primary cause for the struggle, and that the armies of the North were no longer conquering armies, but instead, holy armies of liberation and freedom.

If, prior to January 1, 1863, Southern leadership had clearly seen this eventuality, an eventuality that Lincoln had obviously grasped, how to lose a war might instead have become how to win a war.

If Lincoln's Emancipation Proclamation had been trumped by a Confederate decree, the South most likely would have won the war. The decree could have even been a compromise of sorts with slaveholders not yet willing to face the moral reality that the age of slavery in America had to come to an end.

A hypothetical counter response might have been:

First, that any man of color, free or slave, who was willing to serve in the Confederate army would be greeted as an equal. Free blacks living in the South, those of full or partial African descent, of which there were several hundred thousand, would be greeted in the ranks of the Confederate army with the promise of a bounty upon enlistment (the North was paying up to a thousand dollars a man by this point), and with it, as well, the solemn promise of full and equal citizenship during and after the war, both for themselves and their families. The families of men who died in the gallant Cause would earn the eternal gratitude of the South, and with their deaths, receive the full benefits expected by a family of a fallen hero.

Second, that slaveholders could sell their slaves into the army and receive the bounty as compensation, but with the key stipulation that at that moment, the former slave was now a free man, a citizen, and his family was free as well, with part of the bounty, and all of his pay as a soldier going to their support until the end of the war. Also, that the slave must give a solemn oath that he was joining voluntarily and not under forced servitude. (Ironically, there is a little known fact that a number of black men who served in Northern regiments had actually been sold into the army by their masters; this author has discovered several such statements by black veterans in pension records of soldiers at the National Archives.)

The third step would have to be the full realization that, if several hundred thousand men of African descent did fight for Southern independence, slavery had to end. A possibility being an accelerated program of manumission after the war was over for those whose sons and fathers did not fight, an idea which many subscribed to, such as Lee and General Polk, even before the war, as a way to extract the South from its "peculiar institution."

If such a realization had set in, been grasped and accepted, the South might very well have been able to mobilize 200,000 more men to its cause (and at the same time deny to the Northern armies tens of thousands of recently freed slaves who joined the side of the Union). These numbers could have increased by nearly fifty percent the number of valiant Southern soldiers under arms, presenting the prospect of additional corps of infantry at Gettysburg, or Chickamauga, or for the defense of Atlanta.

Though it is rightly argued that the dreamed-of single "battle of decision" was increasingly delusional by the middle of the nineteenth century, the additional armed strength of the South, combined with the trumping of the moral high ground regarding slavery, most likely would have shattered Lincoln's hopes for reelection in 1864. The peace candidate, former general George McClellan, might very well have become our 17th president, and would have presided over the division of the Union, and the creation of a permanent Confederate States of America.

What might have then been the results? The tragic history of Reconstruction avoided? Could such a decision have not just won the Southern cause, but also then avoided the ugly century-long stain of racism, Jim Crow, the horrid legacy of the KKK, lynchings, and denial of basic rights of citizenship? That instead there would have been an independent South, winning its independence by the sudden onrush of black troops, insuring an equal and far more harmonious society, grateful for those who stood up to defend what was now their land as well, and create a society free of racism after the war?

An exercise in fantasy most likely, for slavery was too deeply imbedded and with it the darkness of racism, for such a proposal to have ever been passed, as history did witness when Confederate Secretary of State, Judah Benjamin, made this exact proposal in 1864, and his words were met with a near riot and disavowal by his own president. Such a proposal finally did pass through the Confederate Congress in February, 1865, but before implementation their capital city fell to Union troops on the morning of April 3, 1865—the vanguard of that charge into the rebel capital led by men of the USCTs, the United States Colored Troops.

How to lose a war? For the South, it was never an issue on the battlefield itself. No one can deny the superior generals of the South, or the stunning valor of her soldiers. It was never about a battle lost. Instead it was about a blindness, created by racism, and the economic greed of a few, that pre-ordained their defeat, once their opponent came to realize the moral high ground, and then seized it first. On the day the Emancipation Proclamation went into effect, without an equal counter reply honoring the promise that "all men are created equal," the South was doomed to lose a war.

There are a number of unfortunate and rather insulting jokes about the French military. While these comments overlook the incredible courage shown in WWI, they were reinforced by the rapid collapse of France in WWII. But the comments stem from when France lost sight of its legacy from Napoleon and suffered a defeat as devastating and total as the blitzkrieg two generations earlier. But the price paid by the victor of this war is just as noteworthy.

THE FRANCO-PRUSSIAN WAR

France, 1870

PETER ARCHER

History repeats itself," Karl Marx declared in the opening lines of *The Eighteenth Brumaire of Louis Bonaparte*, "first as tragedy, then as farce." His observation concerned the ushering in of the Second Empire and the reign of Napoleon III. The "tragedy" to which Marx alluded was Napoleon I's triumphant coup in 1799. The "farce" was the coup of Napoleon's hapless nephew Louis nearly fifty years later. His rule would last for eighteen years, until 1870. At the end, Louis would lose his empire in the most ignominious fashion possible—defeated by the German forces of Helmuth von Moltke at the Battle of Sedan—and find himself taken prisoner. When the news reached Paris, the empire was promptly toppled by rioting mobs. The struggle against Germany continued under the government of Adolphe Thiers.

For the French the war was effectively lost; what played out was, perhaps, the most painful face of the farce as described by Marx's observation. Another interpretation that has been often adopted by later historians is that the French defeat of 1870 was a precursor of the events of 1914 and even those of 1940 rather then the end of the Napoleonic wars.

It was a curious turn of events, since the French had begun the war with Prussia as the odds-on favorites. The Franco-Prussian War was among the first fought with thoroughly modern weapons, and the best of these were in the hands of the French. In 1866, their infantry took up the Chassepot rifle, a mass-produced gun with an accuracy of 1,600 yards, while a primitive version of the machine gun, the *mitrailleuse*, provided mass fire. The Chassepot was a considerable step forward from the antique muzzle loaders, which were unable to hit a target with any accuracy at more than 400 to 500 yards.

The Prussians had switched to breech loaders as early as 1843, a fact that spurred the French development of the Chassepot, in an early version of the arms race. The French initially seemed to have the advantage in artillery; their muzzle-loaded, rifled cannon had been used in Italy to deadly effect. Unbeknownst to French military strategists, however, the Prussians had arranged for the manufacture of steel breech-loading cannon at the great Krupp works. This gave them, ultimately, a sound advantage in the coming war.

Seen from one perspective, the Franco-Prussian War was merely another step in the drive of Otto von Bismarck to unite the disparate German states into a single entity. This aspiration had been at the center of German political life for centuries and had been frustrated by the Peace of Westphalia in 1648 at the end of the Thirty Years' War. That conflict ended with the German states still divided and weak. Bismarck had a vision of a united Germany, one to which he dedicated his political life.

The first step in his plan was the Austro-Prussian War of 1866. Prussia's victory gave Bismarck a taste of success. His policies now turned from the East to the West. He set his considerable political powers to the provocation of war with Napoleon III's France.

He did so with an army in the service of the state few would have

guessed was capable of victory. Built up during the reign of Frederick the Great, the Prussian army officer corps had, for years, been
a bedrock of conservatism. The professional army corps remained
small. A military crisis in 1831 in Poland, and an internal revolt in
1848, forced the army to rely on the militia (*Landwehr*), which it
distrusted politically. France, on the other hand, had fought successful campaigns in Africa and in the Crimea. Their tradition of
glorious military service dated back to Napoleon I. The army, in
the thoughts of the government, *was* the nation, not something
apart from it.

Yet to the discerning, fault lines could be found in the French
military machine. Its generals were ill-educated compared to their
Prussian counterparts. The Germans imposed universal military
service on all males; the French drew their conscripts from the
general population by lottery, which was hardly a reliable guarantee of martial fervor.

Nonetheless, observers in the late 1860s must have found Bismarck's obvious maneuvering toward a war with France puzzling.
It seemed a conflict in which the result was a foregone conclusion,
and that conclusion a French victory.

Though France was the immediate aggressor in the events that
led to the outbreak of war, her actions were contrived by Bismarck.
This he undertook with the full knowledge of his military leaders.
Von Moltke, from 1866–68, was busy training the army for a coming
conflict he saw as inevitable and supported Bismarck in provoking
the war.

The immediate issue that brought about the war was the throne
of Spain—a subject of conflict in Europe since the time of the first
Napoleon. Isabella II was deposed in 1868, and when the Spaniards
sought a replacement, the name of Prince Leopold of Hohenzollern
was put forward. Though a member of the Prussian royal house,
Leopold was a Catholic, a family man, and was related to prominent French families such as the Murats, descendants of Napoleon
I's marshal.

In point of fact, the French objected, on the not unreason-
able grounds that Leopold was obviously Bismarck's candidate and

would be beholden to him. This, of course, was precisely what Bismarck intended them to think. He was helped considerably by the partisan braying of French newspapers. "Prussia has forgotten the France of Jena," one observed, "and we must remind her." France mobilized her army, Prussia followed suit, and war was formally declared on July 19, 1870.

Prussia and Bismarck entered into the war with an infallible sense of rightness. In one sense, they saw it as a war of national pride, an opportunity to humble the mightiest nation in Europe and to show how much they had grown in the past 200 years. France's mobilization was undertaken with the kind of off-hand casualness that characterized most, if not all, of Napoleon III's actions. The emperor himself assumed command over his armies, little realizing how disastrous this decision would become.

Napoleon's first move was to launch an occupation of Saarbrücken, a border town. French forces occupied the town after an uneasy spat of fighting, one that showed that despite the superiority of French armaments, the Germans were more than capable of giving a good account of themselves.

On August 4, German forces attacked the town of Wissembourg. The French, under the command of General Felix Douay, initially refused to believe this was a serious attack and ascribed the shells falling around them to an unusually aggressive reconnaissance. They were soon disabused of this notion. Two Prussian corps struck at the town, and the French (minus Douay, who had been killed by a shell burst) staged a hasty withdrawal. The people of Wissembourg surrendered in the first major German victory of the war.

Marshal Patrice MacMahon, commander of the French forces in the area, observed the collapse of his subordinate's position, but reacted slowly. The sluggishness of the French response doomed any counterattack, and the Germans successfully held the town against all attempts to dislodge them. (There was, as commentators remarked later, a peculiar failure on either side to take advantage of light horse for reconnaissance. This is all the stranger since both sides could look to the remarkable example a decade earlier of Stonewall Jackson's cavalry maneuvers in the American Civil War for the decisive role light cavalry could play in the outcome of a campaign.)

The battle of Wissembourg was, in some respects, decisive in the campaign. It showed there would be no question of France invading the German states and inflicting defeats upon them as Napoleon I had done at the height of his power. Rather, now, the tables were reversed, and France lay open to German attack.

Two days after the collapse of the French at Wissembourg, the forces met at Froeschwiller, only ten miles away. The French were heavily outnumbered now and demoralized from their defeat at Wissembourg. Despite French efforts to hold the town, the Germans succeeded in taking it, thanks in part to the deadly accuracy of German artillery fire. It was in some respects a decisive moment in Western military history. Artillery was crowned the king of battles, a coronation some thirty years in the making.

News of the defeats in Paris caused an explosion of rage. Leading newspapers demanded an explanation, seeking an answer in treachery and defeatism among the Army's upper corps. Some politicians demanded that the citizenry be armed; others suggested a state of emergency be declared and avowed themselves willing to vote the emperor even more extraordinary powers than those he already possessed. Politically, France announced itself a nation of newspaper editors.

Meanwhile, among the Germans, von Moltke's mind struggled free of all entanglements and contradictory stratagems. The chance was before him to launch an invasion of France, and he took it. The Prussian army struck across the Moselle and into French territory.

Now in their own territory, the French army slowed its retreat and showed signs of steadying. By mid-August, both armies had formed into battle lines near Mars-la-Tour.

In this battle, in an odd twist of fate, the Prussians were vastly outnumbered. The French forces were perhaps 130,000. The Prussians, commanded by General Konstantin von Alvensleben, had no more than 30,000 troops. But other Prussian forces were already in motion and approaching. The French attempted a maneuver to leave the area and join other forces massed at Verdun. Despite the heavy odds stacked against him, Alvensleben attacked with the III Corps of the 2nd Prussian Army. The heavily outnumbered German forces fought the French to a standstill and prevented them from escaping the trap.

Now at a standstill, the French still vastly outnumbered their Prussian counterparts. A capable general might have rallied them and led them to a decisive victory, one that could have ended the war. But the French possessed no such general, and the Prussians were determined to hold on to their gains. On August 18, they fought against the force of the French vanguard (under the mistaken impression, initially, that it was the French rear guard, thus proving the point that the best decisions in battles are often taken from the most misdirected of motives) and held them back.

At the height of the battle, Alvensleben sent a message to the commander of the 12th Cavalry Brigade, Major General von Bredow, commanding him to silence the French artillery. It was remarkably similar to the command given by Lord Raglan during the Crimean War that had sent the Light Brigade to its doom at Balaclava. Yet here, the Prussian cavalry charged and was successful. Shielded by gunsmoke, they burst upon the French artillery and dispersed them while themselves taking only moderate casualties. Alvensleben successfully disengaged his force from the French and withdrew, having inflicted heavy casualties upon his opponent and thoroughly demoralized them into the bargain. The inability of the French forces at Mars-la-Tour to join with their counterparts at Metz was to prove a decisive element in the coming campaign. The battle also established once and for all that whatever their numerical superiority over the Prussians, the French forces were by far inferior on the field of battle.

One of the curious facts of the Franco-Prussian War is its remarkable speed of its development. The decisive battle of the war, the battle of Gravelotte, was fought only two days after the conflict at Mars-la-Tour and effectively settled the issue of the war. This was also the first battle of the war in which von Moltke himself commanded the Prussian forces.

This, the largest battle of the war, was fought just west of Metz. The Prussians under the command of von Moltke numbered about 188,000 men, comprising the First and Second armies of the North German Confederation. The French army was about 112,000 strong and was further weakened by the impact of its defeats at Wissembourg, Froeschwiller, and Mars-la-Tour.

In the face of the German advance, the French replied with fire from trenches they had dug during the night, thus anticipating the course of warfare during the next fifty years. The Germans hurled their troops forward, while the French replied with heavy fire from their covered positions, inflicting enormous casualties. They were successful in turning the attack of the German First Army, and victory appeared to be favoring the French.

By 6 p.m. divisions of the II Corps of the Prussian Second Army were advancing, however, and the XII Corps had captured Roncourt. Fresh Prussian forces were brought up and the French began a slow, steady, reluctant retreat. The battle ended at 10 p.m. with growling indecision, instead of decisive victory or defeat. Sniping continued along the line for much of the night. Matters might have been resolved in the morning light of August 19, but the French, rather than resuming the battle, retreated to the fortress city of Metz, where they surrendered to the besieging Germans two months later on October 29, losing 180,000 soldiers to captivity.

The casualties of the fighting that followed the Battle of Metz in August did not reflect the victors: the Germans lost more than 20,000 killed, wounded, or missing in action. The French suffered no more than 12,000 killed or taken prisoner.

The shattering defeat at Metz galvanized the French. Napoleon III himself took command of the army and led it near the Belgian border. Von Moltke replied by launching a pincer movement that caught the French army at Beaumont on August 30. Under Napoleon's orders, the French army attempted to break out of encirclement. The result, on September 1st, was the Battle of Sedan.

As was becoming usual during battles of the nineteenth century and would remain the case through World War I, Sedan began with an artillery barrage seemingly designed to shatter the opponent's morale as well as his power. Soldiers under fire from artillery agree that the ground grew so hot under their feet they could only walk on tiptoe, and any sort of thought was impossible as shells crashed and roared around them.

The French attempted on at least three occasions to break out of the German encirclement and failed each time. The French lost more than 17,000 killed or wounded, while the German forces reported losses at less than 3,000 killed. The following day, the French emperor surrendered.

It was a shattering moment. The French had begun the war with absolute confidence in victory. Now their emperor stood with bowed head before the Prussian generals, offering himself as representative of the nation, shorn of victory. Sedan was a shattering defeat, destroying the Napoleonic myth of the army's invincibility.

The defeat at Sedan also ended the Second Empire. A group of politicians led by Jules Favre and Leon Gambetta declared in Paris that the glittering rule of Napoleon and his empress was no more, and proclaimed the foundation of the Third Republic. Napoleon III went into exile, dying in England in 1873, unlamented and all but unremembered, despite the glittering image of power he had built during his rule. The Third Republic would endure, with ups and downs, until it was crushed under the heels of the Nazi invasion of 1940.

One last challenge remained. When Bismarck offered moderate surrender terms to the new French government, the republic declined to consider the possibility of surrendering French territory. The war, they declared, would go on.

The German forces did what would become the pattern throughout the following sixty years: they struck at the heart of France. They struck at Paris.

In truth, by this time the German armies themselves were weary of the war. Yet the French, under siege in Paris, saw no hope. Other European powers, seeing in the crisis an opportunity to enhance their political strength, began to meddle in the war.

The Germans, having no sympathy for a wider European conflict, tightened their grip, and by January 1871, the Parisian govern-

The Franco-Prussian War   299

ment had surrendered. The peace was proclaimed on January 28th at Versailles.

As the German armies withdrew, the tension between the French government and the people over whom it ruled exploded. By March, crowds had seized the government buildings in Paris and declared a commune. Marx and Friedrich Engels, in London, hailed this development as the beginning of their hoped-for revolution. Yet, though the commune enacted numerous social measures that Marx and Engels and their followers greeted with joy, tragedy was gathering at the gates of the city. Clashes between the republican National Guard and the army increased in violence and frequency. The French army broke through, shattered the barricades erected by the communards, and scattered the forces of the commune.

Thousands upon thousands of communards were rounded up by the victors. They were tried, some executed, many thousands sent into exile. Eventually it would be estimated that as many as 50,000 rebels lost their lives in the fighting and reprisals that followed.

The Franco-Prussian War ended in tragedy for France. The defeat of its armies showed the vulnerability of the great military machine built by the first Napoleon seventy years previously. Twenty-five years later, the Dreyfus Affair would again expose the fault lines in the army and leave it wounded, open to the catastrophe of 1914. If nothing else, the Franco-Prussian War showed that mere military technology—the Chassepot rifles, the *mitrailleuse*—could no longer guarantee victory. Military tactics such as speed, persistence, and above all, maneuverability would be key to the wars that were being fought now upon the European continent. In this respect it must be said that the French were slow to learn the lessons that had been taught ten years before during the American Civil War by the Army of Northern Virginia under the command of Robert E. Lee. Lee and Stonewall Jackson had demonstrated that a small, mobile force, despite an inferiority of equipment, could pin down and destroy a larger army that was indecisive in leadership and confused in its movement.

The French were, to some degree, the victims of their success in wars such as the Crimean conflict. Striking against the Russians, they concluded that victory was possible through sheer weight of arms. Von Moltke showed them otherwise. That the Prussian military memory was long was given terrible force by the onslaught first of August, 1914, and then by the blitzkrieg of 1940.

For the Germans, on the other hand, the war was an unadulterated success. Bismarck might have regretted that the war itself was dominated by Von Moltke, but there could be no question of its political director. King and now Kaiser Wilhelm I had shown himself to be merely a puppet, and Bismarck the master who pulled his strings. He referred to himself as the "midwife" who brought into being the new German Reich. "This imperial birth was a difficult one," he wrote to his wife.

Yet at the height of his triumph, some voices of warning spoke out. "Bismarck has made us great and powerful," said Crown Prince Frederick of Prussia. "But he has robbed us of our friends, the sympathy of the world, and—our conscience."

For three quarters of a century more, those words would haunt the consciousness of the German people.

This war is perhaps the most classic David and Goliath conflict of modern times. It pitted the tiny Finnish army against more than ten times its number of Russian attackers. At first the Red Army made just about every mistake they could. This is less than surprising when you remember that Stalin had purged the Red Army's officer corps only a few years earlier and the best way for those remaining commanders to stay alive was to not attract attention. That takes nothing away from the Finns, whose valiant, if doomed, defense had far reaching consequences in WWII.

WAR IN THE WINTER

A Schooling in the Snow:
Finland, 1939

DOUGLAS NILES

Large, militarized countries taking over smaller, weaker countries: in late 1930s Europe, it was all the rage. By autumn of 1939, Italy had gulped up Ethiopia and Albania, and Germany had swallowed the Rhineland, Austria, western Czechoslovakia, and finally Poland. Josef Stalin, chairman for life and absolute dictator of the USSR, got involved with the conquest of Poland by "virtue" of the Molotov/Ribbentrop Pact. This was a breathtakingly cynical agreement, in which the foreign ministers of Nazi Germany and the USSR agreed to divide up the country along a prearranged border. When Germany invaded Poland at the beginning of September, 1939, the

Soviets simply waited a few days and then moved in to claim their half of that hapless country.

But war between the two great powers still loomed as likely, even inevitable. To further protect the USSR, Stalin imposed "mutual defense pacts" upon the Baltic states of Latvia, Lithuania, and Estonia; Soviet troops moved into those small countries during October and November. Together with eastern Poland, these occupied states created a buffer zone between Nazi-controlled territory and the Russian heartland.

But Stalin wanted to extend this buffer zone to include Finnish territory, including islands in the Gulf of Finland, and part of the Karelian isthmus, which was the land route connecting the key city of Leningrad to Finland. When the Soviets proposed a pact with Finland similar to those they had used to claim the Baltic states, Finland rejected Stalin's demands, and mobilized to face a potential Soviet invasion. Some 300,000 troops, the vast majority of them hastily called up reserves, formed Finland's defensive army. They were under the command of the elderly, but very capable, Marshal Baron Carl Mannerheim, who had been the leading Finnish military commander in two wars (the 1917 Civil War, and the war for independence from Russia in 1919 and 1920).

Stalin reacted to this mobilization with an order to attack. On November 30, 1939, hostilities erupted when the Red air force bombed Helsinki, the capital of Finland, and Viipuri, the key city on the Karelian isthmus, without warning or declaration of war. That same day, the Red army attacked with something approaching 1,000,000 men. The Soviets launched a series of amphibious invasions across the Gulf of Finland, and attacked across the border in locations ranging from Leningrad to the far northern coast, where the two countries met the Arctic Ocean.

Every one of the amphibious assaults was repulsed by the vigorous Finn defense. In the north, the Soviets seized the border city of Petsamo, then started a southward drive along the Arctic Highway. The Soviet force of three divisions was halted after less than a hundred miles by a reinforced battalion of Finnish troops entrenched around the city of Nautsi.

In the central border region, the Soviet Ninth Army, comprised of some five divisions, thrust into Finland's forested terrain along a series of narrow roads. South of the Ninth Army, the Eighth Army attacked with six divisions and an armored brigade, also plunging into wooded country that was broken up by numerous large lakes and wetlands. Both of these massive offensives found the going slow, as the freezing cold and deep snow impeded the Soviet columns, while the Finnish defenders—equipped for winter temperatures with warm clothing and winterized weaponry, white camouflage, and skis—utilized hit and run tactics to inflict casualties and slow down the attack, all the while nimbly avoiding the heavier guns of the Russians.

The main attack moved from Leningrad directly up the Karelian Isthmus, with the city of Viipuri as its main objective. This offensive consisted of two armies, the Thirteenth and Seventh, totaling thirteen divisions of infantry and five armored brigades. The massive onslaught came to a halt almost immediately when the Soviets smashed into a well-prepared, deeply fortified position known as the Mannerheim Line. The line consisted of a series of WWI-type trenches and pillboxes, cleverly designed to make good use of the hilly, forested terrain. Lake Ladoga, to the east, and the Gulf of Finland, to the west, ensured that the line could not be flanked. After suffering heavy casualties during a massive set-piece attack in late December, the attack against the Mannerheim Line ground to a complete halt.

While the deep snow and frigid temperatures in the far north caused the Red army immense problems because of inadequate clothing, frozen weapons and vehicles, and snow drifts blocking supply lines, they were faced with a different challenge in southern Finland. Here it was not cold enough to freeze the rivers and lakes to an extent that allowed mechanized units to cross—though lighter ski troops could maneuver there with relative ease. Furthermore, the weather remained cloudy, with a heavy, low overcast that prevented the Red air force from utilizing the Soviet advantage in air power.

In the forested wilderness of central Finland, the Soviet columns advanced along the roads, but were unable to support each other.

A key objective was the town of Suomussalmi, where two of these roads converged. Temperatures dropped to forty degrees below zero (Fahrenheit), and the Soviet troops, many of whom hailed from the Ukraine and other relatively temperate areas, were unprepared for the killing frost. Their lightweight uniforms were inadequate, and their vehicles with virtually no anti-freeze and with heavy oil that turned to sludge functioned poorly, if at all.

Meanwhile the Finns, wearing white uniforms and swooping silently along on their skis, continued to harass the supply trains and logistical support of the advancing Soviet units. A full division of Finnish troops, the 9th, arrived at Suomussalmi ahead of its artillery, but immediately attacked, and was able to fully surround the Soviet garrison in that small town. A second Soviet mechanized rifle division tried to come to the relief of the trapped garrison, but it too was blocked, ambushed, and surrounded on its forest-cloaked road. By now, the 9th Division's artillery had reached the scene, and in a coordinated attack from December 27th–30th, the Soviet division in Suomassalmi was completely wiped out. The Finns continued on, and during the first week in January, they obliterated the second rifle division. All together, the Soviets lost some 30,000 men, as well as 50 tanks, in the Battle of Suomassalmi; Finnish losses were less than a thousand men killed.

France and England, both at war with Germany but currently occupied in the "Sitzkrieg" wherein both sides stared at each other, with neither attacking, tried to mount a relief force to come to Finland's aid. Neutral Sweden and Norway refused to allow the force's passage, however, so the rest of the world could only stand aside and watch in awe as tiny Finland's army seemed to bring the mighty Soviet Union to its knees.

And, indeed, the Russians had suffered humiliating defeats along the entire length of the border. None of their attacks had met with anything other than a few initial successes, and in every place their spearheads had either ground to a halt, or had been repulsed with heavy losses.

But, of course, it was too good to last. The Soviets learned from their mistakes, and used the rest of January, 1940, to prepare for a massive and well-coordinated offensive. Russian troops were finally equipped properly for the winter conditions, and the Red army concentrated its strength for a conventional assault up the Karelian Isthmus, which was a confined route of attack in which defensive maneuvering would of necessity be held to a minimum. By January 29th, Finland sensed the inevitable and began to put out diplomatic feelers to Moscow, seeking an end to the conflict.

Nevertheless, the Soviets commenced a massive attack on February 1st, sending more than fifty divisions directly into the teeth of the Mannerheim line. Massive artillery bombardments accompanied these attacks, and the infantry plunged forward against a hail of machine gun and shellfire. Soviet losses were terrible, but the outcome was inevitable, as the Russians gradually pushed their way through the Finnish defensive line. On February 13th the Mannerheim Line was fatally breached, and the Finns conducted a fighting withdrawal to Viipuri. When the Soviets entered that city at the beginning of March, the Winter War was over.

The Treaty of Moscow was signed on March 2nd. With that agreement, Finland ceded territory to the Soviets pretty much along the lines of what Stalin had initially demanded: the border on the Karelian Isthmus was pushed farther away from Leningrad, and a few border regions in the central and northern portions of Finland became Soviet territory. The Soviets also gained control of the key islands in the Gulf of Finland, and the right to post troops at one Finnish port, Hanko, which guarded the approach to the gulf.

The legacy of the Winter War was far reaching, for Finland, the USSR, and Germany. The Finns developed a deep hatred of their Soviet neighbors, which pushed them toward the Nazi camp when they needed an alliance to stand against their powerful foe. The Soviets learned much about modern warfare, and began to correct mistakes in their ground and air operations that would serve them in good stead when the next war began, with the German invasion of the USSR in June of 1941. As for the Germans, they saw how poorly the Soviets fought against Finland, and decided that Russia would be an easy target for the lethal blitzkrieg tactics of the Wehrmacht.

They were wrong.

Today it seems inevitable that Germany would lose WWII.
After all it was a relatively small country taking on virtually
the rest of the world. A foredoomed venture in history,
as were many empires started by small states conquering
larger ones such as the Hittite Empire, the Persian Empire,
Alexander the Great's Macedonia, Rome, the Mongol Empire,
the British Empire . . . or perhaps not. After all, at one point
Germany controlled the resources of almost all of Europe.
The Nazi empire was not inevitably bound for defeat.
Certainly history shows it was not, but they did lose.
Here noted historian and novelist William Forstchen points
out the Reich's fatal flaw that, more than bombers
or invading Russia, doomed the Nazi empire.

GERMANY IN WWII

Europe, 1941

WILLIAM R. FORSTCHEN, Ph.D.

I have been teaching a college-level course on WWII for nearly twenty years and without doubt the most popular topic within the course are the great "what-ifs" of that conflict, first and foremost being: could Germany have won the conflict?

It is the subject of numerous alternate histories and even scholarly articles. If ever there appeared to be, on the surface, a nation so organized, and so disciplined as to win, it was Nazi Germany of the late 1930s.

All of the Western "democracies" were at best pacifist, and at worst moribund and outright craven in the face of fascist and com-

munist aggression throughout the twenties and thirties. It was chic
in intellectual circles to openly declare that surrender was better than another conflict, that the centuries-old concept of liberal
democracy was dead, and collectivism, either from the left or the
right was the wave of the future.

Small wonder, given the horrific cost everyone had endured
in the cataclysmic Great War. After that nearly primordial bloodletting, if any positive hope were to come out of it, there was a
belief that so horrible had war become that no one would dare
risk another bloodbath, which many believed would be the end of
civilization.

Those of us born after 1945, especially we who grew up under the shadow of a thermonuclear holocaust, believed that we
were the first to face true global extinction. Our popular culture,
with movies like *On the Beach*, *Fail-Safe*, and even the *Terminator* series,
portrayed the next war as Armageddon. Look back, however, to
popular culture post-WWI and one will find the same fears. H. G.
Wells' remarkably prophetic work *The Shape of Things To Come*, which
was released in Great Britain as a book in 1933 and a movie in 1936,
prophesied the next great war would be waged with massed air
armadas, blanketing cities in clouds of poison gas, and what was
left of civilization would collapse into a new dark age. The postwar
scenes look like something straight out of the *Road Warrior* series.
Prophets of doom projected that London, under aerial bombardment, would sustain upward of a million casualties within the first
week of attacks. As Germany and the Soviet Union raced toward
rearmament, the rest of the world stood impotent with fear.

The fears were not ill founded. Wells had already written of bal-
listic missiles tipped with atomic warheads. The use of chemical
warfare in WWI meant all the European nations were traumatized
by such weapons and labs in many countries had already developed
chemical weapons so potent that a single droplet could kill almost instantly, and when sprayed over civilian populations would
slaughter thousands within minutes, along with biological weapons that might very well wipe out all of humanity. Wells based
his civilization-ending apocalypse on gas weapons, not bombs. It

sounds familiar to us, this fear of weapons of mass destruction. The fear was as real then as it is now—made more potent by the memory of but a few years past when millions had died in the fighting on the Western Front.

A great misperception is that Germany was somehow immune to this fear of total annihilation. Our own wartime propaganda has shadowed our collective memory of WWII, creating an image of a nation mindlessly lock-stepped toward war, either willingly or driven by fear of the Gestapo. Nothing could be farther from the truth.

In the Soviet Union, there was every reason for all "comrades" to live in constant terror of their regime and, if need be, fight. A true psychotic madman was in the driver's seat, who made Hitler look like a rank amateur when it came to terrorizing, torturing, and murdering his own people. At least so far as the "Germanic" population went Hitler showed some restraint in his brutality.

The Nazi regime, at least when it came to the ruling of its own "Aryan" peoples prior to 1939, was a government that moved cautiously and was highly conscious of public opinion. The administration even had its own secret "Gallup Poll," weekly reports garnered through overheard conversations on the street, in beer halls and opera houses and factories, keeping a careful finger on the public pulse and its support of the regime. Yes, thousands "disappeared," but it was not the millions, perhaps tens of millions, as it was several hundred miles to the east in the Soviet Union.

Hitler himself, a decorated veteran of four hard years on the Western Front, feared another such war, and with good reason, knowing that his Reich could not sustain such a brutal years-long effort. The wars he sought were to be quick, relatively bloodless, and fought with an adroit mix of a "butter and guns" economy.

There was never a plan, or even contemplation of a conflict that might last for years, one indicator being that after the victories in Poland and later in France, a fair part of the German army was actually demobilized to return to the fields and factories, with a belief that the conflict was nearly over.

So on one side in 1938 was a once-mighty array of Western alliances terrified that a new conflict could very well be the last war, and on the other side, a Soviet Union focused on its own internal mass murdering, and finally a Germany that, when it contemplated war, saw it as limited in time and space to short, sharp conflicts of but a few weeks or months at most.

No one was prepared for what was to come, and therein can be seen one of the two root causes for the German loss.

It is popular in my classes on WWII for students to speculate as to how Germany or the Axis powers in general might have won and there is a whole list of potential turning points, the failure of which is usually laid at a convenient doorstep: Adolf Hitler's decisions and supposedly psychotic leadership.

A few are at least worth mentioning briefly. One of the favorites is the failure to take England completely out of the war in 1940–41, especially before turning attention on Russia. Some speculate that the famed stopping short of Dunkirk was actually a subtle signal to the British government that it could withdraw from the mainland unhindered, with some of its pride and power intact, hoping that bellicose Churchill's brief tenure as PM would collapse and an armistice be reached. This theory ignores the logistics of armored warfare in 1940. The bulk of the German army was not mobile nor would it ever be. Throughout the war, it was a force still as dependent on the horse and shoe leather, especially for infantry movement and logistical support, as the armies of Napoleon. The tanks of 1940 were little better than slightly beefed up armored cars with a maximum range of but several hundred miles before needing major stand down time for overhaul and maintenance. After reaching the Channel, the armored columns absolutely needed several crucial days to refit, and for supplies to catch up across their tenuous link back into Germany, before resuming the offensive. Even air support was increasingly stretched, given the short range of fighter aircraft in 1940, which still had to sortie from fields in Germany to support the advance.

There was no throwing away of a total victory in June, 1940. Even as the ring finally closed on Dunkirk, there was fear that France could still rally a defense, and common sense mandated that Germany's overstretched military first take their primary foe of WWI out of the fight. What German arms actually did achieve in that six-week campaign stands as one of the most remarkable achievements in military history, knocking France out of the war and forever crippling Britain as a continental force. No small achievement, given how tenaciously both had fought in so many previous wars.

As for the assertion that the Battle of Britain was a lost chance, maybe so, but again logistics played a key role. Poor staff work had not properly prepared for the need to rapidly acquire airfields, refit and re-supply them to handle the aircraft of the Luftwaffe, and move up a sufficient strike force to air fields on the French coast prior to opening an air offensive. It was not just the simple flying in of planes, and the following day loading them up to take on England. Trained mechanics had to be put in place, long-delayed maintenance for aircraft after the conquest of France had to be seen to, thousands of different spare parts and supporting machinery had to be moved from Germany to the new airfields, along with sufficient stockpiles of everything from the correct weight of engine oil to tens of millions of rounds of ammunition and thousands of tons of bombs. While at the same time the Royal Air Force, though beleaguered, prepared for battle at their home bases, which they had operated out of for decades. The fact that the Luftwaffe was able to begin offensive operations little more than a month after completion of the campaign in France is a remarkable achievement in and of itself.

Though the stuff of legend and indeed a near-run thing, chances of a successful invasion after a successful air campaign, especially against a proud island nation aroused to a near suicidal fighting pitch by the defiant counter challenge of Winston Churchill, was highly problematic. Any landing attempt by the Germans would, unlike France, have been met by a *levée en masse* that would have fought the Germans to a standstill, with London, Portsmouth, Manchester, and Liverpool turned into Stalingrads and Leningrads. Recall Churchill's famous promise that if England was invaded, they would rather see London reduced to ruins and ashes, than for the

British people to tamely and abjectly submit—a very pointed put-down of the bloodless surrender of Paris, and a near taunting challenge for Hitler to just try and then see what happens.

Russia? From a strictly military standpoint, before going into the real reasons for losing a war, the month-long delay which pushed the invasion date back from May 15 to June 22, 1941, triggered by the need to come to Italy's aid in the Balkans, might have been a factor. Next was the utter failure of German military intelligence to draw up a true order of battle of Soviet forces in June, 1941, which if accurately documented might very well have forced Hitler and the General Staff to think twice about invasion. In every key area, the German intelligence services underestimated Soviet strength by at least fifty percent, and in some cases, by over ninety percent. Later there was the failure to drive straight on to Moscow and occupy Leningrad when the chance was there, and finally, the million-plus casualties (most of them weather related) created by the infamous standfast order of December, 1941, can be seen as turning points and each would be worthy of a book in itself, if this article was focused strictly on how a single battle or decision might have been the turning point.

There were other moments that are often cited: Hitler's reckless decision to declare war on America, the neglect to build an overwhelming force of U-Boats, failures in seizing the technological edge that was in the palm of their hands with jet aircraft that could have been operational in 1942. All of these added up to defeat. But these are almost tactical in nature when compared to the two root causes of defeat, root causes that, though at first glance might not seem related, in fact are indicative of a deep fundamental flaw in the entire Nazi system which all but foredoomed it to defeat.

The root cause was an utterly incompetent organization system modeled more on the rivalry of medieval barons than a modern industrial state fully mobilized for war, made even worse by the blindness created by a fundamental tenet of National Socialism—and that is racism.

For some reason, most likely a fair part of it being our own stereotyping, we tend to think of Germans as thorough, organized,

HOW TO LOSE A WAR

ruthlessly efficient, and highly obedient to a central authority. As far as World War II goes, in some sense this was indeed true, especially when it came to their army's at times stunning ability to improvise on short notice, and with flexible thinking and command, pull off some incredible comebacks, such as the rebuilding of a southern front in Russia after the defeat at Stalingrad and their incredible delaying actions on all fronts under relentless assault by vastly superior numbers.

In a more general sense though, on a complex societal level, the Nazis created a system that was like a medieval fiefdom of corrupt rival barons and competing warlords, rather than a smooth-working management team designed to fight a protracted war. Throughout the war, the Nazi party was at odds with and deeply mistrustful of its own military, both actually hating each other, industries often worked at cross purposes, vying for government contracts and largess rather than driving toward a common goal of victory, and various agencies created a vast bureaucratic sprawl, loyal only to itself rather than the greater goal of national survival.

This intense system of mutual mistrust between various government agencies was part and parcel of the Nazi system in its early days of organization, designed thus by its chief architect, Adolf Hitler, in order to insure his own survival by never letting one of his followers gain enough power to threaten his own. The destruction of Ernst Roehm and his Brown Shirts, with Himmler's SS acting as the executioners, was but a foreshadowing of all the bloody rivalries and mutual mistrust to come. Not one of his underlings was ever to gain hegemony over the other underlings, or potentially his own leadership, and therefore Hitler openly played all the various factions, the party, the SS, the Gestapo, the army, and the industrialists, against each other, and never was there a common, unified, and most important, an efficient system aimed toward the singular goal of winning the war.

Therefore Himmler would deliberately derail efforts by Goering and vice versa. Bormann plotted against all. The General Staff silently prayed the whole rotten lot would collapse even while feeding from their table. And the crucial agencies for intelligence and counterintelligence were working for one or the other subgroup, and finally against the state itself.

Granted, all bureaucratic agencies, as shown so aptly by Parkinson and so many others, are ultimately self-serving, but in times of war, there has to be some semblance of mutual cooperation if the nation is to survive. Our own Navy, Army, and Army Air Force were often at bitter odds with each other over allocations of resources, building programs, which front to fight on first, the question of strategic versus tactical use of our vast air armada, etc., but there was still a team effort toward the final goal.

In America, prior to the war, there was the incredible and now-forgotten fiasco of failure to come up with a single unified inter-service version for Plan Rainbow Five, America's plan to fight a global war, a lack of inter-service cooperation that directly led to the abandonment of our army in the Philippines, and set the war effort back by a year or more.

Throughout the war in the Pacific, the Army and the Navy, led by Nimitz and MacArthur, could barely conceal the contempt each held for the other, both with vastly different plans for victory over Japan, but the adroit hand of FDR kept the team together, by the classic example of going along with both plans to a certain extent, in order to create a cohesive campaign for ultimate victory. The same stood true of the grand alliance of America and Great Britain, so heralded now as the supreme team effort of the Greatest Generation, though beneath the surface, the Western alliance came close to fracturing more than once. But ultimately they did pursue a unified plan for victory even though Eisenhower, Patton, and Montgomery could barely conceal their mutual contempt at times. The Grand Alliance, as well, managed to at least pull along with it a certain level of mutual support from the corrupt Chinese leadership, the arrogant and self-serving Free French forces, the so often betrayed Poles, and managed even to keep Stalin from pursuing a separate peace. As for the lesser allies, a dozen oppressed and captive nations stood with the alliance as well.

No matter how vicious the infighting at times, outright sabotage and murder of political rivals was never an option (at least outside the Soviet Union) as it was in Germany. Final victory was the watchword and even while some self-aggrandized, this goal was still first and foremost.

Several examples are in order as to the insanity of the German system. The most glaring and sickening was the obsession of the SS with fulfillment of the "Final Solution." In the coldest of practical terms, it bore no relationship whatsoever to the winning of the war. It was a doctrine-driven madness that, in the eyes of the head executioners, came to transcend the war itself, a higher goal even than victory and self-survival. Even if we lose the war, the logic finally ran, at least we'll have killed off the Jews, and in a perverse sense, have won after all. The entire transportation grid of the Reich and its conquered territories was put at the disposal of the SS to transport its victims. Highest priority, higher than troop movements, supplies, ammunition, rations, even their own wounded, went to the movement of victims on their way to extermination.

In the final extreme, during the last year of the war, after the Soviet breakthrough of June, 1944 and the destruction of Army Group Center, with Soviet armored columns advancing fifty to seventy-five miles a day toward eastern Germany, priority was actually escalated, with orders to speed up the "operation." Utter madness when army commanders were screaming for the tools to hold back the Soviet onslaught and for trains to evacuate their wounded and, finally, German civilians as well.

The SS became a nation unto itself, creating a mirror army, the Waffen SS, which always received highest priority (after mass murder of civilians) for shipments of supplies, replacements, and new equipment. Command structure turned to a blur that made the rivalry between Patton and Montgomery, Nimitz and MacArthur look like a tempest in a teapot.

Goering aggrandized to himself whatever power he could seize, far beyond the scope of his command of the Luftwaffe. Army commanders rose and fell based upon whether they curried favor with Bormann and any attempt at coordinated effort between theaters of operation were hopeless.

It is in the industrial base of their war effort that this surreal medieval hodgepodge was even more apparent. Amazingly, not until the defeat at Stalingrad was there actually an attempt to turn all of Germany's capabilities toward the war with full mobilization to a 24/7 work effort. Compare this to the very public mobilization of America's war effort, starting on the morning of December 8, 1941, or the Herculean effort by the Soviets to evacuate entire factory complexes, and move them two thousand miles to the east. Many of the factories were then rebuilt under open air sheds, in the middle of Siberia since there was no time, energy, or resources to waste making fully enclosed and heated factories during that first terrible winter of the war. As millions struggled in such factories, working seventy- and eighty-hour weeks in sub-zero conditions, back in Germany middle- and upper-class *hausfraus* still expected to stay at home and have Ukrainian and Polish servant girls as part of the booty of the war.

What Albert Speer was able to accomplish, within a year of becoming the *Fuehrer* of production after Stalingrad, was stunning and showed what Germany might have been able to achieve if Hitler and his henchmen had accepted the harsh reality of a long and protracted war back in 1940, or even as late as 1941. In spite of the now-relentless bombardment from the air and the collapse on all fronts in 1944, production of fighter aircraft increased several hundred percent under Speer's guidance, but by then it was too late.

Another glaring example of Nazi self-deception is the bizarre opinion, held well into 1942, that the war was still one of limited duration, and to invest in longer-term research and development for weapons several years off was a waste of effort at that moment.

The most famous examples of this are the squandered leads in high technology weapons. In many cases, German technology was three, five, even ten years ahead of the Allies, but the potentials of this were never brought to bear, and realization of this utter folly, fortunately for us, came too late.

Within days after the start of the war, the first combat jet aircraft was test flown by Heinkel. With the right developmental effort, it could have been combat operational by 1941. Time and again, resources to this effort were held back, since the party line was that the war would be over long before then, they already had air superiority with the ME-109; therefore production resources should focus on models already on the assembly line, or which would be available within a year or less. Beyond that, the various manufacturing firms within the Reich often worked at cross purposes to each other, half a dozen firms siphoning off what little resources were available for their own jet and rocket projects, duplicating research and development and thereby squandering resources and time. In their self-centered rivalries, whoever was in favor with Goering at the moment would actively seek to block an opponent's project, a project that might very well have been crucial to winning the war. Imagine Lockheed or Douglas, doing everything possible to block the development of the B-29 in 1942–43, and succeeding in setting back the delivery schedule, simply because it was not "their baby."

Granted there was intense industrial competition in America at times, but a firm hand by the government and the war production board, kept everyone's eye on the final target: victory first.

Meanwhile, in Germany, inter-corporate rivalries came into play, with various aircraft manufacturers pushing for their own particular models. Heinkel, Messerschmitt, Fokker, Arado, and others all had their pet project, all gobbling up the limited research-and-development money that was forthcoming. And then finally, there was interference by Hitler himself, demanding that an aircraft obviously intended for air superiority was not really needed since the war would be over before deployment, but at the moment a good fast tactical jet bomber was needed instead. The result is well known. Perhaps five hundred fighter jets and a couple of hundred twin engine bombers became fully operational in 1944, rather than five thousand in 1942.

In contrast, throughout the war, the American system of manufacturing trumped the Germans. Our manufacturing system was simple and straightforward. The government would announce specs for a next generation weapon after consultation with the military as to what it needed, strategic planning as to what would be the next step for winning the war, and with industrial firms as to what might be feasible. There would be a short deadline of competitive design, sometimes as short as ninety days. A review board would select the winner, and a runner-up. And here then is the crucial factor: the mass production of various subcomponents and sometimes the entire weapon system would be farmed out to numerous rival companies who would each gain part of the pie, and in so doing, generate a flood of production and also crush the winner-take-all mentality of firms in Germany. Dozens of companies, and not just Boeing, were building B-17s, and 29s or their subcomponents during the war. The runner-up design would be held in reserve with a limited production run, in case of unforeseen difficulties developing with the primary contract, a classic example being the mass production of the most expensive plane of the war, the B-29, while at the same time, the lesser known B-32 was produced in limited numbers as a backup if the teething problems with the 29 were not solved in a timely manner.

For ground transportation, Ford, GM, Studebaker, all produced the standard Deuce and a Half truck, with fully interchangeable parts between manufacturers, while by the end of the war it is estimated that Germany had over fifty different types of trucks in the field, creating a replacement parts nightmare. Simple rugged reliability was always a keynote of our designs, along with ease of production and maintenance in field, time required for manufacturing, and cost. The legendary P-51 was one-fourth the cost of a P-47, and could be manufactured in a fraction of the time, was easier to maintain, and by 1944 was creating an "aluminum overcast" above Germany. Though a legendary aircraft, it did have its faults. While it was the best air superiority plane of the war, most pilots still preferred the older "Jug" for its ability to take punishment. The answer: assign the P-47 for ground support and the attack of heavily defended targets, while the more fragile 51 fought it out far above and in support of the bomber streams.

While the folly of wasted time and lack of effort with jet aircraft was played out in Germany, on the other side of the ledger, incredible levels of resources were devoted to the Vengeance weapons, the pet project of the Fuehrer, which any pragmatic analysis would have shown was a true waste of effort and a pipe dream as far as winning the war. If the identical effort for the V weapons had, instead, been put into surface to air, air to air, and air to ground missiles, the results against our bomber fleets, and for that matter, invasion fleets would have been devastating. Germany had a ten-year lead in this technology and squandered it. The remarkable Henschel television-guided rocket bomb, a true smart bomb, developed and deployed in small numbers in 1943, could have shattered the D-Day fleet under a blizzard of precision-guided weapons, but the lack of a coherent planning system, and the mad system of fiefdoms for production, fortunately kept that weapon from anything beyond a few dozen drops during the entire war. Guided missiles, radar, and infra-red homing missiles, both SAM and air launch, could have been realities by 1944, instead of the incredible waste of thousands of V-1s and V-2s that could barely hit a target within a ten-mile radius.

So on one side, advance technologies were dismissed since the war would be over before they could be deployed; on the other side, the equivalent of billions was wasted on but one of Hitler's pet projects and in other areas when development was given a go-ahead, it usually was in rivalry with ten, twenty, even fifty other rival plans. Allied inspectors were awed, at war's end, to find mock-ups and even flying prototypes for mass production of cheap jet fighters, stealth bombers, intercontinental recon aircraft that looked amazingly like the U-2, and even supersonic fighters, the likes of which would not be seen in American and Soviet arsenals for another ten years (all modeled on captured German designs). All of it too late, far too late, and more frightening, nearly all of them potential realities a year or two earlier, if only the proper team effort and logical application of resources had been applied in a timely manner.

Even that most terrifying lead of all, atomic weaponry, was squandered. In the late 1930s, Germany might very well have had a five-year lead on the West in this area. Though the effort strained even the American war effort, nevertheless Manhattan did go forward, first and foremost as a counter to the feared German development. Lack of foresight, again the belief that this stage of the war against European-based powers would be over long before such a weapon was ready, and effort could be postponed to a later date, ruled the day. That, and the second component for how to lose a war played into this field—and here is, in this author's opinion, the true root of how to lose—Germany was blinded by its own mad doctrine of racism.

Racism was not a disease unique to Germany of course. America, much to its shame was still a two-tiered society. Wherever German forces marched, especially in the East, there was, in general, willing support by many in occupied countries for the treatment of the Jews. The Holocaust could never have been carried out to the frightening level it achieved without the willing support of far too many Poles, Ukrainians, and others, and many in England and America turned a blind eye to the reality of it.

Even before the war, however, anti-Semitism acted as a brake on the development of the Nazi war machine. Ironic to note that, of any subgrouping within Germany when Hitler came to power, German Jews had served at a higher, disproportionate level in the Kaiser's army of WWI, eager to show their patriotism and German-ness, in much the same way Americans of Irish, Italian, and even German descent had rallied to the flag in 1917.

Many of the best brains in Germany for military planning, industrial development, and especially scientific advances, fled their homeland with the rise of Hitler; those who stayed were marginalized out of any ability to contribute, and in the end murdered or forced to flee Germany, the most famous refugees case being that of Einstein and many of his inner circle. When discussion did come to the table about the physics of atomic weapons, Nazi officials, in their "know-nothingism" dismissed it as "that Jew science."

The seeds of how to truly lose a war did not just rest on this tragic issue, it went far deeper with the open disdain of all Slavic races as inferior, corrupted by Jewish Marxism, and at best, in a postwar world, fit only for serfdom. Goering joked that once peace came, a Slav's education should be limited, at most, to how to drive a truck and read road signs. The new masters had already carved up the vast eastern territories into fiefdoms, acting like hungry barons, willing to serve their king as long as they got a piece of the booty once victory was achieved.

Thus with the invasion of the Soviet Union in 1941, Germany threw away its one great chance for an absolute victory, never realizing just how close they were to a triumph that could have taken them to the Urals.

The Soviet Union was a vast gulag, a slave empire, held together by ethnic Russians who subjugated all other groups beneath them. There were Balts, Baltic Germans, and Volga Germans, "white" Russians, various Tartar, Mongol and eastern races, remnants of the great invasions of the thirteenth century, and above all else the Ukrainians. If you ever want a quick entry into a fight, even today, dare to make the mistake of referring to a Ukrainian as a Russian; you will be set straight real fast.

One should not forget that even the Poles could have been potential allies once the war turned on Russia. Poland has a unique and forgotten history. In the sixteenth century, it was perhaps the most powerful nation in Europe. To this day, Austrians recognize that it was the Poles who lifted the siege of Vienna in 1683 from the Turkish onslaught. If not for one of the strangest forms of government in history, which allowed but a single baron to block necessary laws, and their equally strange desire to import foreign kings, since none could agree on one Pole to rule them all, the nation would have survived. But by the late 1700s, Poland's friendly neighbors Prussia, Austria, and Russia collaborated to carve the nation up.

Napoleon set an example Hitler should have considered. Playing to the unfair treatment of a now-defunct Poland, evilly destroyed by its neighbors, the French emperor created a protectorate, with promise of full independence once his wars of liberation were complete. In so doing, he created a fierce alliance and sentimental attachment between France and Poland that survived to the twentieth century and in some ways helped to trigger WWII. It was Poland that remained steadfast to the last in its alliance with Napoleon and in so doing, went down to defeat with him, and saw itself divided up yet again. With the collapse of Germany, Austria, and

Russia in 1918, Polish nationalists created a new nation and actually came within a hairsbreadth of destroying Lenin and Trotsky in an all-but-forgotten Polish-Soviet War fought out in the early 1920s. Though knifed in the back by Germany in 1939, Poland was knifed by the Soviets, as well, when Stalin occupied the eastern half of the country in September, 1939, and immediately embarked on his traditional purges with the mass murder of tens of thousands of Polish POWs.

It is feasible that if Germany had managed Poland differently, fanned its natural mistrust of the Soviets, and offered independence, as Napoleon did, Hitler might have found hundreds of thousands ready to come to his side in a great crusade of liberation against the godless Soviet empire.

When German troops marched into the Ukraine in 1941, they were greeted by cheering throngs and thousands of German soldiers found themselves to be liberating heroes, helping to reopen shuttered churches, accepting gifts of flowers and bread from cheering Ukrainian throngs who shouted that the Germans were their saviors, and begged to join in the fight.

Here was the trump card that could have been played but never was because of the insanity of racism.

Slavs were inferior peoples, the invasion was not one of liberation, it was for territorial hegemony. And the "golden pheasants," as the rank and file of the Wehrmacht so sarcastically called them, the party elite, saw the vast open steppes as their new fiefdoms, to be farmed by a re-enslaved Slavic peasantry, as if they were again the Teutonic Knights of old. Before the invasion of June, 1941, the now-infamous secret orders had been posted to the SS, and to some in the army high command, that not only would special battalions of SS move behind the advancing lines for the purpose of murdering all Jews, party commissars, and potential leftists and leaders, but that the ultimate goal, to be enacted across the next several years, was to strip the land clean of food, and drive the civilian population in the conquered territories into a medieval state of servility, with the intent that at least one-third of the entire populace die of starvation and disease, thereby making way for German settlers in the postwar world. It was the most evil, corrupt plan for mass murder in the history of humanity—and it cost Germany the war.

Idiocy. This racism is made even more ironic if one looks at what transpired in Yugoslavia, Trans-Jordan, Syria, and Iraq at the exact same time. Himmler came up with the bizarre racial doctrine that Arabs were not an inferior race, but instead were distantly related to Aryans, and therefore actively recruited into the SS. Bosnian/Albanian/Muslim SS detachments were formed, fully accepted into the SS (complete to a fez for their uniform and mullahs for religious services) and then cut loose on the civilian Christian and Jewish population of the region with murderous results. Some of the crisis in that region, even today, and for that matter in the Middle East in general, is an echo of the embrace by the SS of these ethnic groups, while others who could have contributed a hundred times more to the German war effort were slated for mass slaughter because of racial guidelines. That thinking would make even Kafka shake his head with disbelief.

Imagine, instead, a scenario for how to win a war, rather than how to lose a war.

If only they had dumped the racism and engaged in a realistic, and yes, if need be, cynical analysis of the geo-political/social/religious situation in Eastern Europe, circa 1930. Poland had fought a bitter and darn near successful war against Trotsky's international movement, and nearly driven the stake into the heart of the Soviet Union in the early 1920s. The territory it held to the east had once been part of the old Russian empire and the proud Polish military government knew that there would come a day of reckoning with Stalin and his henchmen. Next in significance were the three Baltic states, Latvia, Lithuania, and Estonia, culturally linked to Germany via the centuries-old Hanseatic League. First and foremost though was Ukraine, which had been ceded to Germany at the treaty of Brest-Litovsk in March 1918, and then lost within the year due to Germany's military collapse at the end of WWI. For a brief period, Ukraine, Lithuania, and Poland had even sought to establish a commonwealth, or at least a mutual defense agreement against the Soviet Russians, but the attempt failed through mutual mistrust, and again that old ugly plague of eastern Europe and the Balkans, ethnic mistrust. Ukraine managed to briefly hold out on its own during the bitter Civil War in which one needed a score card to keep track of who was fighting whom, but was finally betrayed by communists within its own ranks and "sold" back to Russia to be forced into the Soviet Union, while Lithuania and Poland managed to maintain their independence. Stalin, upon coming to power, turned his wrath upon Ukraine, which he feared held enough manpower and the motivation to try to break away. The tool was mass starvation, the looting of all food harvested for three years (primarily to feed Moscow and those Russian cities firmly within the communist fold), and at least nine million died.

Concurrent were the purges, collectivization, the destruction of religion, the takeover by ethnic Russians. Ukraine in 1941 was a "nation" seething with hatred for their Soviet overlords and sensing that the ever-expanding war just might be the vehicle for their own liberation.

The "liberators" came on June 22, 1941, and in the opening weeks were greeted as such. A moral stain that Ukraine has not come to terms with even now is that, in the beginning, they did not just collaborate with the Nazis, but instead a fair percentage of the populace was more than happy to aid in the destruction of the Jewish population of that region. The grisly murder of more than a hundred thousand Ukrainian Jews, at Babi Yar, just outside of Kiev, was an action in which thousands of Ukrainians lent a hand.

But for the sake of the scenario, how to win a war, victory for Germany was indeed at hand on June 22, 1941. The German high command and Hitler had grossly underestimated total Soviet strength in nearly all departments in terms of divisions, amount of armor, industrial capability, and once Stalin had staggered back from the initial shock, his adroit shifting of the war aim from defending communism to defending the violated motherland.

But for the Ukrainians, it was not about "their" motherland. Ukraine has always seen itself as an entity separate from Russia, a subjugated people, betrayed into joining the Russian empire and then dragged back in after Lenin's lying statements that the former

Russian empire was dead and the various "peoples" were free to go their own way.

So, how to win a war:

Declare the invasion of Eastern Europe to be a war of liberation from communism, the sadistic madness of Stalin, and even turn it into a religious crusade, to return to subjugated people the right to their religion. This author and an editor of this series have walked through some of the "killing fields" of Stalin's brutal regime, remnants of destroyed Volga German settlements, annihilated by Stalin in 1942, ruined and defaced churches, empty abandoned villages by the score where forced collectivization had pushed millions of peasants into military-style barracks, and evidence of the vast betrayal of the "kulak class," small landholders who had been encouraged by Lenin with his limited capitalistic approach to boost farm production, and then after his death, their base betrayal and murder by Stalin as a class of people who were enemies of the state.

If Hitler and his henchmen had but set aside their loathing of Slavic peoples (and it is doubly ironic, for those of the Ukraine claim that their blood, in part, descends from the Varangians, Nordic settlers who traversed the rivers of eastern Europe and first established the trade city of Kiev), they would have won the war. Rather than persecute and, in the end, find millions of Ukrainians either passively resisting or taking up arms, these same people, if promised a free and independent Ukraine, would without doubt have rallied to the anti-Russian cause. A hundred divisions could easily have been raised from their ranks, dozens more from the Poles, the Moldavians, the Crim Tartars, and the peoples of the three Baltic states.

The battle of Stalingrad would have seen Ukrainians fighting alongside German, Italian, Hungarian, and Romanian troops. They might not have been the first line elite, but they certainly would have fought with passion and conviction, knowing their national survival and liberation were on the line.

Or let us even take a more cynical tack. Promise them liberation, self-determination, or even insist upon their joining a postwar commonwealth, and once victory against the hated Russians was achieved, turn against them. That irony is a technique as old as recorded history.

Instead, the anti-Slavic racism of the Nazis, their feudal lords' lust to divide the rich Ukraine into fiefdoms long before the battle was won, took from their hands an almost-guaranteed victory on the eastern front, if not in 1941, most definitely by the winter of 1942. Imagine a levy of sixty, eighty Ukrainian divisions to bolster the thin line holding the salient to Stalingrad, perhaps expanding the front, and supporting the crucial drive toward the Caspian to seize the true sinew of this war, the vast oil supplies Germany so desperately needed, the loss of which would bring the Russian war machine to a halt.

With the Ukraine, the Baltic states, and even Poland at their side, the war in the East would have been won in 1942, long before the vast American buildup of 1943 began to flood into England. That island fortress would have again been under siege, perhaps facing bombardment in 1944–45, not with puny V weapons, but with atomic weapons instead. The Germans' own continental empire protected by jet aircraft, smart bombs, and the vast resources of the East were a match for anything America and an England under siege could ever mount in reply. The twentieth century would have ended, not as the triumph of Western liberalism, but instead, as Churchill had warned, a Europe descending into a new dark age, made more sinister by the lights of a perverted science.

Thank heavens we fought an enemy so blinded by self-serving aims, and barbaric racism—otherwise this would not be an essay on how to lose a war, but instead, on how a war was won.

If ever there was a lesson of how the blindness of racism contributed to how to lose a war, it was here. There is only one other such glaring example, in that same war, on the far side of the Asian continent.

For Japan, winning World War II was always a question of negotiating a beneficial treaty with the USA. With millions of soldiers already bogged down in China, Manchuria, and other Far Eastern nations, there was never going to be an invasion of California. Japan did not have the resources to even dream of such an endeavor. The goal of a treaty was less unrealistic than we might suspect, viewed from the perspective of today. With war against Germany almost inevitable, the window was there for military and diplomatic success. Appeasement was still in vogue and her ally, Germany, had occupied most of Europe. But even so, one part of the military character of the Japanese nation had a profoundly negative effect on not only the outcome of their war, but it also changed, even today, the way that nation is viewed by its neighbors.

JAPAN IN WWII

Asia and the Pacific

WILLIAM R. FORSTCHEN, Ph.D.

There has been much speculation across the years about the potential of Germany winning WWII, and rightly so, for it was indeed within their grasp, and their debacle is a classic example of how hubris and a fatally failed system created defeat. But Japan? Common wisdom is that their defeat was foredoomed, from the moment the first bomb fell on Pearl Harbor, that ultimately all that attack achieved was to awaken the "sleeping giant," and then fill us with a terrible resolve.

That might not be the case. There are scenarios where Japan

might very well have achieved a victory, perhaps a stunning victory. Some of the roots of their failure are mirror images of why Germany lost the war; others are, for lack of a better term, walking backward into a war for all the wrong reasons.

Since the end of WWII, Germany at least has attempted to come to terms with the horrors unleashed by the Nazi cult. Their educational curriculum sixty years later, though originally imposed by the victors, nevertheless takes a hard look at what happened at Auschwitz, and has attempted to inculcate not just realization but atonement for its crimes against humanity. Sadly, that is not fully the case with Japan. Its brutalities, execution of prisoners, the mass slaughters in China that are little known in the West, the ghastly treatment of Korean women taken into medieval bondage, are things that have yet to be fully faced and are still the cause of tension in East Asia today.

It is an anomaly, for this level of brutality was not "part and parcel" of Japanese culture, and for a brief period during the Meiji reforms and Japan's entry onto the world stage, the behavior of their armed forces was considered exemplary.

Japan was a medieval kingdom until the late 1860s, the only major Pacific nation in the world to successfully resist Western "white" imperialism. The Emperor Meiji, seeing the inevitable advantages that Europe and America were achieving through industrialism, and the inability of their social/military system to resist this wave of the future, ordered the modernization of his country. What was wrought in little more than thirty years was stunning. In one generation, Japan leapt from the seventeenth into the twentieth century. With British aid it created a modern navy, with German aid an army, and with American advice, a modern economic industrial system.

The first testing of this modernization came in 1904–05, when Japan went to war against the Russian Empire, and achieved a stunning success. The war was limited in nature, a fight to prevent Russian imperial advances into northern China and the Yellow Sea, and to achieve for Japan hegemony over the Yellow Sea and secure the foundation of its own imperialistic designs on Korea and China.

In other words, Japan felt confident enough to begin to play the "great game" with white imperial powers. The Russo-Japanese War of 1904–05 climaxed at the famed battle of Tsushima, where Admiral Togo annihilated the Russian fleet (and a young officer named Yamamoto was wounded).

It was noted by British, German, and American observers that though tough, the Japanese army fought according to the new rules of war being codified at Geneva, that Russian prisoners were treated humanely, and in general that the Japanese fought honorably. England was so impressed as to seek closer ties with Japan as conflict with Germany began to loom. As loyal allies, when World War I started, Japan did declare war on Germany, provided the bulk of the forces to take out the small German imperial strongholds in China and the Pacific, and provided a flotilla of modern ships for action alongside British ships in the Mediterranean. At the end of the war, Japanese troops were the bulk of the forces deployed in the east as allied intervention into civil war-wracked Russia (though tensions between Americans and Japanese stationed side by side in Siberia nearly brought them to blows).

The brutality Japan displayed during WWII was therefore not at all pre-evident in the same way it was not pre-evident with Germany of World War I (in spite of the British charges about the "rape of Belgium"). What did transpire next, though, exactly as with Nazi Germany, was one of the two root causes that stole victory from Japanese arms 1937–45, and that is, yet again, the insanity of racism.

Many historians argue, this one included, that World War II actually started in 1931, with the Japanese seizing Manchuria in a nearly bloodless coup, and turning it into a puppet state, Manchukuo. It is an area rich in natural resources, especially iron and coal, essential ingredients for an emerging industrial state, and some hoped it could serve as their "lebensraum"; however, anyone who has been to the region knows it is one of the more inhospitable locations on the face of the earth.

The complexity of Japanese political/military infighting during the 1930s, which took them from a tacit ally of the Western democracies into outright war, is a complex study. In short, the militarists in Japan, using the emperor as a mystical religious cult figure, came to seize control of the government. Their public relations agenda to their own people was: since the emperor was indeed the direct descendant of a god, then Japan held a unique position among all humanity. Their race therefore had in its presence a divine blessing—the living presence of a god, and Japan's ultimate destiny was to achieve its own "place in the sun," a place, of course, sanctioned and mandated by that divine blessing.

For the more pragmatic, this was a front for imperial ambitions. Japan felt a real threat, as did Germany and the Western democracies, from the Soviet Union. With the purging and exile of Trotsky, the radical rhetoric of the International had been suppressed for the moment, Stalin claiming that communism first had to be perfected inside his own empire, and then naturally their "religion" would expand around the world. Japan, one must realize, is a neighbor of Russia, separated only by a narrow strait of water, not much wider than the North Sea separating England from Germany. Russia had been humbled in the 1904–05 war, and it was fairly assumed at some point that Stalin would seek payback. The bold seizure of Manchuria, carving it away from a moribund China, in a very real sense blocked Soviet designs on that region, and did indeed poise a dagger at Soviet-held Siberia. There was a real potential here that someday war would explode again.

The realists in Japan knew that they lacked the resources for a protracted land struggle with Russia, that their own industrial base and access to resources had to be expanded. After all, they were now "players." More than one Japanese expansionist argued that was not their goal identical to the British creation of the Raj, or America's own imperialistic wars in 1846 against Mexico and in 1898 against Spain, which had carved out a nation. One person's manifest destiny can easily be argued as another person's imperialism and quest for hegemony, which America had indeed achieved. When looking at it in the cold light of history, it is an argument hard to deny.

China was a giant, convulsed by a brutal civil war (1927–1949) which had claimed millions of lives. After the collapse of the last dynasty and the brief moment of hope under Sun Yat-sen, had come the chaos of rival war lords, the emergence of the so-called "Nationalist" government under Chang Kai-Shek, and his communist rival, the Moscow-supported Mao. China was the obvious, natural point of Japanese expansion. Some Japanese moralists even argued that a strong force could finally bring about peace in the region and finish off the communists, and ultimately, the Nationalists might even bow to the inevitable and agree to an alliance in a commonwealth-type arrangement. The pragmatic imperialists argued that here was a limitless supply of nearly every natural resource needed by a modern industrial state, and yet again, the zealots maintained that this was finally Japan's religious destiny—a holy crusade to unify the Oriental races and block white European imperialism and exploitation.

It was a mixture of all of these reasons that pushed the militarists in the army to argue that intervention in China was essential if Japan was to survive, if Stalin was to be blocked, and a proper balance established with the West. China was ripe for the taking and if Japan did not move swiftly and forcefully, it would fall into someone's lap sooner or later, either the Western powers would carve it up under puppet rulers, or Mao would eventually gain the upper hand and the Soviets would move in. Besides, their taking of China was no different than England's of Burma, France's of Indochina, Holland of the East Indies, and America taking the Philippines.

And so they moved at last in the summer of 1937. There had been earlier expansion across the edge of the Gobi Desert, north of the Great Wall, and a lodgment in Peking (old spelling). A minor incident at the Marco Polo Bridge at the edge of Peking became the pretext, first for a full scale sweep into northern China, and then shortly thereafter, a million men were committed into operations along the coast region and a major drive to seize Shanghai and nearby Nanking.

How to lose a war. Here it is, for the Sino-Japanese War 1937–45, though all but forgotten in the West today, was a genocidal blood-fest unmatched in history. Even the brutality of the SS in occupied Russia and the Ukraine pales in comparison. To sound devoid of all human empathy, at least the SS attempted to justify their actions by claiming it was to suppress counter-rebellion, or in the "only following orders" defense, that the high command demanded that the region's population be slashed by one third to make way for Germanic settlement. The behavior of the Japanese army, in contrast was one of systemic bloodlust and madness, the casual murder, torture, rape, and brutalization of tens of millions of innocent civilians trapped under their dominion.

This author studied the campaign as preparation for a novel about the war in the Pacific. One of the works I heavily relied upon was *The Rape of Nanking*, a remarkable study published by a brilliant young scholar, Iris Chang. A descendant of survivors of those "days of infamy" in China, 1937, the author produced a brilliant, terrifying work that so overwhelmed her with its horrors that she committed suicide shortly after release of the book, trapped in a cycle of revulsion and severe depression.

Nanking briefly served as the Nationalist capital, the government abandoning the city in the second week of December, 1937. The Japanese commander in charge of capturing the city, in a fit of rage that the Chinese Nationalist government had dared to resist and then escaped, declared the revival of the medieval tradition that a city which resisted would be given over to three days of pillage—and cut his troops loose from all discipline. Rape, of great-grandmothers of eighty to children of six, was widespread. Chinese historians estimate that nearly every woman in the city endured rape, and then suffered gross mutilation if they were allowed to survive at all. The book contained one photo of what was left of a woman that was so horrific that this author, used to the images of war, hid the book so his teenage daughter would not stumble upon it and see the depths of human depravity.

Several hundred thousand civilians were not just executed, they were tormented and tortured to death. Tethered to long ropes, they were used for bayonet and target practice, allowed to run just enough to make the sport enjoyable. Children were impaled in front of their parents, human beings were slowly roasted alive, there were even reports of acts of cannibalism (a practice documented as being practiced against American POWs as well). A Japanese army newspaper actually ran a boastful front page commentary about a competition between two officers to see who could catch and behead the most victims in one day, complete with photographs of the two with a stack of their trophies. (The winner had murdered over a hundred victims.)

An ironic side note. There was a hero at Nanking. A European trade representative who was so outraged by the horrors he was witnessing that he quickly painted the symbol of his national flag onto bedsheets, cordoned off a dozen or so blocks, placed his national flag at the intersections and, along with a handful of others, moved over a quarter of a million terrified civilians into this sanctuary, then defied the Japanese commander to dare to break into the sealed-off area, with the threat that his nation would declare war. The Japanese commander backed off. The hero, Herr Rabe, who used his flag to save a quarter of a million lives was a member of the Nazi Party. Only in 2008 has the communist government of China officially recognized his heroism and erected a statue in his honor.

Here, forever, is how to lose a war. A warring nation can wage war with aggression, but beyond a certain line, in this organized system of murder we call war, too much transpires, and unless a conqueror can murder every last person and erase all living memory of their brutality, there will forever be resistance, for generations if need be. In the twentieth-century world of mass communications, the Japanese were so inept, stupid, or just so plain arrogant that they publicized their brutality and allowed others to witness and document it as well. Only weeks after Nanking fell, *Life* magazine published photographs of the mass murder, forever hardening American public opinion, though not to the point of a call for intervention (only one in twenty Americans would have been willing to take that step in 1937).

All of China, the entire world, knew of the rape of Nanking, whereas the Nazis and Stalin at least tried to keep their horror shows secret. From that date forward, China could never be conquered.

It seems that history is replete with pre-war announcements by various warring nations that the entire affair will be over in six days, six weeks, or six months. So it was in China. Japan invaded with its war lords promising that the campaign would be over by the end of the year, six months. Four years later they were still trapped in a quagmire. If one looks at the economic analysis run by the Japanese government in 1940–41, a threadbare, emerging modern state which had invaded China to provide the resources necessary for their firm establishment as a major "player," was heading to full collapse by 1942 at the latest, and would have to abandon their campaign. The war effort in Japan was not just bleeding China to death, it was draining the Japanese economy as well. A crisis point was being reached. Either the war in China had to be won, or abandoned. And thus the horrid logic that war must be supported by yet more war took hold. The militarist argued that in order to win in China, Japan needed to seize essential resources elsewhere, the sinews of modern war being aluminum, nickel, rubber, and, above all else, oil. And all these resources could be found in European-held colonies. Colonies held by France and Holland, which had collapsed under the Nazi blitzkrieg, or by England, whose back was against the wall, or by America.

We were an enigma to them. Imperialists who had seized the Philippines but were now promising it independence. A powerful nation that seemed to wish to avoid war at all cost. A great myth is that the Japanese in general viewed us as weak, effete cowards who hid behind others, totally lacking in the spirit of *bushido*. Nothing could be farther from the truth. A whole generation of Japanese officers, especially navy personnel, had been educated in America, the most famous of whom was Yamamoto. They knew of our vast size, any of their economists could easily draw up a chart comparing industrial strength. Those familiar with us counseled loudly against war, even as they planned for it.

Here is the second ingredient for "how to lose a war." Never, ever dismiss your enemy; never dismiss the counsel of those who intimately know your potential enemy before you engage him. The weird insanity of Japan, circa 1941, is that nearly everyone in the upper levels of the power structure, especially the navy and the surviving civilian government, realized that fighting America was all but a forlorn hope, but then did so anyhow. The logic is well-known to nearly anyone who studies the Pacific War. Destroy the American fleet on the first day of the war (for so it was taught by the great American naval prophet, Alfred Mahan, read by all Japanese naval academy students), then engage in a quick campaign of "snatch and grab," sweeping up the British and Dutch colonies (the French had already conceded Indochina to them). Once this was an accomplished fact, finish off any American counterstrike, and the Americans would logically view this as a war of limited interest to them and then seek an honorable peace. The defeat of Russia in 1905 was the model they wished to apply to us. So little did they understand that, at least until the middle of the twentieth century, Americans had no concept of *limited* war, and if engaged, especially if attacked first, would see the conflict as a moral crusade and press it to an inevitable conclusion.

And so the war came.

There was a third ingredient to this formula of how to lose a war and it directly harkens back to the blood frenzy in China in 1937, and that is the inherent racism of the Japanese militarists. There was a potential, stunning in its power and scope, which if properly employed might very well have guaranteed them if not a final victory (given America's technological superiority by 1943, and atomic weapons by 1945), at least a protracted fight which might very well have gone on till the end of the decade or even longer, and the potential of nearly half the planet as their allies.

When Japan sprang forth on its war of aggression against America, Great Britain, and Holland in December, 1941, they trumpeted that they were sweeping across Asia and the Pacific as liberators of the oriental race against white imperialism and oppression. Their feeble propaganda ministry heralded this as the Greater East Asian Co-Prosperity Sphere. The propaganda machine churned out the rhetoric to greet the advancing Japanese army as liberators and friends.

They came instead as plunderers, murderers, and rapists. It is a harsh thing to say of a people who today stand as one of our firmest allies and international friends, a people who this author personally admires, both now and for their legendary past before World War II, but the history of 1937–45 cannot be denied. Ask any Korean, Filipino, Vietnamese, Indonesian, Mongol, and especially the Chinese (or for that matter any American Marine) who endured those bitter years and the animosity, the bitter memories are just below the surface. Certainly there were many in the Japanese army, and to a greater extent their navy and air forces, who fought with nobility and honor, like the samurai of old, who treated the innocents with chivalry, their opponents in war to be fought with skill and cunning, but to treat fairly if wounded or captured. But far too many sank to the lowest levels of brutality. Here was how to lose a war perhaps even more extreme than the behavior of Germany in the Ukraine.

Imagine instead a different, far more sane, and yes, cunning approach to this conflict. The legendary Steven Ambrose so adroitly observed that throughout World War II, be it the village, town, or city of a friend or foe, all knew that when the American GIs marched in, or fought their way in street by street, civilians were protected, be they French, Belgium, German, or Japanese. And the same stood true for the British. That as soon as the fighting ceased, and at times while the fighting still raged, Americans would risk their lives to save the innocent, would lift their fire if an enemy medic crawled out to rescue a fallen comrade, and in many cases our own medics would go to the aid of a fallen foe. Our own forces would place themselves at risk to protect others, even as the world devolved into madness, and once the fighting stopped, the innate good will of the battle-weary GI would cause him to share his last bit of rations with the abandoned and starving. To this author the most heart-rending image of that war is a drawing by Bill Mauldin of his two dogfaces, Willie and Joe—hungry, ragged, and exhausted, wearily looking at starving children while holding their full mess tins, the reader knowing that a second later the food would be shared with the starving innocents and they would go back into battle hungry.

Impossible as it is, imagine the Japanese army had advanced in conquest with a similar humane philosophy and training for its officers and enlisted men. All studies have shown this was a fundamental flaw in the training of the Japanese army. Physical brutality was the norm, up to summarily executing soldiers who had displeased their officers, without benefit of trial. Physical brutality was the norm in their army. Officers beat and even executed those who displeased them. In turn this brutality worked down the chain of command, from officers brutalizing NCOs, and in turn, NCOs brutalizing their line infantry. Civilians were next. It had a schizophrenic quality to it, GIs taken prisoner would describe how one officer would approach them with sympathy and compassion, announcing how he had been educated at USC or Purdue, offer the last bit of money in his pocket and rations in his haversack, and then but minutes later that same prisoner would be summarily executed by an enraged guard when these few precious goods were found.

Imagine instead an army trained to behave humanely and with chivalry, coming as liberators from the "white man's" imperial oppression. That upon the conquest of Malaya, Sumatra, Burma, Japanese troops had acted with decorum. That Japanese administrators offered liberation and self-determination, the only caveat being that during the duration of the conflict they would ask the local populace for help, that children would be fed and given medication, that local leaders be treated with respect, even if at the start they displayed hesitation, and yes, that white captives be treated with respect as well. Unfortunately for the Japanese, usually within hours, days at most, the supposed white oppressors were no longer seen as imperialist overlords but instead a longed-for past, no matter how exploitive, and then for long smoldering years their return was dreamed of as liberation. Recall that upward of eighty percent of the deaths during the Bataan death march were Filipino troops, not Americans. (There were about 66,000 Filipinos and 12,000 American prisoners on the infamous march.) For that matter, even more intense rage was leveled against the Filipino prisoners by the Japanese because they were viewed as Oriental traitors. This nightmare treatment was dished out across the length of that long brutal march in full view of the weeping civilian population, an action which insured that this entire captive nation would remember, and be ready for the day of liberation. MacArthur's proclamation, "I have returned" might have been the bombast of an egotist, but it rang true across the Philippines, who saw their returning over-lords as liberators and not as the enemy, and greeted the returning American troops with jubilation. China and other Asian nations' populations were treated just as badly by Japan. The massacre at Nanking, where tens of thousands were slaughtered, showed just how vicious it was.

There was a real and potent danger in India, burning with a desire for independence, a reality so alarming to the British that the more pessimistic in the government feared that India might explode into a frenzy for independence. Japan was actually able to field an entire division of troops from the Raj ready to fight for that independence. This could have been a hundred divisions from across Asia standing by their side, if they had come as lib-erators rather than oppressors. As the Germans threw away such a chance in their invasion of the Soviet Union, so did the Japanese in their far more vast conquests of 1941–42. By 1944–45, enraged local populations were eager to see their defeat and expulsion—and the hatred has lingered for two thirds of a century.

If there is a third way to lose a war, it is: never fight a war you don't have to fight in the first place, especially against a superior foe. Japanese strategic thinking became fixated upon the notion that, in order to secure their primary prize, the Dutch East Indies, the American fleet would have to be destroyed and the British ex-pelled from their colonial possessions as well. One could raise the question: why? There were only a few voices that raised this basic question as Japan prepared for war against the Western allies, dis-missed with hardly any debate, as to why go to war with America and even Britain at all. It is a scenario that in fact was a secret nightmare of FDR who, in his wisdom, did see that ultimately the Axis powers had to be destroyed, but America would only enter the war if attacked first. What would we have done if Japan simply struck at the Dutch? Could we have then raised a national war effort against them that could be fought with vigor? With England nearly on the ropes in its fight against Germany, could Churchill indeed raise the national will to take on another enemy half a world away? Could Roosevelt have successfully declared war against Japanese aggression, mounted only against the Dutch, and then seen that war fought through to a successful conclusion, which would have cost hundreds of billions of 1941 dollars and a hundred thousand or more dead? It is an alternate history type speculation, but a valid one to consider in this study of how to lose a war. I hardly think a rally cry of "Save the Dutch Colonies" would have resonated with the same power as "Remember Pearl Harbor."

The rationale for the Japanese actions of December 7, 1941, was the desperate need to secure resources that would enable the successful conclusion of the war in China and to secure, as well, Japan's place as an imperial power. Never in their wildest fantasies did they dream that one day their troops would shake hands with invading German troops somewhere along the Mississippi River. Such stuff is the pure dark fantasy of our own propaganda machine at the start of the conflict. Japan always believed that a successful war with America would be a war fought in the older tradition of a limited conflict, with limited objectives, concluded with a successful peace conference. It is even speculated that Japan might have offered the Philippines back to us as a negotiating ploy. Again the model was its victory against Russia in 1905—win just what you need, then make concessions to insure the peace and avoid a protracted war. That war was fought to block Russian expansionism, and secure their own position on the continent of Asia; it was never about Japanese troops eventually storming the Kremlin.

If they had followed a Dutch only policy, or even an attack against the Dutch and England, but left us entirely alone, FDR might have been able to push for a declaration of war, but it would have been war without the passionate fire that consumed us on the afternoon of that day of infamy, a war in which the sleeping giant was filled with a terrible resolve, and therefore sought nothing less than a total, and if need be, annihilating victory. It is hard to imagine America fighting thus, in order to preserve Dutch and British colonialism, hardly the stuff that would cause Americans to flood recruiting stations and storm into withering fire on remote tropical atolls. Our antiquated battleships and few carriers of 1942, if met in open engagement in this far different war, most likely would have been defeated if we had fought, with a resulting prospect of war weariness in America, isolationists screaming it was Roosevelt's war and why are we fighting to defend colonialism, and in short order a settlement sought.

A Japan which had come as liberators rather than mass murderers, a Japan which had more adroitly played a political game with America and better understood how we perceived the nature of war, might very well have secured for itself a true empire, in the same way their tacit allies, the Nazis, could have achieved it in Europe and western Asia. Thank heavens for this generation that the totalitarian regimes of the twentieth century, rather than being the new models of efficiency that they claimed to be, instead proved to be some of the most short-sighted, in fact suicidal, governments ever created, while the traditional democracies they disdained, proved to be far more resilient than any had dreamed possible.

Saddam Hussein commanded a large, well-equipped army financed with lots of oil wealth, had recent military success in a war against Iran, had bought modern weapons from a nearby superpower, and commanded a fiercely loyal personal guard full of members of his own tribe and numbering in the thousands. It just should not have been that easy.

BLOOD, DUST, AND OIL

Operation Desert Storm, 1990–91

JOHN HELFERS

On paper, the largest joint coalition military operation since World War II, against a determined enemy on its home terrain, appeared to be a relatively even fight. However, the force buildup and stunning six-day offensive that shattered Saddam Hussein's force of more than 1.2 million soldiers, including his supposedly elite Republican Guards, would prove that appearances could be very deceiving.

After its protracted war with Iran from 1980–88, covertly aided by the U.S., which remained publicly neutral on the conflict, Iraq was bankrupt and in debt to both Saudi Arabia and Kuwait. In 1989, Kuwait increased its oil output by 40 percent, lowering oil prices even further, and harming Iraq's economy. Accusing the small, oil-rich nation of practicing "economic warfare" against Iraq, dictator Saddam Hussein began amassing a large military force on the border between the two countries when negotiations to alleviate the situation stalled. When Hussein spoke with U.S. ambassador April

Glaspie about the situation during this time, a released transcript of the meeting had Glaspie stating: "We have no opinion on the Arab-Arab conflicts, like your border disagreement with Kuwait. I was in the American Embassy in Kuwait during the late '60s. The instruction from the State Department we had during this period was that we should express no opinion on this issue and that the issue is not associated with America. James Baker has directed our official spokesmen to emphasize this instruction."

Some political historians claim that Hussein took this to mean that the U.S. would not challenge him if he moved against Kuwait. Indeed, Hussein was counting on America's non-involvement, believing the superpower's government and military were still in disarray from defeat in Vietnam more than twenty-five years earlier, and would do anything to avoid a fight. However, if Kuwait was taken over, there would be little to stop Hussein from attacking Saudi Arabia, a firm ally of the U.S. But since the U.S. hadn't stated any opposition to Iraq's invasion of Iran in 1980 (which certainly suited the American government's agenda for the region at the time), there is evidence to believe that Hussein thought he could take over Kuwait relatively unopposed. It is not definitely known whether Hussein had planned to take his incursion into Saudi Arabia, but given his antipathy toward that nation for its alliance with the West, it was a very likely scenario, and one the U.S. could not allow.

On August 2, 1990, roughly 100,000 Iraqi troops entered Kuwait, seizing the nation in one day. Its leader, Emir Jaber al-Ahmed al-Sabah, and his family escaped by helicopter out of the country, but the rest of the populace were now the unwilling subjects of Iraq.

The American response was swift. President George H.W. Bush convened with his advisors, including General Colin Powell (Chairman of the Joint Chiefs) and General Norman H. Schwarzkopf (commanding the U.S. Central Command), who would end up leading the coalition forces into battle. While the U.S. military had scored a minor success with the invasion and liberation of Grenada in 1983 against Marxist hardliners, this was a whole different ballgame, in a region the military hadn't fought in since World War II. Aware of the mistakes of the last protracted conflict, Bush heeded Powell's advice that if they were going to win, they needed to bring all necessary force to bear on the battle. The biggest fear was that Hussein would move to consolidate his position in the region, taking over Saudi Arabia and requiring a much larger mission to remove him.

President Bush decided to take steps to prevent that from happening, but needed time to organize the massive logistics effort that such a mission would entail. To keep not only the American people but also the rest of the world calm, he took his usual three-week vacation at Kennebunkport in August, but planned strategy every day with his National Security Advisor, Brent Scowcroft. It helped that Saddam Hussein didn't make any offensive moves during this time, apparently feeling secure in his takeover of Kuwait. Again, it is unclear why he delayed in moving on Saudi Arabia—perhaps because he feared a backlash among other Arab nations—but for whatever reason, his army did not advance any further during this time.

Bush also used this time to cement a coalition of nations that would eventually remove Hussein's forces, bringing together thirty-three other nations that supplied troops, equipment, or money to prepare for the counterattack. Two days after the invasion of Kuwait, General Powell issued orders that sent fifty U.S. navy warships, including the aircraft carriers U.S.S. *Independence* and U.S.S. *Eisenhower*, to the Persian Gulf. To keep Hussein further at bay, the U.S. military released announcements that famous units—the 82nd Airborne Division, the 24th Mechanized Infantry Brigade, the 1st and 2nd Marine Divisions, the 1st Mechanized Infantry Division, etc.—had arrived in the area, when in fact there was only the barest trickle of troops coming over. However, a huge buildup throughout August and September landed 72,000 personnel and 100,000 tons of equipment, enough for Schwarzkopf to be confident that he could repel Hussein's forces in the event of an attack.

If it actually came down to a battle, the initial plan had been to make a long end run around Hussein's dug-in troops on the Iraq-Kuwait border to engage and destroy his best forces, the Republican Guard, then mop up the weaker front lines afterward. However, before the plan could be enacted, Hussein made some strategic changes of his own. He reinforced his Kuwait occupying army to 250,000 men, and built more defensive fortifications, including placing units near many of the country's 700 oil wells and refineries, a pointed threat to the rest of the oil-needing world. He also moved his Republican Guard farther back into Iraq, placing lesser troops in front of them, creating layers of increasingly tougher and tougher defense—the opposite of conventional military strategy, which would be to place the strongest troops at the front, to prevent an incursion into the country.

His men had also created a deadly killing zone along the hundred-plus kilometers on either side of Kuwait's and Iraq's shared border, a field of mines, oil-filled ditches, looming sand berms, and deep trenches, all to drive the enemy into killing lanes, fields of fire upon which the invading army could be destroyed, as the Iraqis had done to the Iranian army during their war. Finally, there was the looming specter of chemical weapons, which the U.S. knew Hussein had, and had used in the past against the Kurdish tribes to the north. A chemical-fought war would be an even messier affair, and while it would most likely solidify world opinion against Hussein, it would be a nightmarish scenario that could slow the Coalition offensive considerably. For his part, Hussein still planned to use the media against the U.S. military, figuring that if enough U.S. deaths were broadcast to the nation, the populace would turn against the war, as it had against the Vietnam conflict.

Schwarzkopf's response to these obstacles was to keep to the original plan, and simply go farther and deeper around the army, out far enough to outflank the Republican Guard and come at them from an unexpected direction. It would mean coordinating 200,000 men, vehicles, artillery, and supplies to travel nearly 200 miles out, then come back around the defenses, covering the same ground in about two days. In late October, after conferring with General Powell, he got the authorization to enact the plan, even though it meant they would need to build up their strike force to that 200,000-man strength, which wouldn't happen until January 15th. Meanwhile, they would make one last effort to get Saddam to leave Kuwait peacefully.

On November 30th, the United Nations Security Council unanimously passed the authorization to use force to remove Hussein's forces if he would not leave Kuwait peaceably. Bush sent Secretary of State James Baker to meet with Iraqi Foreign Minister Tariq Aziz in Geneva, Switzerland, to hand-deliver a letter warning Hussein to leave Kuwait by January 15th. However, Aziz, following the first directive of politics in Iraq ("Bring no bad news to the Father-Leader"), claimed he could not accept the letter. The U.S.'s final warning to Hussein went unregarded, with his half-brother Barzan Tikriti, who was present at the meeting, calling his brother and telling him there was nothing to worry about, that the Americans were weak, and just wanted to talk, not to fight.

He could not have been more wrong, and on January 16, 1991, he, Saddam Hussein, and the Iraqi Army learned what a fatal mistake they had made.

Just past midnight, a huge fleet of airplanes, from EF-111s that would jam enemy radar and transmitters, to the F-117 Nighthawk—the first time the stealth fighter-bomber appeared in modern warfare—along with a virtual armada of other jets, F-15C Eagles, F-16 Fighting Falcons, F-15 Strike Eagles, Navy A-6 Intruders, and British Tornadoes, all swooped in to knock out communication centers, air-defense systems, military bases, and emplacements for Hussein's notorious Scud missiles, which he used against Israel and Saudi Arabia during the war.

The massive air strike was complemented by a barrage of precision-guided Tomahawk missiles, which used radar guidance to home in on selected targets at 550 miles per hour. Resistance from the Iraqi air force was scattered and feeble, with many pilots taking to the air, only to either be shot down or flee the battle space.

By the time the attacks were over, the Coalition claimed an eighty percent success rate, with many of Iraq's military sites damaged or destroyed. After the initial round of bombing, the Coalition air forces targeted the Iraqi military itself, followed by strikes on the nation's infrastructure. During the course of the war, more than 1,000 missions would be flown each day, with a net result of 100,000 sorties executed during the war, dropping 88,500 tons of bombs. Unfortunately, due to many of the targets being located near civilian populations, there were some inadvertent noncombatant deaths. Even so, when the next morning came, the city of Baghdad wasn't a smoking ruin like the carpet-bombed cities of World War II. For the most part, the strikes had been executed as surgically as possible, and it showed.

Faced with this overwhelming air superiority, and only able to fight back by having his anti-aircraft gunners fire blindly into the air, trying to saturate the sky, Hussein embarked on a strange series of maneuvers, including releasing 1.5 million barrels of oil into the Persian Gulf. It is not known what the dictator was hoping to accomplish with this tactic—it posed no obstacle to an amphibious landing, and only befouled the ocean waters in the largest man-made spill ever created.

Next, during the last week of January, he ordered all of his remaining aircraft to fly to Iran, completely ceding the skies over Iraq to the Coalition air forces. This would turn out to be another deadly mistake, although in retrospect, it's doubtful that his under-equipped, undertrained pilots could have held their own against the Coalition jet fighters for more than another few days.

Without enemy planes to worry about, and with the majority of anti-aircraft defenses neutralized or destroyed, the Coalition planes began concentrating on their next target—enemy armor. Tanks, trucks, personnel carriers, and artillery, all were fair game, and the F-16 Fighting Falcons and A-10 Thunderbolts pounced with deadly accuracy. By mid-February, the Coalition air force was reporting up to one hundred enemy tank kills a day. This was a vital part of their plan, as once the air power had knocked out a sizable portion of Hussein's ground units, the Coalition forces could begin their massive offensive against what was left of the Iraqi army.

When reconnaissance reports indicated Hussein had concentrated his forces in the east in expectation of an amphibious invasion of the coast (and indeed, there were 17,000 Marines out there to do just that, if it became necessary), leaving his western flank relatively exposed, the Coalition saw their chance. Schwarzkopf, along with his corps commanders, including General Fred

Franks and General John Yeosock, laid the groundwork for a three-pronged offensive designed to mislead, confuse, and ultimately lay the enemy open to the now-famous "left hook" maneuver that would bring the XVIII Airborne Corps into the Iraqi's flank.

The plan was relatively simple—once the XVIII Corps was in place in the west, the 1st Cavalry Division would feint at Al Ru'Qua, a city near the borders of Kuwait, Iraq, and Saudi Arabia, hoping to lure even more of the Iraqis over in response to their maneuvers. After the defensive lines were distracted, the 1st Infantry Division—the Big Red One—would attack the main lines in order to create holes for the 2nd Armored Cavalry Regiment to exploit and move forward, allowing the British 1st Armored Division to bring up their heavy equipment transports to help hold the breach for other units to pass through. As for the supposedly formidable defenses of the Iraqis? The plan was to bypass them altogether, filling in the ditches with dirt and avoiding the massed enemy troops altogether. It didn't hurt that many of the front-line Iraqi soldiers were green draftees who would just as soon surrender as fight. Hussein's tougher soldiers were miles to the north, in no position to help on the front lines.

In the early morning hours of February 24th, the main assault began. When the initial assault proceeded ahead of schedule, the entire battle plan was moved up as well. The elements of the VII Corps, commanded by General Franks, performed brilliantly, taking the enemy by surprise and punching a hole twenty kilometers deep into the enemy lines. The 1st Cavalry was still distracting units near Al Ru'Qua, and there were still the offshore Marine units that Hussein had to keep his eye on. At the same time, the XVIII Airborne Corps, which had packed up and moved two hundred miles to the west, swept in across the empty southern Iraq desert, led by the 3rd Armored Cavalry Regiment and the 24th Mechanized Infantry Division. Their flank was protected by the French 6th Light Armored Division, which overwhelmed the Iraqi 45th Infantry Division, then took a position to defend the Coalition flank. With all of the elements in place, the Coalition forces turned east and smashed into the Republican Guard.

To their credit, the Guard fought as fiercely as they could, but they were simply outgunned, outmatched, and outfought on every level. The Coalition tanks, the M-1 Abrams and Challenger, were state-of-the-art for the time, while the Iraqi armor consisted of a mishmash of Chinese T-59s and T-69s, 40-year-old Soviet T-55s, and some T-72s from the 1970s, none of which were well-maintained. The range on the Abrams' and Challenger's main guns was three times that of the Iraqi tanks, and the Coalition gunners' night vision capability meant they could locate and destroy the enemy well before being detected themselves. The Iraqis were also using outdated steel penetrator ammunition, which, when they scored a rare hit, was defeated by the advanced Chobham armor of the British and American tanks. While the battle wasn't completely one-sided, it was pretty close. The total Coalition casualties at the end of the first day of fighting were four killed and twenty-one wounded, compared to hundreds of Iraqi tanks destroyed and most likely several hundred to thousands of enemy casualties.

The lopsided fighting continued for four more days, with the Coalition forces running roughshod over the Iraqis whenever they encountered them. On February 27th, Schwarzkopf briefed the White House that 3,000 of Hussein's 4,700 tanks had been destroyed. With this news, and the fact that the once-proud Iraqi army had been reduced to a powerless shell of its former self, with the remains of the forces fleeing Kuwait, President Bush ordered the suspension of ground operations, exactly 100 hours after the offensive began.

Operation Desert Storm was one of the most stunning victories ever achieved by a military force. Suffering only 148 dead and 513 wounded, the Coalition killed an estimated 100,000 Iraqi soldiers, and took prisoner somewhere between 60,000 and 80,000 troops, forcing the remains of Hussein's army back inside his borders, where they could recover some of their lost equilibrium by crushing a Kurdish revolt to the north, destroyed when promised U.S. support for the tribes never arrived, leaving them to the cruelty of the still-formidable Iraqi army units in the area.

The mistakes Saddam Hussein made, both in the buildup and execution of the war against the Coalition, are legion. First, much like the Japanese at the outset of World War II, he refused to believe that the U.S. would respond aggressively to his invasion, figuring they would still be reeling from the defeat in Vietnam. That was anything but the case, as he soon learned. Second, he did not strengthen his position in the region when he had the chance. It was thought that he had his eye on Saudi Arabia, yet when presented with the opportunity to seize the lightly defended nation, he delayed for three weeks, giving the Coalition vital time to build up their presence in the region, and enable Schwarzkopf and his soldiers to prepare for their own offensive. The lack of accurate information on his enemy would prove to be a huge detriment to planning how to face them—when his generals couldn't bring him any "bad news," how were they supposed to present an accurate picture of the opposition they were facing? Also, placing green draftees at the front lines, ill-trained and poorly equipped men with little motivation and even less of an idea about how to fight a war of this magnitude, was another crucial error, as was later evidenced by the mass surrenders during the offensive. Although opinions varied on the "elite" Republican Guard, there is little doubt that they probably would have been tougher opponents in the first phases of the Coalition offensive. But being pinned down by Coalition aircraft and suffering weeks of intense bombing wore down their morale as well, reducing them to punching bags for the armor and artillery units.

Finally, Hussein made his biggest mistake in thinking he could actually fight a land-based maneuver war, pitting his underequipped, undersupplied, and undertrained forces against a multi-nation coalition that was led by what is still the finest military in the world, that of the United States. In terms of tactics, morale, and ability, the Iraqi army had literally no chance against the superb planning and execution of the multi-pronged offensive enacted by the Coalition, resulting in one of the swiftest defeats in the history of modern warfare.

But Hussein would survive to live another day, until the U.S. returned to Iraq twelve years later, embarking on another campaign that would have a very different outcome from the lightning-fast strike and victory of Operation Desert Storm.

AFTERWORD

In all honesty this afterword has to begin with two statements that lawyers call "exculpatory language." That means a mealy-mouthed explanation of why if everything you say that follows is wrong you really didn't mean it and it isn't your fault anyhow. In this case we felt required to say something because included in this volume are less than two dozen wars out of the hundreds, if not thousands, that have been fought. And more important these wars were, at least partially, chosen because one side lost in an interesting way. So drawing conclusions from a preselected and small list is not considered or being put forward as any sort of valid historical analysis.

That said, here is a sort of historical overview based on these wars on why wars that should have been won were lost. To begin let's look at each war and the underlying cause of defeat.

The Peloponnesian Wars

Athens went from flawed strategy to flawed strategy and Sparta was just as bad. Opportunities for compromise were ignored and, finally, Athens simply outreached itself in Sicily.

Pyrrhus' War

The Greek leader went to war for reasons not connected to his nation's needs and then lost focus on what war he was fighting. Eventually the cost of even victories was too much.

Fall of the Aztec Empire

Too centralized a structure, inability to adapt, religion interfered with the functioning of the military, and abusive policies had antagonized almost all of the subject tribes who joined the conquistadors.

The Spanish Armada

A lack of strategic coordination and making decisions based upon the moment and not the nature or needs of the fleet. Or perhaps if your power is failing when measured against that of your neighbors, don't stake it all on one grandiose gesture.

The American Revolution

Understand the enemy you create. Coordinate your efforts, don't underestimate any opponent fighting with the home field advantage.

Jena Auerstadt

No matter how well they worked during the last war, don't use the last war's tactics and equipment to fight the next war.

The Napoleonic Navy

If you have an expensive arm, either support it or not. Halfway support and making demands it can no longer achieve guarantees defeat.

The Spanish Resistance

Understand how the people of the nation you are fighting will react. Don't underestimate the guerilla as an opponent. Either dominate entirely or get out, don't linger and bleed.

Napoleon's Russian Campaign

Never base your entire strategy on your opponent reacting in the manner you expect. Certainly don't just sit there waiting for the reaction you want when it doesn't come.

The Defense of France 1814

When you are likely to lose, don't turn down good terms and fight until you have lost it all.

Egyptian-Wahhabi War

When you have won what you want, stop. If you are attempting to defeat a popular movement, send troops that can win, and enough of them.

The Mexican War

An unpopular autocrat can cripple your defense, no matter how valiant your soldiers are.

The Confederacy

Even the best generals and the bravest soldiers cannot overcome not using a large part of your potential resources and the other side having the high moral ground.

Anglo-Sudan War

No matter what your technological edge or the experience of your soldiers, you still have to send enough to do the job.

The Franco-Prussian War

All the courage and valiant rhetoric in the world can't overcome bad organization and worse leadership. Just because you won the last war doesn't mean your enemy didn't learn from the defeat. Did you?

The Boer War

Irregulars fighting on home ground cannot be fought with rigid military techniques. Sending enough soldiers early saves having to send even more later.

The Winter War

No matter what your numbers, be ready and equipped to fight the war where and how you have to. Incidentally if you abuse your

officer corps and discourage innovation, then your army isn't going
to handle new situations very well.

Germany 1941

Don't turn potential allies into enemies. The enemy of your
enemy can be an ally, but not if you treat them worse than your
enemy did.

Japan WWII

Don't take on a foe you can't beat. Don't count on early victories
if they can't force the peace. It is always an error to underestimate
the morale and determination of your opponent. Finally, antag-
onizing and abusing hundreds of millions of potentially friendly
people when you are victorious guarantees you will stand alone
in defeat.

Korea

Never underestimate the opposition, especially on racial
grounds. Keep your intelligence up, someone should have known
of the North Korean invasion before it happened. Be prepared for
success. The North Korean army ground to a halt due to a lack
of supply, not allied resistance. If you are vulnerable, watch your
flanks. The enemy hardly ever attacks where you want once you
have lost the initiative. Understand the political consequences of
your military decisions.

Mau Mau Rebellion

If you are going to have an insurrection, prepare first. It also
helps to have at least a good part of the population support you.

Vietnam

If you are going to fight a war, fight it to win. Civilian control
of the military does not mean operational control by civilians. Finally, you can win on the battlefield and lose in the media. Democracies will not support a war the people feel is pointless.

The Six-Day War

Even if you have a massive advantage in every form of weaponry, the skill and morale of your opponents can defeat you. People, such as the Israelis, with nothing to lose will fight as if they have nothing to lose.

Uganda-Tanzania War

If you start a war, get the people in your nation behind it. It also helps to have army units capable of fighting effectively. Madmen do not make good military commanders.

Desert Storm

Don't assume your opponent will not react to your invading a neighbor or similar aggressiveness. Remember you have to win the war to reap the benefits. Don't plan a war of maneuver when you won't have control of the air over the battlefield. Being bombed for weeks and unable to fight back will destroy the morale of any unit. Recruits from populations you have murdered and oppressed don't become motivated soldiers. They have nothing to gain from your victory. It probably is egomaniacal to think your undertrained and underequipped conventional army can defeat the much larger and more professional force of the richest nation in the world.

So to summarize, if you are out to lose a war then here are a few steps demonstrated by the wars discussed here that will ensure your defeat:

1. Keep changing the goals of the war.
2. Fight it just like the last war.
3. Let the leader's ego be more important than military considerations.
4. Oppress and antagonize as many populations as you can.
5. Underestimate irregulars and disregard the support they will get from the populace.
6. Count on courage and morale to overcome deficiencies in weaponry and command.

7. Assume how your enemy will react and look for the one battle that wins it all.

8. Don't send enough forces to win or secure the victory.

In simple language don't be so taken with yourself and your army that you fail to learn from the mistakes others have made before you.

ENDNOTES

The Collapse of the Spanish Armada

1. Lacey Baldwin Smith. *Elizabeth Tudor, Portrait of a Queen* (Boston, Toronto: Little, Brown and Company, 1975), p. 194.
2. http://www.britainexpress.com/History/tudor/armada.htm
3. Elizabeth Jenkins. *Elizabeth the Great* (New York: Coward McCann, Inc., 1958), p. 56.
4. Ibid.
5. Ibid.
6. Mary M. Luke. *Gloriana: The Years of Elizabeth I* (New York: Coward McCann Geoghegan, 1973), p. 48.
7. Ibid, p. 49.
8. Ibid.
9. http://www.loc.gov/rr/rarebook/catalog/drake/drake-7-cadizraid. html
10. http://www.britishbattles.com/spanish-war/spanish-armada.htm
11. Ibid.
12. Mattingly, Garrett. *The Armada* (Boston: Houghton Mifflin Company), p. 321.
13. Ibid, p. 333.
14. Ibid, p. 333.
15. Fair, Charles. *From the Jaws of Victory* (New York: Simon & Schuster, 1971), p. 136.

Lobster Stew

16. Frederic Kidder and John Adams. *History of the Boston Massacre, March 5,*

1770: Consisting of the Narrative of the Town, The Trial of the Soldiers: and A Histori-cal Introduction, Containing Unpublished Documents of John Adams and Explanatory Notes. J. Munsell: New York, 1870.

17. "No Taxation Without Representation: Three Letters of 1754 to Governor William Shirley, with a Preface of 1766 To the PRINTER of the LONDON CHRONICLE," *The London Chronicle*, February 8, 1766. The Writings of Benjamin Franklin: Philadelphia, 1726—1757 Internet Link: http://www.historycarper.com/resources/twobf2/taxation.htm

18. Henry Steele Commager and Richard Morris, eds. *The Spirit of Seventy-Six*, p. 39.

19. Mark Boatner. *The Encyclopedia of the American Revolution*, p. 129.

20. Henry Steele Commager and Richard Morris, eds. *The Spirit of Seventy-Six*, p. 134—135.

21. Liberty: Episode III. Twin Cities Public Television. 1997.

22. Mark Boatner. *The Encyclopedia of the American Revolution*, p. 654.

23. Charles Cornwallis Cornwallis. Correspondence of Charles, First Marquis Cornwallis, Volume I of III, J. Murray: London, 1859, p. 24.

24. Ibid, p. 33.

25. Ibid, p. 28.

26. William Dobein James. *A Sketch of the Life of Brig. Gen. Francis Marion and A History of his Brigade From Its Rise in June. 1780, Until Disbanded in December, 1782*. Project Gutenberg Etext #926. Chapter 2.

27. Ibid.

BOOKS BY
BILL FAWCETT

HOW TO LOSE A WAR
More Foolish Plans and Great Military Blunders
ISBN 978-0-06-135844-9 (paperback)

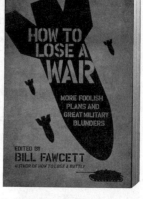

From the ancient Crusades to the modern age of chemical warfare, history is littered with horribly bad military ideas, and each military defeat is fascinating to dissect.

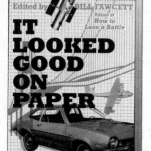

IT LOOKED GOOD ON PAPER
Bizarre Inventions, Design Disasters & Engineering Follies
ISBN 978-0-06-135843-2 (paperback)

This book is a collection of flawed plans, half-baked ideas, and downright ridiculous machines that, with the best and most optimistic intentions, men have constructed throughout history.

YOU SAID WHAT?
Lies and Propaganda Throughout History
ISBN 978-0-06-113050-2 (paperback)

From the dawn of man to the War on Terror, Fawcett chronicles the vast history of frauds, deceptions, propaganda, and trickery from governments, corporations, historians, and everyone in between.

OVAL OFFICE ODDITIES
An Irreverent Collection of Presidential Facts, Follies, and Foibles
ISBN 978-0-06-134617-0 (paperback)

Featuring hundreds of strange and wonderful facts about past American presidents, first ladies, and veeps, readers will learn all about presidential gaffes, love lives, and odd habits.

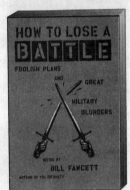

HOW TO LOSE A BATTLE
Foolish Plans and Great Military Blunders
ISBN 978-0-06-076024-3 (paperback)

Whether a result of lack of planning, miscalculation, a leader's ego, or spy infiltration, this compendium chronicles the worst military defeats and looks at what caused each battlefield blunder.

YOU DID WHAT?
Mad Plans and Great Historical Disasters
ISBN 978-0-06-053250-5 (paperback)

History has never been more fun than it is in this fact-filled compendium of historical catastrophes and embarrassingly bad ideas.

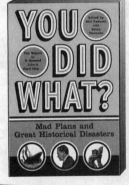

HUNTERS & SHOOTERS
An Oral History of the U.S. Navy SEALs in Vietnam
ISBN 978-0-06-137566-8 (paperback)

Fifteen former SEALs share their vivid, first-person remembrances of action in Vietnam—brutal, honest, and thrilling stories revealing astonishing truths that will only add strength to the SEAL legacy.